Grammar as Science

Grammar as Science

Text by
Richard K. Larson

Graphic design by
Kimiko Ryokai

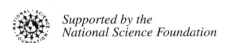 *Supported by the*
National Science Foundation

The MIT Press
Cambridge, Massachusetts
London, England

For information about special quantity discounts, please e-mail special_sales@mitpress .mit.edu.

This book was set in Times Roman and Univers by SNP Best-set Typesetter Ltd., Hong Kong.

Printed and bound in the United States of America.

Library of Congress Cataloging-in-Publication Data
Larson, Richard K.
    Grammar as science / Richard K. Larson ; designed and illustrated by Kimiko Ryokai.
        p. cm.
    Includes bibliographic references and index.
    ISBN 978-0-262-51303-6 (pbk. : alk. paper)
    1. Grammar, Comparative and general—Syntax—Textbooks. I. Ryokai, Kimiko. II. Title.
    P291.L33   2010
    415—dc22

                                                                              2008054058

10 9 8 7 6 5 4 3 2 1

To Kenneth Locke Hale (1934–2001)

Photo by Sabine Iatridou.
Reprinted with permission.

Contents

Preface for Teachers

The undergraduate curriculum has traditionally been viewed as a domain in which students are introduced to broad issues of life, society, and thought, and where skills of general application and utility are developed and strengthened. On the traditional view, the goal of an undergraduate program is not to recruit and train potential graduate students, but to inform individuals about the wider implications of a field, and to foster in them the intellectual skills that that field especially draws upon.

This book arose out of an effort to rethink part of the undergraduate curriculum in linguistics at Stony Brook University in line with the traditional goals of undergraduate education. Specifically, it represents an attempt to reconsider the structure and content of the introductory syntax course from the standpoint of three broad questions:

1. What is the general educational value of studying syntax?
2. What broad intellectual issues are engaged in studying syntax?
3. What general intellectual skills are developed by studying syntax?

The answers embodied in *Grammar as Science* are the following:

1. Syntax offers an excellent instrument for introducing students from a wide variety of backgrounds to the principles of scientific theorizing and scientific thought.
2. Syntax engages in a revealing way both general intellectual themes present in all scientific theorizing and ones arising specifically within the modern cognitive sciences. For example:

   - How does a scientist construct, test, evaluate, and refine a theory?
   - How does a scientist choose between alternative theories?
   - What constitutes a significant generalization, and how does one capture it?
   - When does a scientist propose or assume unseen objects or structure, and how are such objects or structure justified?

- How secure is scientific knowledge?
- Can one study a human phenomenon as a natural object and gain scientific understanding of it?
- What is the nature of a mental object like a language?

3. Syntax offers an excellent medium through which to teach the skill of framing exact, explicit arguments for theories—the articulation of hypotheses, principles, data, and reasoning into a coherent, convincing whole.

This book is intended both for undergraduates who are majoring in linguistics and for undergraduates who are taking linguistics courses through a department of linguistics (as opposed to a department of English or anthropology) but do not plan to become majors. In my experience, such students generally do not have significant science background and hence can especially profit by a course of this kind.

Grammar as Science is not an introduction to scientific theorizing, with syntax serving as a novel domain to illustrate concepts and results. Rather, it is an introduction to syntax as an exercise in scientific theory construction. In view of this, *Grammar as Science* covers a good deal of standard territory in syntax. The teacher will find here discussion of core topics such as phrase structure, constituency, the lexicon, inaudible elements, movement rules, and transformational constraints. At the same time, the broad goal of developing scientific reasoning skills and an appreciation of scientific theorizing has entailed some divergences between *Grammar as Science* and other introductory syntax books.

First, there is less stress here than elsewhere on providing an up-to-date introduction to syntactic theory, employing state-of-the-art technical tools. If the guiding aim is to get students to think precisely and explicitly about natural language structure and to grasp the process of constructing a theory of that structure, then the exact tools used in the construction are not of paramount importance. What is important is that the tools be precise, explicit, and relatively easy to use. I have found traditional phrase structure rules to be a very natural first tool in formal language study, one that students take to readily, and one that permits a very direct grasp of the relation between linguistic rules and linguistic structure. Accordingly, I make free use of phrase structure rules throughout this book, despite their being largely obsolete in current linguistic theory.

Second, this book covers a somewhat narrower range of topics than other books. Again, this is because the primary goal is not to cover the modern field of syntax, but to introduce students to the process of grammatical theory construction as a scientific enterprise. *Grammar as Science* is structured so as to encourage general reflection on this enterprise. The units are organized thematically into sections that bring out important components of the enterprise, such as choosing between theories, constructing explicit arguments for hypotheses, the need for explaining linguistic phenomena (as opposed to simply describing them), and the conflicting demands that push us toward both expanding and constraining our technical tool set. The choice of topics is always guided by this larger programmatic goal.

Grammar as Science was conceived as part of a "laboratory science" course, in which students collect and actively experiment with linguistic data. The book is made up of a large number of relatively short units, each corresponding to a single class session. The main concepts for each unit are typically few, and arise in response to specific empirical questions and challenges that are posed. To aid in making the laboratory experience real for students, *Grammar as Science* is designed for use with Syntactica, a software application tool developed at Stony Brook University that allows students to create and explore simple grammars in a graphical, interactive way. *Grammar as Science* can be used independently of Syntactica as a stand-alone text, but my experience has been that Syntactica adds much to the course. Specifically, use of this tool

- Confers a dynamic character on the process of hypothesizing grammars. Students can "try the rules out" and see what happens.

- Permits an incremental approach to building grammars. Students can add one rule after another and check consequences at each stage.

- Confers a measure of "objectivity" on the issue of whether a rule set does or doesn't generate a given tree. If the rules a student has written are correct, the program will generate the tree. Students find this quite compelling.

- Inculcates habits of precise thinking and expression. Computers insist upon a level of precision in their input that is not negotiable.

- Provides a natural route to asking questions about human syntactic knowledge and its representation. For example, in what way are we or aren't we like a machine in which the relevant rules have been entered?

The text layout of *Grammar as Science* was conceived and executed by Kimiko Ryokai. It follows Japanese design principles, which emphasize visual/graphic organization of material. I have found that this format helps students to understand and retain the material; they also find it enjoyable.

Its good intentions notwithstanding, *Grammar as Science* could doubtless be improved in many ways. I warmly welcome all criticisms, comments, and suggestions for revision.

Richard.Larson@stonybrook.edu.

Acknowledgments

The general theme of *Grammar as Science* draws its inspiration from a remarkable group of educators, including Ken Hale, Maya Honda, Jay Keyser, Wayne O'Neil, and Josie White Eagle. Ken Hale and Wayne O'Neil, in particular, have been central figures in shaping my own thoughts on teaching linguistics as science. It is a great pleasure to acknowledge their influence. I also thank Noam Chomsky for cheerfully consenting to play the special role he does in this book.

The innovative graphic layout of *Grammar as Science* was conceived and executed by Kimiko Ryokai, whose work I acknowledge with admiration. As an undergraduate student, Ms. Ryokai introduced me to the unique aspects of Japanese-style text design, which emphasizes visual presentation and organization of material.

I also express my sincere gratitude to Hiroko Yamakido for extensive initial editing of the manuscript, and my profound thanks to Anne Mark for taking an extremely complex manuscript and bringing it into final form. My thanks also to Franc Marušić for preparing the index.

Sincere thanks to Amy Brand for originally bringing the *Grammar as Science* project to MIT Press, and to Ada Brunstein for overseeing its completion. MIT Press has shown astonishing patience with an author who never once met a deadline.

My profound thanks to the National Science Foundation, which funded the *Grammar as Science* project under NSF grant USE-915041.

Finally, my sincere thanks to the generations of introductory syntax students at Stony Brook University, who, more than anyone else, are responsible for this book.

Acknowledgments

PART I   Setting Out

The study of grammar once enjoyed a central place in education, one going back to the classic liberal arts curriculum of the late Middle Ages. Grammar was, along with logic and rhetoric, one of the subjects in the trivium: the core group in the seven arts students were expected to master. The importance of the "big three" is reflected in our modern word *trivial*, which originally applied to knowledge regarded as so basic that it required no argument. Any educated person could be assumed to know it.

In an earlier time, studying grammar primarily meant studying Latin and Greek. Access to the classical languages meant access to the root cultures of the West, their literature and science. Latin and Greek were viewed as "special languages": models of clarity, logical organization, intellectual subtlety, and economy of expression. Studying how these languages worked was viewed as something very close to studying the principles of logical, coherent thought itself. When other languages were analyzed, they were always analyzed on the model of Latin or Greek.

The curriculum in which grammar held its place of honor is obsolete now; the time when educated people could attend only to the classics of the West is long past. Furthermore, we now know that Latin and Greek are, by any reasonable standard, typical human languages: in no way clearer, subtler, or more logical than, say, Greenlandic Eskimo or Chinese. The old rationales for studying grammar are gone. Is the relevance of grammar behind us, too?

Not at all! In the last five decades, the subject of grammar has been reborn in a very different setting. Grammar has emerged as part of a new science, linguistics, that poses and investigates its own unique and fascinating set of questions, pursuing them with the same rigorous methodology found elsewhere in the study of natural phenomena. This new scientific perspective on grammar owes much to the linguist Noam Chomsky, who introduced it in the mid-1950s and who has contributed centrally to its development ever since.

When we study human language, we are approaching what some might call the "human essence," the distinctive qualities of mind that are, so far as we know, unique to man, and that are inseparable from any critical phase of human existence, personal or social. Hence the fascination of this study, and, no less, its frustration.
—*Language and Mind*, p. 100

Noam Chomsky
Institute Professor
Massachusetts Institute of Technology

The idea of a "scientific" approach to grammar might strike you as odd at first. When we think of "science," we usually think in these terms (see Goldstein and Goldstein 1984):

- Science is a search for understanding.
- Achieving understanding means discovering general laws and principles.
- Scientific laws and principles can be tested experimentally.

How do such notions apply to grammar? What is there to *understand* about grammar? What would general laws and principles of grammar be? And how might we test laws and principles of grammar experimentally, assuming we could find them in the first place? Our puzzlement about these questions suggests a certain implicit view of language, and the kind of object it is.

Language as a Natural Object

From a very early age, children appear to be attuned to the distinction between **natural objects** and **artifacts**. In an interesting series of experiments, psychologist Frank Keil has shown that whereas very young children judge the identity of objects largely on the basis of superficial features, at some point they begin to realize that certain kinds of objects have an inner essence that may sometimes be hidden or obscured (see Keil 1986). For example, before a certain age children will identify a black cat that has been painted to look like a skunk as a skunk, whereas after this age they identify a black cat painted to look like a skunk as a painted cat and not as a skunk. They realize that being a skunk involves more than looking like a skunk; the true identity of an object may be concealed by appearances.

Interestingly, in making this transition, children seem to draw an important distinction between natural objects, like cats and skunks, and artifacts (things made by humans). Although they judge a painted cat to be a cat nonetheless, they understand that an old coffeepot that has been modified into a birdfeeder is now really a birdfeeder. In other words, they see natural objects as having their own defining properties, whereas artifacts are whatever we make them to be, as a matter of convention.

Human language can be viewed in both these ways, as artifact or as natural object; and how we view it strongly shapes our reaction to the facts it presents us with. Language has been seen by many people as an aspect of culture, similar to other basic human institutions and traditions like tool-making or agriculture. In this view, languages are the product of human imagination and development: created by humans, taught by humans, and learned by humans. They are cultural artifacts possessing the properties and obeying the rules that we bestow on them, and the patterns or regularities we find in them are basically just matters of convention. Like the birdfeeder, language is what we've made it to be, and there is no more to say. There is no question of understanding anything, or discovering anything, or testing anything. It is this broad view of language, I believe, that leads to puzzlement when we think about grammar as science.

But language can instead be seen as a part of the natural world. In a series of influential works, Noam Chomsky has argued that human language is more correctly viewed as a natural object, analogous to a limb or a bodily organ (see Chomsky 2000a). True, language arose in the course of human prehistory, but it was no more invented or developed by humans than arms or lungs. Rather, language ability evolved, like other species-specific properties. Likewise, although languages develop in the course of human ontogeny, they are neither taught to nor learned by children, any more than children are taught to grow arms or learn to have hearts. Rather, we humans speak and in so doing provide the environment—the "nutrition," to use a Chomskyan metaphor—in which language can grow and develop in our children.

Under this perspective, languages become objects of the natural world much like quasars or spinach leaves. They are entities whose properties and structure are to be determined by naturalistic investigation. Accordingly, when we are faced with a certain pattern or regularity in linguistic facts, we do not put it aside as a matter of convention; rather, we start to look for a "law" or principle that predicts the pattern and suggests an explanation. And we realize that the explanation may well be hidden to us, and need to be tested for experimentally. Adopting the naturalistic perspective opens up human language as a new domain, a fresh territory for scientific exploration.

The Terrain Ahead

This book is an introduction to the modern subject of grammar (now called **syntax**) from the perspective of language as a natural object. Its goals are twofold:

- To systematically explore some of the ideas and results in the new territory of syntax, and
- To provide experience with rigorous scientific reasoning and argumentation, and the development of scientific theorizing.

Successful exploration requires open eyes and a clear head. You need to be observant about your immediate surroundings (so you won't miss anything). You need to be mindful of how you got there (in case you need to retrace your steps or reconstruct your route for others). And you need to be logical about where you will go next (so you don't just blunder about).

This book consists of short units that usually involve some specific factual point(s) and a small number of ideas or concepts. These will be your "immediate surroundings" as we proceed. Try to read and master each unit in a single sitting. Be observant, and try to see all there is to see.

When the terrain is unfamiliar, where you are and how you got there are sometimes difficult to keep in your head. Maps are useful for this purpose. The units of this book are grouped into parts that form the map of the territory we'll be exploring:

- Meeting the subject and discovering its questions (Part I)
- Constructing a theory that attempts to answer the questions (Part II)
- Choosing between competing theories (Part III)
- Arguing for one theory versus another (Part IV)
- Searching for deeper explanation (Part V)
- Following the many consequences of a theory (Part VI)
- Enlarging and constraining the tools that a theory employs (Part VII)

Since these divisions mark the stages that researchers typically pass through in constructing a scientific theory in any domain, they make a good general "route plan" for us. At the beginning of each part, we will stop and do a "map check" to make sure we know where we've gotten to and where we should go next. Often we will consult a guide, someone more familiar with the area.

Science is tentative, exploratory, questioning, largely learned by doing! —"Rationality/Science," p. 91

You won't need much in the way of equipment to undertake this trip. The presentation assumes no previous experience either with grammar or with the broader discipline of linguistics. All you will need is a healthy sense of curiosity and a willingness to think critically about a subject matter (language) that most of us take for granted in day-to-day life and rarely think about at all. With that much, we can begin.

UNIT 1   **What Is Linguistics?**

Leading Questions

In beginning the study of any field, one good way of orienting yourself is to find out what problems the field works on. What **leading questions** does it seek to answer? In the approach to linguistics we will follow, the leading questions are very easy to formulate.

In day-to-day conversation, we routinely speak of people "knowing English" or "knowing Japanese and Korean." We talk about a language as a body of knowledge that people do or do not possess. The leading questions of linguistics arrange themselves around this commonplace way of talking: they address **knowledge of language**.

Whenever someone can be said to know something, a number of basic questions present themselves.

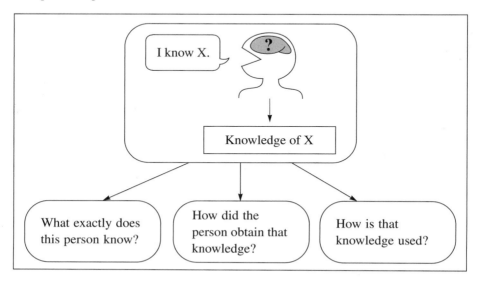

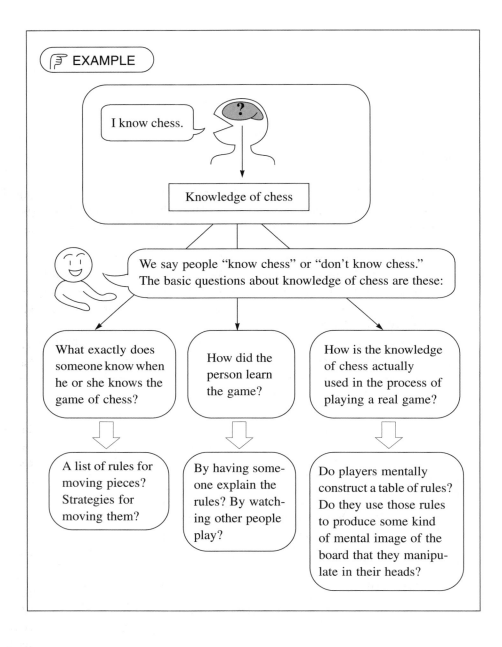

Linguistics is concerned with these basic questions as they apply to knowledge of language. It seeks to discover the answers to these questions:

What exactly do people know when they know a language?	How is knowledge of language acquired?	How is knowledge of language used (e.g., in speech and understanding)?

Viewed in this way—as addressing certain knowledge that we have internalized in the course of growing up—linguistics is basically a branch of **psychology**, broadly understood. Linguistics is trying to find out something about human minds and what they contain.

Studying Knowledge of Language

Trying to find out what's in the mind might seem easy at first. Since knowledge of language is in us—in our minds—shouldn't we have direct access to it? Shouldn't we be able to elicit that knowledge by intensive self-reflection—like remembering something forgotten through hard, careful thought? Sorry, things aren't that simple.

Knowledge of Language Is Tacit

To clarify the problem we face, think about the following sentences, imagining that they are spoken in a natural way, with no word given special emphasis. Concentrate on who is understood as the "surpriser" and the "surprisee" in each:

(1) Homer expected to surprise him.
(2) I wonder who Homer expected to surprise him.
(3) I wonder who Homer expected to surprise.

These sentences are similar in form but curiously different in meaning. Any competent speaker of English will understand sentence (1) to mean that Homer expected to do the surprising and that he expected to surprise someone other than himself. Sentence (2) contains the identical substring of words *Homer expected to surprise him*, but it is immediately understood to have a very different meaning. In fact, it has at least two meanings distinct from that of sentence (1): someone other than Homer ("who") is expected to be the surpriser, and the surprisee ("him") may be either Homer or some third party. Finally, sentence (3) is identical to sentence (2) minus the word *him*, but now Homer again must be the surpriser, rather than the surprisee.

These facts are remarkably intricate and subtle, yet immediately obvious to anyone who has mastered English. But what principles are we following in making these judgments?

In fact, we don't have a clue—not initially, at least. True, we can make complex judgments about sentences like these. But we cannot directly grasp the basis of our judgments. People don't consciously know why, when they say *I wonder who Homer expected to surprise him*, the name *Homer* and the pronoun *him* will be taken to refer to different people.

The knowledge that we possess of our language is almost entirely **unconscious** or **tacit knowledge**. In this respect, language appears to be similar to other important parts of our mental life. Sigmund Freud is famous for having proposed that much of the mind's functioning and contents lies entirely hidden to consciousness. Freud held that unconscious phenomena and processes are no less psychologically real than conscious ones, and that appeal to them is just as necessary for an understanding of human cognition.

> I handle unconscious ideas, unconscious trains of thought, and unconscious impulses as though they were no less valid and unimpeachable psychological data than conscious ones. [And] of this I am certain—that anyone who sets out to investigate the same region of phenomena and employs the same method will find himself compelled to take the same position ...
> —*Fragment of an Analysis of a Case of Hysteria* ("Dora"), p. 232

Sigmund Freud
1856–1939

For the most part, the principles and operations behind knowledge of language lie outside the range of consciousness and cannot be recovered by simply sitting down, staring off into space, and thinking hard.

A "Black Box" Problem

If we can't directly intuit what's in our minds, then our only option is to approach the investigation of internal things (like knowledge and mental states) as we would approach the investigation of external things (like birds and planets). That is, we must formulate explicit theories about what we know, and we must find ways to test, refine, and extend those theories in order to reach a satisfactory explanation of the facts. Since we can't look directly at what's inside the mind, our job will be to figure out what's inside on the basis of what we can observe from the outside.

Problems of this kind are sometimes called **black box problems**. In a black box problem, we have an unknown mechanism that receives observable input data and produces observable output behaviors. The task is to figure out what's inside the box on the basis of inputs and outputs alone.

In the case of human language, the observable input is the speech data that people are exposed to as children, the language that they hear around them. The output is their various linguistic behaviors as children and as adults: the sentences and other expressions that they produce, their judgments about their speech and the speech of others, and so on. By carefully examining this kind of information, the linguist must deduce the language mechanism that lies within the human mind.

A Talking Analogy

To make the black box nature of the problem more concrete, consider a simple analogy (due to MIT linguist James Harris). For many years, toymakers have produced talking dolls of various kinds. Some have a string on their back or neck that you pull. Others have a button on their wrist or stomach. Still others talk when you talk to them (although these must be turned on initially with a switch).

Imagine yourself an engineer who has been handed a particular model of talking doll: say, the kind that has a string on its neck. Your task (as set by your boss) is to discover exactly how the doll talks. In other words, you have to figure out the properties of the mechanism inside the doll that allows it to do what it does. Suppose also that a certain constraint is placed on your work: you are not allowed to open the doll up and observe the mechanism directly. This makes it a black box problem: you can't look inside.

To solve this problem, you would have to use what's observable from the outside as a basis for guessing what's inside. Examining the doll, you would observe things like this:

- The language mechanism is powered exclusively by pulling the string; there are no plugs or batteries.
- The doll has a fixed repertory of ten or so utterances, which come out in random order ("Mommy, play with me now," "I want another drink of water," "I'm sleepy, nite-nite," etc.).
- All repetitions of a particular utterance are identical.
- The doll always starts at the beginning of an utterance—never in the middle, even if you pull the string out only partway.
- Submerging the doll in water damages the language mechanism.
- The language mechanism is apparently about the size of a tennis ball and is located in the abdominal region.

Take a few moments now and write down what mechanism you think is inside the doll, and how these observations imply this mechanism.

Deducing What's inside the Box from the Output

Thinking about the observable properties of the doll, you can make a pretty good educated guess about what's inside, even if you aren't allowed to cut the doll open and look inside. For example, since the doll produces a very limited range of utterances and all repetitons of a particular utterance are identical, it is very likely that the utterances are stored within the doll as whole chunks, not constructed online. That is, it is likely that the doll contains a storage unit loaded with all of its utterances; pulling the string causes a whole, individual stored utterance to be played back from its beginning.

Deducing what's inside humans is vastly more complex than deducing what's inside the doll, but already we can see some things by contrast. For example, since we humans produce an enormous range of utterances, without exact repetitions, it's very unlikely that we have utterances stored within us as whole chunks. Rather, we probably do construct our utterances from smaller parts as we speak, with the parts and their rules of combination being what's stored. With humans, then, something different and more complex is involved. As we will see in later units, the rich complexity of linguistic data—the speech we hear around us, the output we observe—allows us to conjecture a very rich mechanism inside the human mind.

Deducing What's inside the Box from the Input

The data we draw on in solving a black box problem come not only from "output behavior": in our present case, the utterances produced by talking dolls, or the utterances and linguistic judgments produced by talking humans. They also come from the input the mechanism receives. Often we can deduce what kind of mechanism is inside the black box by seeing what kind of information initially went into it.

For example, going back to our analogy, suppose you observe that, for the doll, "learning" the ten or so utterances that it produces involves a human being producing each of these utterances. Perhaps you visit the factory where the dolls are made and you observe a person speaking into a microphone that is connected to the doll by a wire. You observe that the doll's speech exactly repeats that of the person speaking into the microphone, that the utterances the doll ultimately produces are copies of the human's speech. Such evidence would clearly support your hypothesis that the doll contains some kind of storage and playback device— a disk, a tape player, or something similar. So, the circumstances in which the doll acquires its language can give us information about the mechanism inside it, even when we can't observe this mechanism directly.

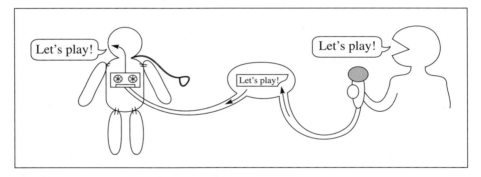

Comparisons with Human Language

Applying this strategy to human language yields surprising results—indeed, some of the most fascinating results in all of the cognitive sciences. Clearly, humans do not learn language like our talking doll, or like a parrot. Although children do repeat expressions that they hear around them in day-to-day speech, often very closely matching the intonation, pitch, and timing of words, their speech goes far beyond what they hear. Children, and indeed humans generally, are extremely creative in their language use, routinely producing utterances they have never encountered before.

Furthermore, the data that form the input to human language acquisition are not clean and precise. Our doll's utterances were "learned" from very precise, careful speech uttered into a microphone, perhaps in the sheltered environment of a sound booth. But these are not the circumstances in which human speech is acquired, with careful models of good sentences presented clearly and coherently. In fact, spoken natural language does not provide particularly good models for a child to follow in acquisition. The speech that children hear is often characterized by fragmentary and outright ungrammatical expressions, interruptions, lapses of attention, errors, burps, you name it. When you are listening, speaking, or holding a conversation, your impression is typically one of connected discourse. But that is by no means the reality. The data that children must draw upon in learning a language are remarkably messy and "defective." (If you need convincing of this, simply lay a tape recorder on a table during a normal daily conversation, and later transcribe three minutes' worth of the speech you have recorded. How many complete, coherent, and grammatical sentences do you observe?)

Finally, the evidence that children draw upon in learning language is at best extremely indirect. Recall our three example sentences (repeated here):

> (1) Homer expected to surprise him.
> (2) I wonder who Homer expected to surprise him.
> (3) I wonder who Homer expected to surprise.

The judgments we make about "surpriser" and "surprisee" are intricate and subtle, but obvious to anyone who knows English.

How did we learn the principles that underlie these judgments? Surely they were not taught to us directly or explicitly. They are not found in any English grammar textbook; they have never even been noticed, except by a minuscule circle of specialists, and indeed, they are still not known with absolute certainty even by specialists. Yet every normally developing English-speaking child masters them at an early age with no special effort.

Universal Grammar

From these reflections, it is clear that language learning and its outcome present a surprising picture. Our resulting knowledge of language has these properties:

- It is **tacit**; we come to know many things that we don't know that we know.
- It is **complex**; it underwrites very subtle and intricate judgments.
- It is **untutored**; the vast bulk of it was never taught to us directly.
- It is **gained in the face of very impoverished input**.

One plausible explanation for this picture—perhaps the only plausible explanation—has been proposed by the linguist Noam Chomsky. Chomsky suggests that children come to the task of language acquisition with a rich conceptual apparatus already in place that makes it possible for them to draw correct and far-reaching conclusions on the basis of very little evidence. Human language learning involves a very powerful cognitive system that allows learners to infer their grammar from the meager data they are presented with in day-to-day speech. Chomsky terms this cognitive system **Universal Grammar**, or **UG** for short.

We may think of Universal Grammar as the system of principles that characterizes the class of possible grammars by specifying how particular grammars are organized (what are the components and their relations), how the different rules of these components are constructed, how they interact, and so on. ... Universal Grammar is not a grammar, but rather ... a kind of schematism for grammar.
—*Language and Responsibility*, pp. 180, 183

Noam Chomsky
Institute Professor
Massachusetts Institute of
Technology

Photo by Donna Coveney/MIT.
Reprinted with permission.

UG in humans is very roughly analogous to the mechanism inside our talking doll. Although the doll's device is not a deductive conceptual mechanism, it is one that allows dolls equipped with it to "learn" or at least be made to "speak" any language. By simply recording utterances in one or another language on the disk, drum, tape, or whatever device the mechanism uses for storing its messages, dolls can be made to utter sentences of German, Hindi, Maori, and so on. Furthermore, just as the doll's mechanism is part of its basic physical structure, is specific to that kind of doll, and is found in all dolls of that kind, so too the basic mechanism that makes it possible for humans to learn language is apparently part of our physical structure (our genetic endowment), is peculiar to the human species alone, and is found in all members of our species (putting aside cases of pathology).

Evidence for Universal Grammar

Evidence for basic linguistic endowment in humans comes from at least three sources:

- The acquisition process is surprisingly uniform for all children, even though the languages being learned may seem wildly different.
- Although the languages acquired by children are superficially diverse, deeper investigation reveals significant, shared design features.
- With equal facility and with no special training, all children, of whatever ethnic or genetic background, learn whatever language or languages they have significant contact with. No one has a racial or genetic predisposition to learn one language more readily than another.

These facts would be all but impossible to understand if normally developing human children did not come to the task of native-language acquisition equipped with a single standard acquisition device, provided by their biological makeup.

The Task of Linguistics

Given these results, we can reformulate the task of linguistics in investigating knowledge of language. Linguistics must accomplish the following:

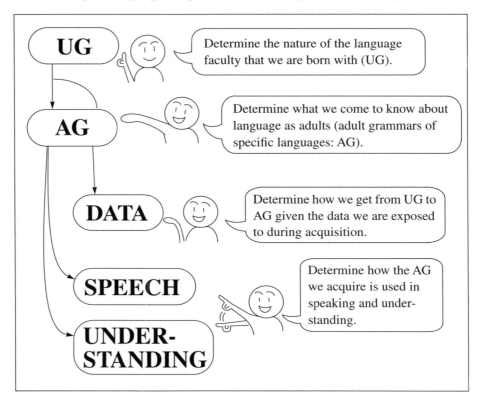

What Is Syntax About?

Review

1. Linguistics addresses knowledge of language. It seeks to answer three basic questions.

- What exactly do we know when we know a language?
- How do we acquire that knowledge?
- How do we use that knowledge?

2. We figure out what's in people's minds by deducing it from the data they are exposed to and the behavior they exhibit.

It's a black box problem!

3. We know many complicated things about our language that we were never directly taught. Moreover, the data from which we draw our knowledge are often defective.

This suggests that some sort of mechanism must already be in place that supports language acquisition.

4. Part of language we know as children, prior to experience. It is with us at birth, as part of our genetic endowment as human beings.

It's called **Universal Grammar (UG)**!

Dividing Up the Problem Area

In studying people's knowledge of language, modern linguistics follows a general methodological principle set down by the French philosopher René Descartes. Descartes counseled that in approaching any problem, we should begin by trying to divide it up into smaller, more manageable parts.

We should divide a problem into as many parts as admit of separate solution.
—*Discourse on Method*, p. 92

René Descartes
1596–1650

When you study a new language, there are a number of things you must master, including pronunciation, vocabulary, and grammar. These can be viewed as separate parts of your developing linguistic knowledge, and they correspond approximately to the parts of linguistic knowledge studied by the modern field of linguistics:

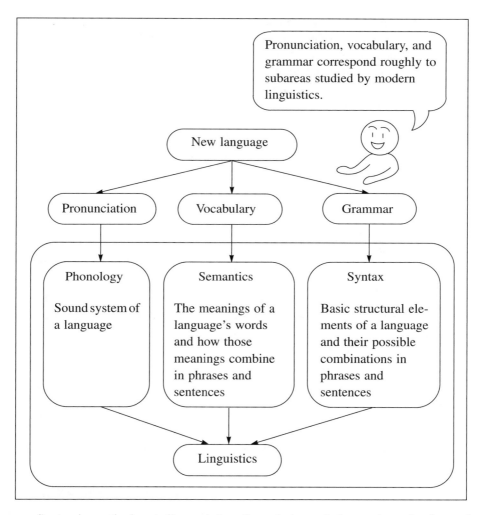

Syntax in particular studies and describes what people know about the *form* of the expressions in their language. It studies the basic grammatical patterns of language and what gives rise to them.

How do we go about describing what people know about grammatical patterns? To gain some insight into this, let's start with the broader question of how we capture patterns in any domain. We'll pursue it in relation to a question that's always close to our hearts (and stomachs): what's for dinner?

Capturing Patterns: What's for Dinner?

We're all used to eating meals on the fly these days: a quick sandwich and soda at a deli, or perhaps a fresh salad from a salad bar if we're eating healthy. In casual meals of this kind, there are few constraints on what can be eaten or the order in which it's consumed. Pretty much anything goes. However, when it comes to a real "sit-down meal"—the sort of thing you might invite a friend over to your house for—most people have definite feelings about what constitutes a proper dinner: what it can and should include, and what form it should take.

For example, depending on your nationality or cultural heritage, here are some possible meals that you might feel to be acceptable:

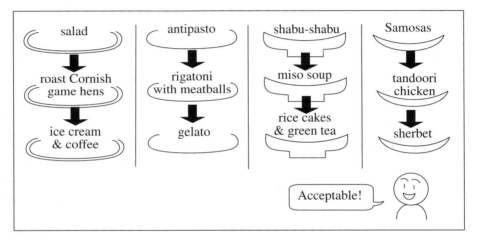

By contrast, most people would reject menus like these (marked with an asterisk "*"—sometimes called a "star" in linguistics—to indicate that they are unacceptable):

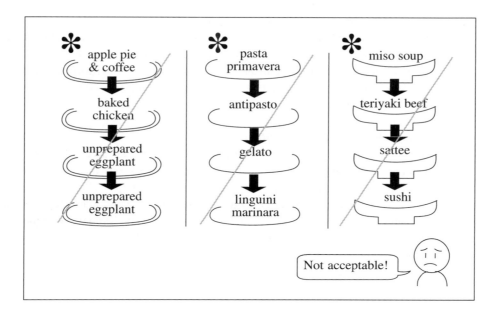

What? In What Order? In What Combinations?

Some of our intuitions about what makes an acceptable meal concern *what* we eat. For example, traditional American meals don't include unprepared vegetables of certain kinds like eggplant or parsnips. Nor do they include raw fish—fish that isn't cooked, smoked, or salted in some way.

Other intuitions about what makes an acceptable meal concern the *order* in which we eat various dishes. For example, whereas the first menu here is acceptable, the second isn't:

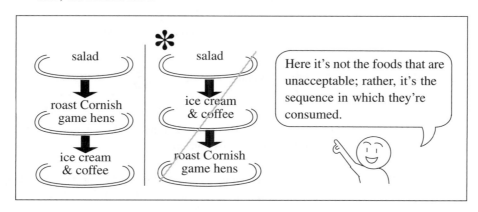

Finally, there are constraints on what *combinations* of things should appear together in a single meal. For example, while sattee, sushi, and teriyaki beef are all fine items on a Japanese menu, in Japanese culture they probably wouldn't be eaten all together in a single meal. In the same way, in American culture baked chicken and hot dogs wouldn't be eaten together—a meal would include one or the other, but not both.

Categories and Arrangements

Suppose you were asked to describe what constitutes an acceptable or "well-formed" traditional American meal—that is, to work out the pattern behind possible American dinners. How would you go about it?

One natural idea would be to divide the various foods into categories and subcategories. If you look at the suggested menus in a traditional cookbook, you will find terms like *appetizer*, *main course item*, and *dessert* (categories). The various foods (subcategories) can be classified according to these categories:

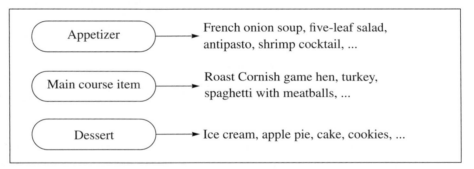

With this classification, you could then state the pattern of an acceptable American meal in terms of the arrangements of these general categories. For example, you might say that a possible dinner has the following general pattern:

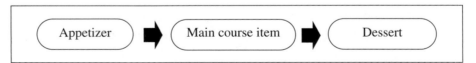

This strategy would capture what is eaten (the things in the categories), the order in which they are eaten (expressed by the order of the general categories), and the combinations.

Of course, many subtleties could come into play at this point. For example, some foods can occur in more than one category. Many main course items like shellfish can also be served as appetizers as long as the portion is small enough. You might want to classify such foods as both appetizers and main course items:

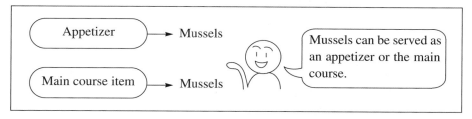

A very formal meal might include a first course or a fish course before the main course and possibly liqueur after dessert. This means that you would have to add items to the general pattern:

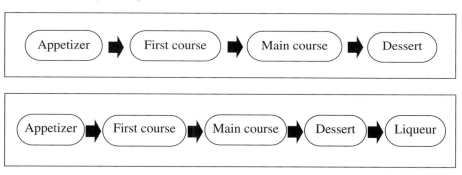

To summarize: there are numerous factors to consider in describing an American meal completely. Foods have to be cross-classified to some extent, and there is a (potentially large) number of patterns to account for. Nonetheless, the basic procedure used here appears sound and capable of being extended to these other cases without too much difficulty.

Capturing Syntactic Patterns

The example of eating patterns suggests a general strategy for capturing all patterns that hold for some collection of objects. We proceed as follows:

- Classify the objects into general categories.
- State the possible patterns that we observe as arrangements of the general categories.

Let's try applying this lesson to sentence patterns using the following simple grammatical data. The three lists contain both acceptable and unacceptable sentences; the unacceptable ones are marked with an asterisk.

I	II	III
Bart ran.	Homer chased Bart.	Homer handed Lisa Maggie.
Homer sleeps.	Bart saw Maggie.	Marge sent Bart SLH.
Maggie crawls.	Maggie petted SLH.	*Sent Marge Bart SLH.
*Ran Maggie.	*Chased Bart Homer.	*Marge Bart SLH sent.
*Crawls Homer.		

Following the strategy suggested above, we might begin by classifying the expressions in I–III into different general categories. Just as traditional cookbooks separate foods into different menu items like appetizer and main course, traditional grammar books separate the words into different **parts of speech**. Parts of speech represent general categories of words. Traditional parts of speech include categories like noun, verb, preposition, adjective, and article. For present purposes, the two traditional categories of noun and verb will suffice for dividing up all the words in I–III:

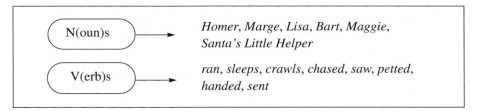

N(oun)s → *Homer, Marge, Lisa, Bart, Maggie, Santa's Little Helper*

V(erb)s → *ran, sleeps, crawls, chased, saw, petted, handed, sent*

Next, just as we analyzed acceptable patterns of meals into sequences of general categories of foods, we analyze the acceptable patterns of English sentences into sequences of our general categories of words:

Acceptable English sentences (I):   N V

Acceptable English sentences (II):   N V N

Acceptable English sentences (III):   N V N N

As in the case of meals, these rules state what can appear (the words in the categories), the order in which they appear (expressed by the order of the general categories), and their possible combinations (expressed by what's in the separate categories).

Once again, there are many additional points and subtleties. Just like some foods, certain words seem to occur in more than one category. For example, the sequence of sounds that we pronounce "saw" can appear as a noun, as in *The saw was old*, or as a verb, as in *Bart saw Maggie*. Furthermore, just as there are additional menu items and patterns beyond appetizer–main course–dessert, there are many additional categories of words (adverbs, intensifiers, conjunctions, determiners, etc.) and many patterns of categories beyond those just considered.

These don't seem to raise any problems of principle, however. As before, the basic procedure appears sound and capable of being extended to other cases. We simply introduce new words, new categories, and new patterns.

Speakers Know Patterns

The results above allow us to formulate an explicit hypothesis about what speakers know when they have systematic knowledge of some structured domain. We could hypothesize that they know **categories** and **patterns**. In the case of sentence patterns, we would be making the following conjecture:

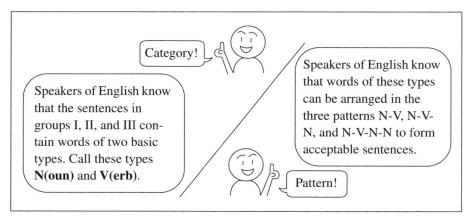

Category!

Speakers of English know that the sentences in groups I, II, and III contain words of two basic types. Call these types **N(oun)** and **V(erb)**.

Speakers of English know that words of these types can be arranged in the three patterns N-V, N-V-N, and N-V-N-N to form acceptable sentences.

Pattern!

This would be the kind of knowledge that a syntactician might reasonably attribute to speakers of English. Attributing this type of knowledge to speakers constitutes an explicit proposal about (part of) what those speakers know about the structure of their language.

Internal Structure

The hypothesis that speakers know categories and patterns entails that their knowledge of syntax is structured in a certain way. Our explanation for how English speakers are able to recognize well-formed sentences involves seeing those sentences as divided into parts that are arranged in certain definite ways. The hypothesis states that a well-formed sentence of English is composed of nouns and verbs, and it is the way these parts are arranged that determines well-formedness.

There is strong evidence that our grasp of syntax must be like this: structured out of parts. To appreciate this, recall the properties distinguishing a human's linguistic behavior from that of a talking doll:

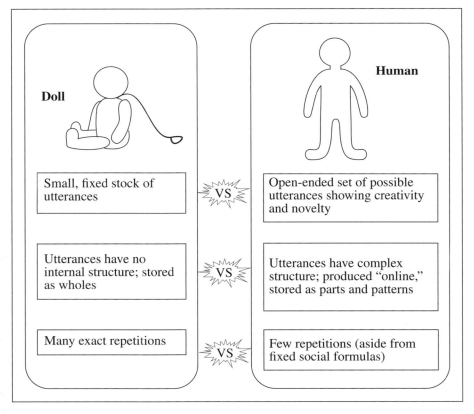

Doll

Small, fixed stock of utterances

VS

Human

Open-ended set of possible utterances showing creativity and novelty

Utterances have no internal structure; stored as wholes

VS

Utterances have complex structure; produced "online," stored as parts and patterns

Many exact repetitions

VS

Few repetitions (aside from fixed social formulas)

As we saw, a talking doll produces a small number of utterances, usually no more than ten or twelve; and each repetition of a given utterance is identical to any other (ignoring wear and tear on the doll). On this basis, we quickly concluded that the doll's linguistic mechanism must be some form of playback device, in which each utterance the doll can produce is stored as a separate unit.

Human linguistic capacities are nothing like this, however. For one thing, human linguistic competence allows us (at least in principle) to produce infinite collections of well-formed sentences. Consider, for example, this set of sentences (from Platts 1979, p. 47):

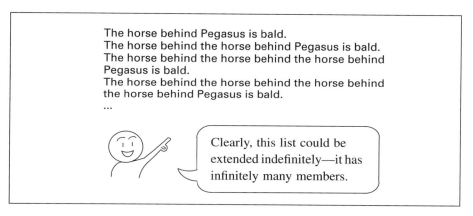

The horse behind Pegasus is bald.
The horse behind the horse behind Pegasus is bald.
The horse behind the horse behind the horse behind Pegasus is bald.
The horse behind the horse behind the horse behind the horse behind Pegasus is bald.
...

Clearly, this list could be extended indefinitely—it has infinitely many members.

Although this set of sentences is infinite, English speakers recognize that every sentence in the set is a well-formed sentence of English. Of course, our actual capacity to produce or process sentences like these is limited in certain ways. When the sentences get too long, we can't get our minds around them: we forget how they began, or we get distracted, or we simply lose track. Consequently, we can't show our mastery of them in the usual ways. But it seems that these limitations reflect constraints on such things as memory and attention span and have little to do with specifically linguistic abilities. If we had unlimited attention spans, life spans, memories, and so on, we would presumably be able to produce all the sentences in the set.

The infinite size of such collections shows that unlike the doll's mechanism, our minds don't simply store the sentences that we produce and understand as separate units. Our brains are finite objects with finite storage capacity. One simply cannot get an infinite object into a finite brain. On the other hand, if sentences are structured, and built up out of smaller parts, then our ability to produce an infinite number of sentences can be explained. Suppose we know a basic stock of words and a basic stock of patterns for combining them. Suppose further that we are able to reuse patterns in the process of constructing of a sentence. Then this will be enough to produce an infinite set:

The horse behind	Pegasus is bald.
Art N P	N

The horse behind	the horse behind	Pegasus is bald.
Art N P	Art N P	N

The horse behind	the horse behind	the horse behind	Pegasus is bald.
Art N P	Art N P	Art N P	N

Notice that our infinite collection of Pegasus sentences involves reusing the Art-N-P pattern!

By drawing on this pattern over and over again, we are able to construct sentences of greater and greater length—indeed, of potentially any length. Again, all of this points to the central importance of categories and patterns—parts and structures—in a sentence.

EXERCISES

1. Give four important properties that distinguish human linguistic abilities from those of a talking doll like Chatty Cathy® or Teddy Ruxpin®.

2. Human knowledge of language shows four key properties. What are they?

3. What is our strategy for capturing the syntactic patterns that hold across the sentences of a language?

4. State the categories found in sentences (1)–(4) and the pattern(s) of combining these categories:

    (1)   Homer came home tired.

    (2)   Homer heard Maggie clearly.

    (3)   Lisa picked Maggie up.

    (4)   Marge thinks Bart chased Lisa.

5. The following set of sentences is potentially infinite, making use of a recurring pattern. What is the pattern?

    (1)   Bart laughed.
          Bart laughed and-then Bart laughed again.
          Bart laughed and-then Bart laughed again and-then Bart laughed again.
          Bart laughed and-then Bart laughed again and-then Bart laughed again and-then Bart laughed again.
          . . .

6. The following examples are from Japanese. Assume that the Japanese parts of speech are the same as the parts of speech of the English gloss. What is the pattern? (Note: The little particles *-ga*, *-o*, and *-ni* are used in Japanese to indicate a word's status as a subject, direct object, or indirect object, respectively.)

    (1)   Taroo-ga   Pochi-o   mita.
          Taroo-NOM Pochi-ACC saw
          'Taroo saw Pochi.'

    (2)   Taroo-ga   Hanako-ni   Pochi-o   ageta.
          Taroo-NOM Hanako-DAT Pochi-ACC gave
          'Taroo gave Pochi to Hanako.'

PART II Grammars as Theories

It's time for our first "map check"—a stop to consider where we are in the larger landscape, and what to look for in the landscape ahead.

The urge toward science typically starts with **phenomena that raise questions**. We observe something that surprises us and makes us curious. We want to know more. We start asking questions. The phenomena that surprise us needn't be exotic or technical—things found only in laboratories or observed with complex apparatus. The everyday world presents us with many puzzles.

It is important to learn to be surprised by simple things. ... The beginning of a science is the recognition that the simplest phenomena of ordinary life raise quite serious problems: Why are they as they are, instead of some different way?
—*Language and Problems of Knowledge*, p. 43

Human language is like this. Language is something that surrounds us and that we take for granted in daily life. But as we have seen, when we reflect carefully on our knowledge of language and pose even the most basic questions about it, we become surprised and puzzled!

- What do we know when we know a language?
- How did we come to know it?
- How do we use that knowledge?

A certain intellectual effort is required to see how such phenomena can pose serious problems or call for intricate explanatory theories. One is inclined to take them for granted as necessary or somehow "natural."
—*Language and Mind*, p. 24

Surprises, puzzles, and questions unsettle us. They capture our attention and occupy our thoughts. They press us to **construct a theory** (or story) about what is going on—one that will solve the puzzles, answer the questions, and put our minds at rest. Science does not end with theory construction, however. A hallmark of science is its drive to **test theory against experience**.

A scientist, whether theorist or experimenter, puts forward statements, or systems of statements, and tests them step by step. In the field of the empirical sciences ... [the scientist] constructs hypotheses, or systems of theories, and tests them against experience by observation and experiment.
—*The Logic of Scientific Discovery*, p. 27

Sir Karl Popper
1904–1994

Theories that survive repeated testing (what Popper called the "clash with reality") are theories in which we gain increasing confidence.

These points chart the general path ahead for us. We have identified some puzzling and intriguing questions about our knowledge of language. Our task now is to begin constructing a theory that will address these questions and illuminate the phenomena that raise them. Furthermore, we must find ways of testing our theory against experience, to see whether it's correct. Indeed, we have already begun this process. Our initial observations of human language have already ruled out a theory in which it consists of a store of complete sentences, like the talking doll's "language."

A natural starting point is one of the questions raised earlier: exactly what do we know when we know the syntax of our language? To anticipate slightly, this part of the book will develop the idea that **people know a grammar**, conceived of as a set of rules and principles. In this view, **a grammar constitutes a scientific theory about (a part of) human linguistic knowledge**. The general questions confronting us will therefore include these:

- How do we systematically construct a grammar?
- How do we test it?
- How and when do we revise and extend it, in response to our tests?

To aid their investigations, scientific researchers often construct tools (physical or conceptual) to make inquiry easier, more efficient, or more precise. In the next unit, we will look at some basic tools that will assist us in grammar building.

Introducing Phrase Structure Rules

Review

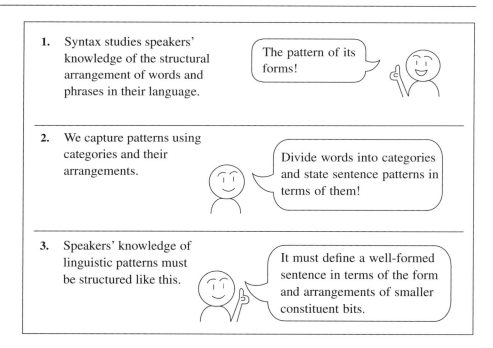

1. Syntax studies speakers' knowledge of the structural arrangement of words and phrases in their language.

   The pattern of its forms!

2. We capture patterns using categories and their arrangements.

   Divide words into categories and state sentence patterns in terms of them!

3. Speakers' knowledge of linguistic patterns must be structured like this.

   It must define a well-formed sentence in terms of the form and arrangements of smaller constituent bits.

Generating Sentences

So far we've described syntactic patterns by writing out statements like "N V N is an acceptable pattern for a sentence of English." Let's now start using some simple notation for this purpose. We will adopt the arrow notation on the left-hand side below as a shorthand way of saying what is written out on the right-hand side:

Notation	English prose
N → *Homer*	"*Homer* is a noun."
N → *Marge*	"*Marge* is a noun."
N → *Lisa*	"*Lisa* is a noun."
N → *Bart*	"*Bart* is a noun."
N → *Maggie*	"*Maggie* is a noun."
N → *Santa's Little Helper*	"*Santa's Little Helper* is a noun."
V → *ran*	"*Ran* is a verb."
V → *sleeps*	"*Sleeps* is a verb."
V → *crawls*	"*Crawls* is a verb."
V → *chased*	"*Chased* is a verb."
V → *saw*	"*Saw* is a verb."
V → *petted*	"*Petted* is a verb."
V → *handed*	"*Handed* is a verb."
V → *sent*	"*Sent* is a verb."
S → N V	"A noun followed by a verb is a sentence (of English)."
S → N V N	"A noun followed by a verb followed by a noun is a sentence (of English)."
S → N V N N	"A noun followed by a verb followed by a noun followed by another noun is a sentence (of English)."

One virtue of this arrow notation is brevity. It's a lot quicker to write "S → N V N N" than it is to write out "A noun followed by a verb followed by a noun followed by another noun is a sentence (of English)."

Patterns as Rules

Another virtue of the arrow notation is that it suggests a kind of "recipe" or procedure for constructing English sentences. That is, we can view the statements above as rules that can be followed to construct well-formed English clauses.

Consider the following procedure:

1. Write down the symbol "S". Interpret a statement "X → Y Z" as an instruction to replace or rewrite the symbol X with the symbol Y followed by the symbol Z.

2. Whenever you have two or more rules for rewriting the same symbol, choose freely among them.

With this procedure, we can use our rules to produce a large number of well-formed English sentences by a series of rewritings:

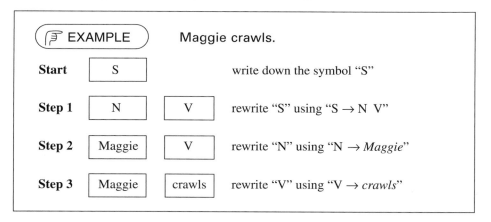

☞ EXAMPLE   Maggie crawls.

Start	S		write down the symbol "S"
Step 1	N	V	rewrite "S" using "S → N V"
Step 2	Maggie	V	rewrite "N" using "N → *Maggie*"
Step 3	Maggie	crawls	rewrite "V" using "V → *crawls*"

☞ EXAMPLE   Homer chased Bart.

Start	S			write down the symbol "S"
Step 1	N	V	N	rewrite "S" using "S → N V N"
Step 2	Homer	V	N	rewrite "N" using "N → *Homer*"
Step 3	Homer	chased	N	rewrite "V" using "V → *chased*"
Step 4	Homer	chased	Bart	rewrite "N" using "N → *Bart*"

The end product in each case is a well-formed English sentence. The rules furnish a procedure for generating English sentences: a **generative procedure**.

Phrase Structure Rules

Rules of the kind given above are called **(context-free) phrase structure rules** (or **PS rules** for short). They have the general form shown below:

$$X \rightarrow Y1 \ Y2 \ Y3 \dots Yn$$

The mother   The daughters

This says that the single symbol X can be rewritten as the string of symbols Y1 Y2 Y3 ... Yn. Since the symbol X is understood as giving rise to the symbols Y1 Y2 Y3 ... Yn, the former is sometimes spoken of as the **mother** of the latter; alternatively, the latter are spoken of as the **daughters** of the former.

The phrase structure rules listed above can be divided into two basic kinds:

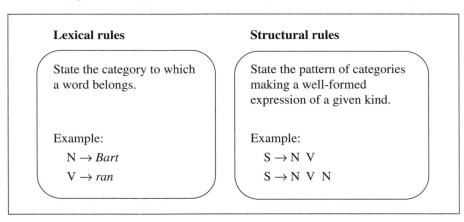

Lexical rules

State the category to which a word belongs.

Example:

N → *Bart*

V → *ran*

Structural rules

State the pattern of categories making a well-formed expression of a given kind.

Example:

S → N V

S → N V N

Tree Diagrams and Derivations

We have seen that the generative procedure yields a derivation like this for *Maggie crawls*:

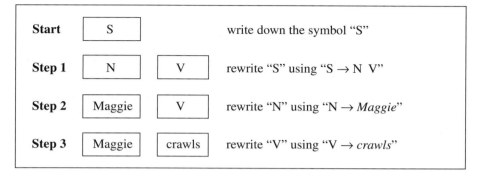

Notice that in deriving this sentence we could have applied our rules in a different order:

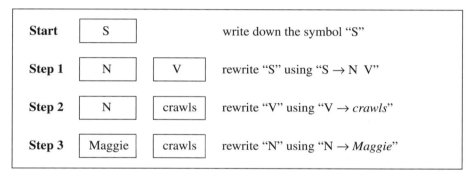

If you think about it, you'll see that any set of rules will produce a **family of derivations** that differ by applying the rules in different orders. Thus, *Maggie crawls* has two different derivations under our rules. *Homer chased Bart* has nine different derivations. And so on.

Generating Tree Diagrams

There is a useful way of abbreviating the derivations for a sentence produced under a set of rules: with a **phrase marker** or **tree diagram**. Suppose we do this:

1. Write down the symbol S.
2. Pick any rule that can be used to rewrite S (any rule of the form "S → ...").
3. Write the symbols that appear on the right-hand side of the rule beneath S and connect them to S by lines.
4. Repeat the procedure with the symbols that now appear beneath S (that is, pick a rule that can be used to rewrite them; write the symbols occurring on the right-hand side of their rules beneath them and connect with lines).
5. Continue this way until no more symbols can be added.

The result is a tree diagram with S at the top, with branches in the middle, and with words at the bottom.

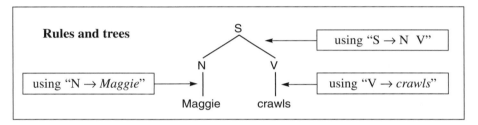

The string of words at the bottom of the tree is the sentence that we are trying to generate. It is sometimes called the **terminal string** of the tree.

Tree diagrams display how a grammar generates a given sentence like *Maggie crawls*, ignoring the order in which the rules are applied. A tree diagram therefore abbreviates the family of alternative derivations that differ only in order of rule application.

Some Terminology

We will be using tree diagrams a great deal in the units that follow, so it is useful to have some terminology for talking about them. The points in a tree that are labeled by categories like S, N, and V or words like *Homer* and *Lisa* are called the **nodes** of the tree. The lines that connect nodes are called the **branches** of the tree. The single node at the top is called the **root node** of the tree. And the nodes at the very ends of the branches—the words—are called the **terminal nodes** or **leaf nodes** of the tree.

We also need terminology for talking about a given node in relation to other nodes in a tree. The node that appears immediately above a given node is its **mother node**. The nodes that appear immediately below a given node are its

daughter nodes. As in real genealogical trees, a node can have at most one mother, but it can have more than one daughter. Two nodes that have the same mother—two daughters of the same mother—are called **sister nodes**:

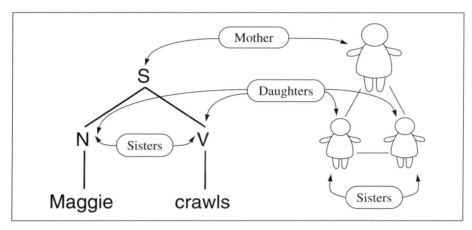

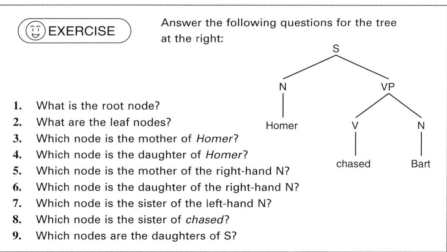

EXERCISE   Answer the following questions for the tree at the right:

1. What is the root node?
2. What are the leaf nodes?
3. Which node is the mother of *Homer*?
4. Which node is the daughter of *Homer*?
5. Which node is the mother of the right-hand N?
6. Which node is the daughter of the right-hand N?
7. Which node is the sister of the left-hand N?
8. Which node is the sister of *chased*?
9. Which nodes are the daughters of S?

Tree Diagrams and Rules

There is a close correspondence between trees and the rules that are used to produce them. If you are given a set of rules and a tree, it's easy to determine whether the rules generate the tree. Likewise, if you are given a tree, you can easily determine a set of rules that would generate it.

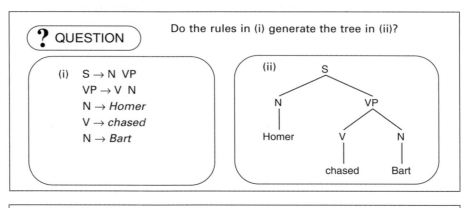

? QUESTION   Do the rules in (i) generate the tree in (ii)?

(i) S → N VP
     VP → V N
     N → *Homer*
     V → *chased*
     N → *Bart*

(ii)

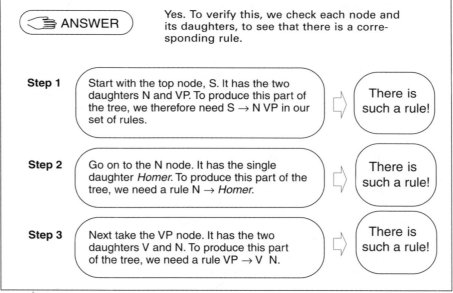

ANSWER   Yes. To verify this, we check each node and its daughters, to see that there is a corresponding rule.

Step 1 Start with the top node, S. It has the two daughters N and VP. To produce this part of the tree, we therefore need S → N VP in our set of rules.   ⇨ There is such a rule!

Step 2 Go on to the N node. It has the single daughter *Homer*. To produce this part of the tree, we need a rule N → *Homer*.   ⇨ There is such a rule!

Step 3 Next take the VP node. It has the two daughters V and N. To produce this part of the tree, we need a rule VP → V N.   ⇨ There is such a rule!

Applying this reasoning to the remaining two nodes, you'll see that they check out too. Since every mother-daughter part of the tree corresponds to a rule in the list, the tree can be generated by the list.

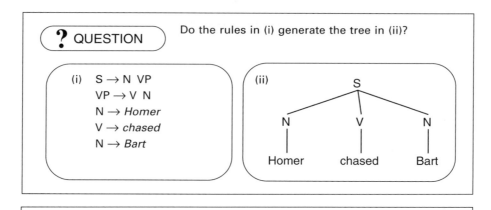

? QUESTION   Do the rules in (i) generate the tree in (ii)?

(i) S → N VP
     VP → V N
     N → *Homer*
     V → *chased*
     N → *Bart*

(ii)

ANSWER   No! Which mother-daughter parts of the tree fail to correspond to rules in the list?

Syntactic Ambiguity

We've seen that sentences can have more than one derivation under a given set of rules if we simply apply the rules in different orders. This is not the only way for multiple derivations to arise, however. Consider the following set of rules and the sentence beside it:

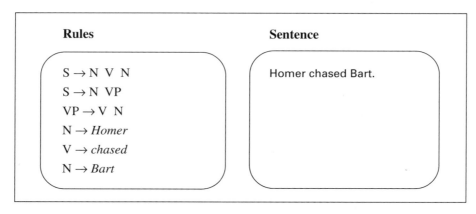

Rules

S → N V N
S → N VP
VP → V N
N → *Homer*
V → *chased*
N → *Bart*

Sentence

Homer chased Bart.

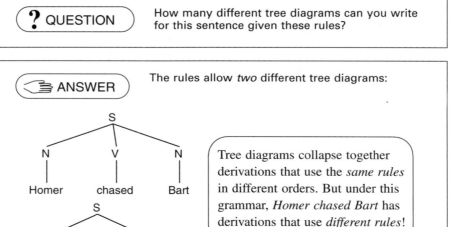

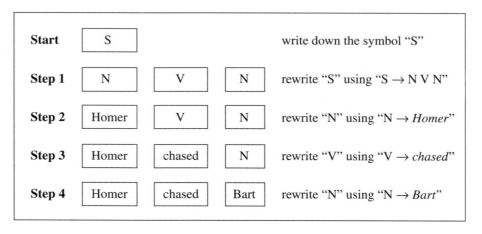

There is a (family of) derivation(s) in which we use the rule S → N V N to rewrite the S symbol:

Start	S			write down the symbol "S"
Step 1	N	V	N	rewrite "S" using "S → N V N"
Step 2	Homer	V	N	rewrite "N" using "N → *Homer*"
Step 3	Homer	chased	N	rewrite "V" using "V → *chased*"
Step 4	Homer	chased	Bart	rewrite "N" using "N → *Bart*"

But there is also another (family of) derivation(s) in which we use the rules S →
N VP and VP → V N:

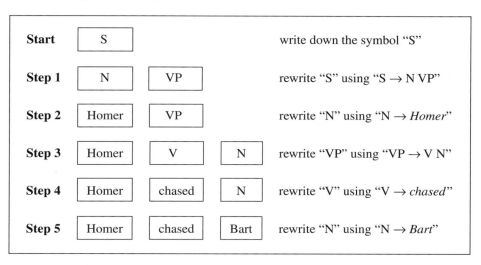

Start	S			write down the symbol "S"
Step 1	N	VP		rewrite "S" using "S → N VP"
Step 2	Homer	VP		rewrite "N" using "N → *Homer*"
Step 3	Homer	V	N	rewrite "VP" using "VP → V N"
Step 4	Homer	chased	N	rewrite "V" using "V → *chased*"
Step 5	Homer	chased	Bart	rewrite "N" using "N → *Bart*"

These two different (families of) derivations correspond to two different tree
diagrams because they use different rules. Specifically, the rule set contains two
different ways of rewriting the category S, both of which result in the same string
of words. We will see in Unit 6 that when we have different rules or rule sets that
generate the same sentences, we must find ways to decide which rule system
represents the best theory.

Sentences that have more than one tree diagram under a given set of rules
are said to be **syntactically ambiguous**: the grammar provides more than one
way of generating them. Syntactic ambiguity, having more than one tree, is
different from **semantic ambiguity**, having more than one meaning. As we will
see later on, sentences with more than one tree often do have more than one
meaning, but this isn't always true.

Grammars

Review

1. Syntax studies what speakers know about the structural arrangement of words and phrases in their language.

   The pattern of its forms.

2. Speakers' knowledge of syntax allows them to ...

   Construct phrases and sentences out of smaller parts.

3. Phrase structure (PS) rules provide a way of generating sentences. These rules introduce words and tell how those words combine in well-formed strings.

   Lexical rules and structural rules.

4. PS rule derivations are conveniently represented with ...

   Tree diagrams!

Grammars as Theories

Suppose we have some expressions from a language—a collection of phrases, sentences, and so on. Any set of rules that generates those expressions is called a **grammar** for those expressions.

These sentences were given in Unit 2:

Bart ran.
Homer sleeps.
Maggie crawls.
Homer chased Bart.
Bart saw Maggie.
Maggie petted SLH.
Homer handed Lisa Maggie.
Marge sent Bart SLH.

This set of rules is a grammar for the sentences:

S → N V	V → *ran*
S → N V N	V → *sleeps*
S → N V N N	V → *crawls*
	V → *chased*
N → *Homer*	V → *saw*
N → *Marge*	V → *petted*
N → *Lisa*	V → *sent*
N → *Bart*	V → *handed*
N → *Maggie*	
N → *Santa's Little Helper*	

When the set of expressions generated by some rules includes all of the expressions of a language, we'll call the rules a **grammar for the language**.

People Know Grammars

The notion of a grammar provides a natural guiding hypothesis about what people know about the syntax of their own language.

> Guiding hypothesis   What humans internalize in the course of acquiring their native language is a grammar—a set of rules.

Under this proposal, the grammars that we write down become scientific theories of people's (tacit) syntactic knowledge—candidate solutions to our "black box problem." As such, they become something to be tested, corrected, refined, and extended, just like any other scientific theory:

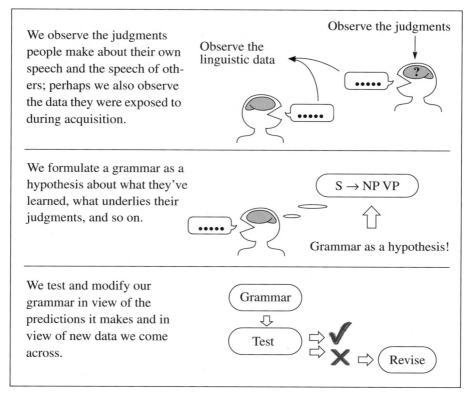

We observe the judgments people make about their own speech and the speech of others; perhaps we also observe the data they were exposed to during acquisition.

Observe the linguistic data

Observe the judgments

We formulate a grammar as a hypothesis about what they've learned, what underlies their judgments, and so on.

S → NP VP

Grammar as a hypothesis!

We test and modify our grammar in view of the predictions it makes and in view of new data we come across.

Grammar

Test

Revise

We'll look at the third step more closely in the next unit. For the moment, let's look at the first two steps in more detail.

The Data of Syntax

Your knowledge of your native language gives you the ability to judge whether certain strings of words in that language are or are not sentences of the language. Linguists use such well-formedness judgments as a data source in constructing a theory of what speakers know. Native speaker intuitions and judgments are in fact a primary source of data in linguistics.

Judging Well-Formedness Is Not Simple!

Judging well-formedness may seem an easy thing. To determine whether the rule for English sentences is S → N V or S → V N, we just speak sentences with these patterns and listen to whether they sound good or not. What could be simpler? In fact, matters are not so direct.

Well-Formed ≠ Sensible or Natural

Judging whether a sentence of English (or any other language) is well-formed is not the same thing as judging whether it "makes sense" or whether it could ever be used naturally in conversation. Consider examples (1) and (2), due to Chomsky (1957, p. 15):

> (1)   Colorless green ideas sleep furiously.
> (2)   Revolutionary new ideas happen infrequently.

(1) is clearly nonsensical. We don't know what it would be like for an idea to be green, never mind for it to be both green and colorless. Likewise, we don't know what it would mean for ideas to sleep, never mind to sleep furiously. Nonetheless, even though (1) is nonsensical, we recognize it as following an English pattern. (1) has the same grammatical pattern as (2), which is a fully sensible and meaningful sentence of English. In this respect, (1) and (2) contrast sharply with (3), which is not a sentence of English at all:

> (3)   Colorless sleep furiously ideas green.

The pattern that we are detecting in (1) and (2) is clearly something independent of what those sentences say or express. It concerns the pure form of these sentences. English speakers know that (1) and (2) share a common formal pattern and that it is a possible pattern for English sentences.

Well-Formed ≠ Proper or Educated

Judging whether a sentence of English (or any other language) is well-formed is also not the same thing as judging whether the sentence sounds "proper" or "correct." Consider the pairs in (4)–(6):

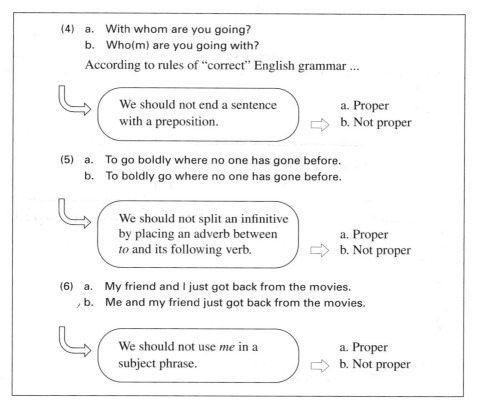

(4) a. With whom are you going?

    b. Who(m) are you going with?

According to rules of "correct" English grammar ...

> We should not end a sentence with a preposition.

a. Proper

b. Not proper

(5) a. To go boldly where no one has gone before.

    b. To boldly go where no one has gone before.

> We should not split an infinitive by placing an adverb between *to* and its following verb.

a. Proper

b. Not proper

(6) a. My friend and I just got back from the movies.

    b. Me and my friend just got back from the movies.

> We should not use *me* in a subject phrase.

a. Proper

b. Not proper

Even though they may have been taught in school that the patterns in (4b), (5b), and (6b) are "improper" or "incorrect," many English speakers nonetheless follow these patterns, and understand others who follow them as well. Proper or not, these patterns are part of these speakers' internal grammar; their linguistic production and comprehension draws on them. As linguists, we are interested in the linguistic patterns that are actually in people's minds, not in the patterns they are "supposed" to follow but may not. Accordingly, the judgments we are interested in are the ones reflecting the language that people actually speak, not ones reflecting some variant that may be regarded as proper or educated. That is, we are interested in describing the linguistic patterns that speakers actually know, the ones they follow in their own speech. We are not interested in externally prescribed patterns: canons of good English, good French, good Hindi, and so on, that individuals may be aware of and may have been taught in school, but do not really follow. So, again, when we ask others or ourselves whether a given expression is well-formed, we are not asking whether it is grammatically "proper" or "correct."

Ungrammatical versus Unacceptable

To simplify our discussion, let's adopt a useful terminological distinction. When a speaker rejects a given sentence *for whatever reason*, we'll say that she judges the sentence to be **unacceptable.** When a speaker rejects a sentence because its structural pattern fails to conform to one from her internalized grammar, we'll say that she judges it to be **ungrammatical** or **ill-formed**. Evidently, determining whether a sentence is ungrammatical/ill-formed is much trickier than determining whether it's unacceptable. In the case of unacceptability, we simply ask the speaker whether a sentence is good or not. In the case of ungrammaticality, we must find out whether the unacceptability arises from a particular source. Sentences can be unacceptable for many reasons. Ungrammaticality is a narrower concept.

like not sensible, not proper, etc.

> A sentence rejected by a speaker for whatever reason ...
>
> Unacceptable.

> A sentence rejected by a speaker because its structural pattern fails to conform to one from her internalized grammar ...
>
> Ungrammatical!

Covering the Data

When we go about formulating a grammar, we begin with the judgments that people make about their own speech and about the speech of others. An initial data set might be a list of sentences marked with well-formedness judgments. We looked at a collection of sentences like this in Units 2 and 3. The sentences without stars (asterisks) are ones that English speakers would judge to be grammatical, or **well-formed**. The ones with asterisks are ones that English speakers would judge to be ungrammatical, or **ill-formed**.

N V	N V N	N V N N
I	II	III
Bart ran.	Homer chased Bart.	Homer handed Lisa Maggie.
Homer sleeps.	Bart saw Maggie.	Marge sent Bart SLH.
Maggie crawls.	Maggie petted SLH.	*Sent Marge Bart SLH.
*Ran Maggie.	*Chased Bart Homer.	*Marge Bart SLH sent.
*Crawls Homer.		

We next formulated a set of rules that generate the unstarred sentences:

$S \rightarrow N\ V$ $V \rightarrow ran$
$S \rightarrow N\ V\ N$ $V \rightarrow sleeps$
$S \rightarrow N\ V\ N\ N$ $V \rightarrow crawls$
            $V \rightarrow chased$
$N \rightarrow Homer$ $V \rightarrow saw$
$N \rightarrow Marge$ $V \rightarrow petted$
$N \rightarrow Lisa$ $V \rightarrow sent$
$N \rightarrow Bart$ $V \rightarrow handed$
$N \rightarrow Maggie$
$N \rightarrow Santa's\ Little\ Helper$

Judgments of grammaticality are data. But so are judgments of ungrammaticality. Our theory must cover both!

Notice that although we concentrated on the unstarred sentences, in the sense that those were the ones we aimed at generating, the starred sentences are really just as important. Judgments of grammaticality/well-formedness are data. But so are judgments of ungrammaticality/ill-formedness. Our theory must cover both!

What does that mean, exactly? In what sense can rules cover or account for sentences that aren't grammatical?

In saying that a speaker has internalized a set of syntactic rules, we're claiming that those are the rules the speaker draws on in judging well-formedness and ill-formedness. We're saying that those rules account for the judgments. Accordingly, when we attribute a set of rules to a person, we expect that the person will judge sentences generated by the rules to be well-formed and sentences not generated by the rules to be ill-formed.

Sentences generated by the rules will be judged by the person to be well-formed.

AND

Sentences not generated by the rules will be judged by the person to be ill-formed.

Both kinds of data are relevant and important. Both represent *facts* that we must account for in constructing our theory.

Formulating a Grammar

So far our grammars have been very simple, consisting of just two basic kinds of PS rules:

——— **Lexical rules** ———

Classify particular words into specific grammatical categories (N, V, etc.).

——— **Structural rules** ———

State possible arrangements of grammatical categories in a language.

This means that when we are formulating a grammar (or revising one), these are the two kinds of rules we have to think about.

We add lexical rules to increase the stock of words in our theory.

We add structural rules to increase the stock of structural patterns.

When we must introduce both new words and new patterns, we add both kinds of rules.

Building Systematically

When you are trying to formulate a grammar, or any other scientific theory for that matter, there are always a number of ways to proceed. For example, you might simply eyeball a collection of data like this and write down all of the necessary rules in one go:

I	II	III
Bart ran.	Homer chased Bart.	Homer handed Lisa Maggie.
Homer sleeps.	Bart saw Maggie.	Marge sent Bart SLH.
Maggie crawls.	Maggie petted SLH.	*Sent Marge Bart SLH.
*Ran Maggie.	*Chased Bart Homer.	*Marge Bart SLH sent.
*Crawls Homer.		

While this may be reasonable when you are dealing with a few simple pieces of data, it is often useful to follow a more systematic strategy. Here is one "cookbook" recipe for building a grammar:

1. Start with a single piece of data.

2. Build enough of a grammar to account for that one piece of data.

3. Extend your grammar by adding just enough rules to account for the next piece of data.

4. Check to see that your new grammar also accounts for all previous data.

5. Repeat, starting from Step 3.

Notice that when your piece of data is that a certain expression is ill-formed, what you check (then and subsequently) is that your rules *don't* generate this expression!

The idea behind this procedure is simple and obvious. You start with a grammar that covers one fact. You then extend it step by step, always checking to see that, when you add new rules, you haven't lost the ability to generate any well-formed sentences considered previously, and you haven't gained the ability to generate any ill-formed sentences considered previously. This procedure keeps everything under control for you. You build the grammar systematically. For example:

☞ **EXAMPLE**   Let us apply this procedure to the data in I, II, and III.

First sentence: Grammar needed
`Bart ran.`   to generate it:

$$S \rightarrow N\ V$$
$$N \rightarrow Bart$$
$$V \rightarrow ran$$

Second sentence: Extend grammar:
`Homer sleeps.`

$$S \rightarrow N\ V$$
$$N \rightarrow Bart$$
$$N \rightarrow Homer$$
$$V \rightarrow ran$$
$$V \rightarrow sleeps$$

⇨ Check that *Bart ran*
   is still generated:

   ⇩

   Yes, it is!

Third sentence: Extend grammar:
`Maggie crawls.`

$$S \rightarrow N\ V$$
$$N \rightarrow Bart$$
$$N \rightarrow Homer$$
$$N \rightarrow Maggie$$
$$V \rightarrow ran$$
$$V \rightarrow sleeps$$
$$V \rightarrow crawls$$

⇨ Check that *Bart ran*
   and *Homer sleeps*
   are still generated:

   ⇩

   Yes, they are!

Fourth sentence: The same grammar:
`*Ran Maggie.`

....

⇨ Check that *Ran
   Maggie* isn't generated
   by the grammar:

   ⇩

   No, it isn't!

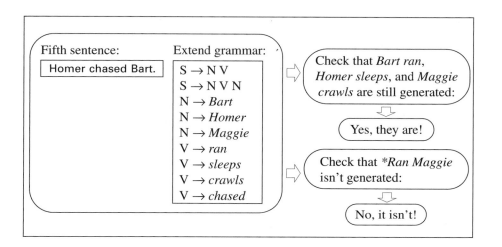

Fifth sentence:

| Homer chased Bart. |

Extend grammar:

S → N V
S → N V N
N → *Bart*
N → *Homer*
N → *Maggie*
V → *ran*
V → *sleeps*
V → *crawls*
V → *chased*

Check that *Bart ran*, *Homer sleeps*, and *Maggie crawls* are still generated:

Yes, they are!

Check that **Ran Maggie* isn't generated:

No, it isn't!

Working with Grammars

Review

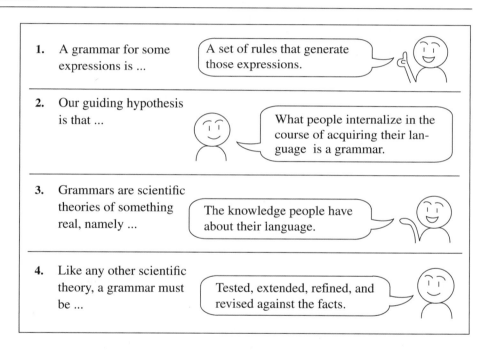

1. A grammar for some expressions is ...

   A set of rules that generate those expressions.

2. Our guiding hypothesis is that ...

   What people internalize in the course of acquiring their language is a grammar.

3. Grammars are scientific theories of something real, namely ...

   The knowledge people have about their language.

4. Like any other scientific theory, a grammar must be ...

   Tested, extended, refined, and revised against the facts.

Testing a Grammar

Testing a grammar is partly a matter of checking whether its rules generate the expressions you want and don't generate the ones you don't want. For example, suppose we've collected the following data from some individual, Jones:

Data Set 1

Bart ran.	Homer chased Bart.	Homer handed Lisa Maggie.
Homer sleeps.	Bart saw Maggie.	Marge sent Bart SLH.
Maggie crawls.	Maggie petted SLH.	*Sent Marge Bart SLH.
*Ran Maggie.	*Chased Bart Homer.	*Marge Bart SLH sent.
*Crawls Homer.		

Suppose further that we come up with the following grammar:

Grammar A

S → N V	N → *Homer*	V → *ran*
S → N V N	N → *Marge*	V → *sleeps*
S → N V N N	N → *Lisa*	V → *crawls*
	N → *Bart*	V → *chased*
	N → *Maggie*	V → *saw*
	N → *Santa's Little Helper*	V → *petted*
		V → *sent*
		V → *handed*

Part of testing Grammar A will be to check whether its rules generate all the unstarred sentences and none of the starred ones. We do this by attempting derivations for each sentence.

This is not the end of it, however. Notice that Grammar A generates sentences beyond those listed in Data Set 1. It also generates all of the expressions in Data Set 2:

Data Set 2

Homer ran.	Bart chased Lisa.
Bart sleeps.	Marge handed Lisa Maggie.
Lisa crawls.	

These sentences are relevant to our testing, too! In claiming that Jones knows Grammar A, we are making the following predictions:

- Sentences generated by Grammar A will be judged to be well-formed by Jones.

- Sentences not generated by Grammar A will be judged to be ill-formed by Jones.

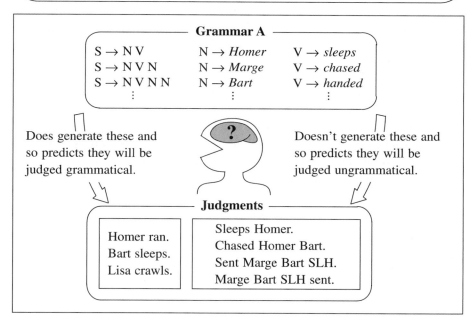

Thus, well-formedness and ill-formedness judgments become **predictions** of the theory. Given that Grammar A generates the additional sentences, we predict that they too will be judged to be well-formed by Jones, even though they go beyond our original data set. They are additional data on which we must test our theory. So the situation is this:

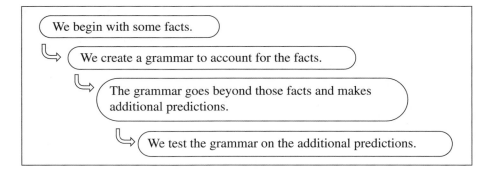

Revising a Grammar

When we test our grammar against additional data, there is of course no guarantee that it will predict correctly. It may well be that the grammar generates sentences that are judged ill-formed by the speaker whose grammar we are trying to model. In this case, we say that our grammar is **incorrect**, or that it **mispredicts** the data.

When a grammar is incorrect, we must **revise** it so as to avoid generating expressions we don't want. Consider Data Set 3 and check whether Grammar A generates these sentences:

Data Set 3

*Bart crawls Maggie.   *Homer ran Bart.
*Maggie sleeps Bart.   *Maggie handed.

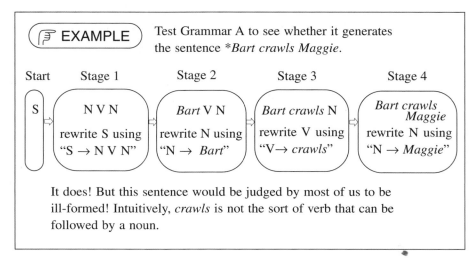

☞ EXAMPLE   Test Grammar A to see whether it generates the sentence *Bart crawls Maggie.*

Start	Stage 1	Stage 2	Stage 3	Stage 4
S	N V N	*Bart* V N	*Bart crawls* N	*Bart crawls Maggie*
	rewrite S using "S → N V N"	rewrite N using "N → *Bart*"	rewrite V using "V→ *crawls*"	rewrite N using "N → *Maggie*"

It does! But this sentence would be judged by most of us to be ill-formed! Intuitively, *crawls* is not the sort of verb that can be followed by a noun.

Given this result, we must refine Grammar A so that it does not generate this undesirable example (and others like it). How should we do this?

One idea might be to distinguish among types of verbs. That is, we might divide our verbs into two different kinds and assign them to different categories. There would be verbs like *crawls*, which don't take a following noun, and verbs like *saw*, which do take a following noun. Let's call verbs like *crawls* **intransitive verbs** and assign them to their own category Vi. (We'll talk about verbs like *handed* in the next unit.) So we change our lexical rules for intransitive verbs as follows:

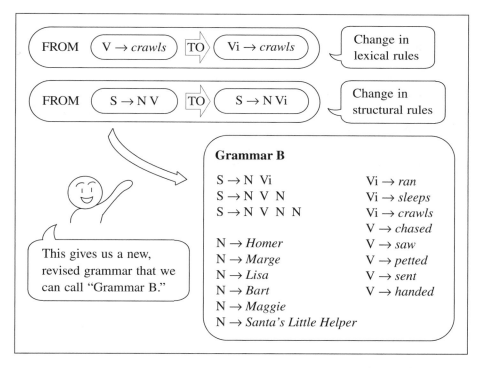

FROM (V → *crawls*) TO⟩ (Vi → *crawls*) — Change in lexical rules

FROM (S → N V) TO⟩ (S → N Vi) — Change in structural rules

This gives us a new, revised grammar that we can call "Grammar B."

Grammar B

S → N Vi   Vi → *ran*
S → N V N   Vi → *sleeps*
S → N V N N   Vi → *crawls*
                                 V → *chased*
N → *Homer*   V → *saw*
N → *Marge*   V → *petted*
N → *Lisa*   V → *sent*
N → *Bart*   V → *handed*
N → *Maggie*
N → *Santa's Little Helper*

If you check, you will see that *Bart crawls Maggie is no longer generated. We have revised Grammar A so that it no longer mispredicts the data in question.

A Note on Checking Predictions

Remember that when you are checking predictions with speakers, you always have to be careful in evaluating their judgments. Remember that *ill-formed* is different from *senseless*, *unnatural*, *incorrect*, or *improper*. To use terms from Unit 4, *ungrammatical* is different from *unacceptable*. If you present a sentence to someone and he objects to it, saying, "That sentence sounds bad," you must be sure about what exactly he is objecting to. Is it the content of the sentence? Its naturalness? Its usefulness? Its status as "proper" English? Its structural form? Only the last constitutes a judgment of ungrammaticality. If the speaker rejects a sentence simply on the grounds that it's "improper," you may not want to classify it as ungrammatical.

Extending a Grammar

We've seen that a grammar may produce expressions that we don't want. It may predict expressions to be well-formed that are actually ill-formed. In this case, the grammar is incorrect. A grammar may also fail to generate sentences that we do want. It may fail to predict expressions to be well-formed that are in fact well-formed. In this second case, we say the grammar is **incomplete** or **fails to cover the data adequately**.

When a theory is incomplete, we must **extend** it to generate the expressions that we want. Both Grammars A and B are radically incomplete: they produce only a minuscule part of the full range of English sentences. To develop a grammar that covers anything like the real range, we would have to extend Grammar A or B in at least two ways:

Include more lexical rules	Include more structural rules
EXAMPLE	EXAMPLE
Test Grammar B to see whether it generates the sentence *Bart likes Maggie*.	Test Grammar B to see whether it generates the sentence *Bart walked to Maggie*.
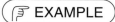 No, it doesn't.	No, it doesn't.
To generate this sentence, we would need the rule V → *likes*, which is not in Grammar B.	To generate this sentence, we would need lexical rules for the words *walked* and *to*, which are not currently in Grammar B. Furthermore, we would need a structural rule to introduce the word *to*, which Grammar B lacks.

We will look at the issues that arise in extending a grammar in much more detail in Unit 6.

EXERCISES

1. Consider the sentence *Homer saw her duck*. It has two meanings, which correspond to two different sentence patterns. What are the two patterns?

2. Here is a set of phrase structure rules for English:

S → N V	V → *ran*
S → N V N	V → *saw*
S → N V N N	V → *sleeps*
	V → *fed*
N → *Homer*	V → *crawls*
N → *Marge*	V → *gave*
N → *Lisa*	V → *chased*
N → *Bart*	V → *sent*
N → *Maggie*	
N → *SLH*	

   These rules generate the sentences in (1):

   (1) Bart ran.   Homer chased Bart.   Marge gave Homer Maggie.
        Homer sleeps.   Lisa saw Maggie.   Homer sent Bart SLH.
        Maggie crawls.   Maggie fed SLH.

   A. What tree diagram do the rules give for the sentence *Maggie fed SLH*?

   B. Give four other sentences of English that these rules generate (i.e., find examples different from the ones in (1)).

3. The sentences below show new patterns, different from the ones in (1) of Question 2:

   (1) Homer talked to Marge.
        Homer talked about Bart.
        Maggie crawled to Lisa.
        SLH ran from Homer.
        Homer talked to Marge about Bart.
        Maggie crawled from Lisa to Marge.

   A. What new rules must be added to the rules in Question 2 in order to produce these sentences?

     B.   What tree diagram do your new rules give for the sentence *Homer talked to Marge about Bart*?

4. The sentences in (1) show yet another sentence pattern, different from the ones in Questions 2 and 3.

    (1)   Homer talked to Bart yesterday.
           Marge gave Homer Maggie quickly.
           Homer chased Bart recently.

     A.   What new rules must be added in order to produce these sentences?

     B.   What tree diagrams do your new rules give for the sentences *Homer talked to Bart yesterday* and *Homer chased Bart recently*?

5. *Bart chased Lisa* is a sentence (S) with the pattern N V N. Now consider the sentence *Marge thinks Bart chased Lisa*. One way to state the pattern of this sentence is N V N V N. But there's a better way. What is it?

6. Below is a set of phrase structure rules for English. (Ignore what *CN* and *Art* stand for.)

S → NP V NP	N → *Bart*
S → NP V NP NP	N → *Marge*
NP → Art CN	N → *Homer*
NP → NP *and* NP	N → *Lisa*
NP → N	V → *bought*
	V → *saw*
Art → *a*	V → *sent*
CN → *beer*	
CN → *gift*	

     A.   These rules generate a tree for the sentence *Homer bought Marge a gift*. Give the tree.

     B.   These rules generate a tree for the sentence *Homer sent Marge Bart and Lisa*. Give the tree.

7. Below is a grammar for a small part of English. (Again, ignore what the new category symbols may stand for.)

S → NP V NP	Art → *the*
S → NP V NP PP	CN → *man*
S → NP V NP AP	CN → *vase*
NP → Art CN	CN → *judge*
NP → NP AP	N → *Homer*
NP → N	N → *Marge*
AP → A	V → *considers*

V → *found*
A → *intelligent*
A → *broken*
A → *guilty*
PP → *there*

A.   This grammar generates a tree for the sentence *The man found Homer there*. Give the tree.

B.   This grammar assigns two different trees to the sentence *Marge found the vase broken* (that is, the sentence is syntactically ambiguous under these rules). Give the two trees.

C.   To generate the sentences in (1)–(3), you must add a rule or some rules to the grammar. State what rule(s) you must add. (Note: Think of this as a cumulative process, so for each sentence, list only a rule or rules that you haven't added at an earlier point.)

(1)   The man arrived tired.

(2)   a.   A tall man arrived.
       b.   Marge saw a tall man.

(3)   Bart left the party angry at Lisa.

6 Here is a grammar for a small part of English:

S → NP V NP   N → *Homer*
S → NP V PP   N → *Marge*
S → NP V NP P   V → *decided*
NP → Art CN   V → *considered*
NP → N   V → *looked*
V → V P   P → *up*
PP → P NP   P → *on*

Art → *the*
CN → *answer*
CN → *boat*
CN → *present*

A.   This grammar generates a tree for the sentence *Homer looked Marge up*. Give the tree.

B.   This grammar assigns two different trees to the sentence *Marge decided on the boat* (that is, the sentence is syntactically ambiguous under these rules). Give the two trees.

C. To generate the sentences in (1)–(2), you must add a rule or some rules to the grammar. State what rule(s) you must add. (Note: Think of this as a cumulative process, so for each sentence, list only a rule or rules that you haven't added at an earlier point.)

(1) Homer looked Bart over.

(2) Marge looked the new answer up.

7. Here is a grammar for a small part of English:

S → NP Vi	Art → *a*
S → NP Vd NP PP	Art → *the*
S → NP Vt NP	Vi → *ran*
NP → N	Vi → *slept*
NP → Art CN	Vi → *crawled*
PP → P NP	Vt → *chased*
	Vt → *saw*
N → *Homer*	Vt → *knew*
N → *Maggie*	Vd → *gave*
N → *Marge*	Vd → *sent*
N → *Lisa*	P → *to*
N → *Bart*	
CN → *man*	
CN → *woman*	
CN → *girl*	
CN → *boy*	

Extending the grammar

Now, here is a list of sentences:

(1) Maggie left the room after Lisa.   Marge told Lisa about Bart.
Marge put a hat on Bart.   Marge wrote a letter to Bart.
Homer put Maggie near Lisa.   Marge wrote a letter about Bart.
Bart put Maggie in the crib.   Marge wrote a letter about Bart.

A. State what new rules must be added to the grammar in order to generate the sentences in (1).

B. Give the tree diagrams that the grammar plus your new rules assign to these eight sentences. (You will need eight trees.)

Testing and revising the grammar

C.   State whether your new, amended grammar generates the following
      sentences:

(2)   *Marge put a hat to Bart.   *Marge gave a hat near Bart.
       *Marge gave a hat on Bart.   *Marge told Lisa to Bart.
        Marge wrote a letter near Bart.   Marge wrote a letter after Bart.
        Marge wrote a letter on Bart.

D.   If your rules generate any of the ill-formed sentences in (2), revise them
      so that they do not.

Evaluating additional data

Consider the following additional examples:

(3)   Marge wrote.   Marge wrote a letter.   Marge wrote to Bart.
        Marge gave.   Marge gave money.   Marge gave to charity.
       *Marge put.   *Marge put the hat.   *Marge put on charity.

E.   What further questions do these facts raise for your rules?

F.   What analysis should be given for them?

PART III Choosing between Theories

Scientific theorizing has a **hypothetico-deductive structure**. In response to some question, problem, or puzzle, the scientist

1. Thinks up an idea or hypothesis.

2. Deduces conclusions from that hypothesis. (What else would be true if it were correct?)

3. Checks those conclusions against the facts. (Are the conclusions supported by empirical evidence?)

Incorrect conclusions (ones not supported by the facts) call for a change in the hypothesis.

Syntactic investigation has this general hypothetico-deductive character. Our question is, What do speakers of a language know when they know the syntax of their language? Our specific hypotheses come in the form of rules that generate the sentences of that language. We

1. Think up a set of rules.

2. Derive sentences from those rules.

3. Check those sentences against our intuitions. (Are the sentences in fact grammatical?)

Ungrammatical sentences generated by our rules call for a change in those rules.

A set of hypotheses about a certain domain constitutes a **theory of that domain**. Our set of rules thus constitutes a theory of what speakers of a language know about the syntax of their language. We call such a collection of rules a **grammar**. From this perspective, a grammar becomes a scientific theory, and grammar building becomes an exercise in scientific theorizing.

A grammar of a language can be considered, in what seems to me a perfectly good sense, to be a complete scientific theory of a particular subject matter.
—*The Logical Structure of Linguistic Theory*, p. 77

The rules we have come up with so far have been related to the data in a very direct and obvious way. In response to sentences with four words like *Homer handed Lisa Maggie*, we conjectured a sentence rule with four daughter categories S → N V N N. What could be simpler?

We will soon see, however, that things are not so simple after all. As it turns out, for a given set of sentences there will typically be *many* different sets of rules—many grammars—that generate it. In some of these grammars, the relation between rules and sentences is much more indirect than in the example *Homer handed Lisa Maggie*/S → N V N N. This raises an important question: How do we *choose* between alternative grammars? This question will occupy us in Units 6–10.

In science, choice between two theories is usually a complex matter. Broad criteria for favoring one theory over another include these:[1]

1. Coverage of the facts. (The more comprehensive a theory is, the better.)

2. Simplicity. (The easier a theory is to use, or the simpler its deductive structure, the better.)

3. Fertility. (A good theory breeds new ideas about areas beyond those for which it was originally developed.)

4. Depth of understanding. (A good theory not only covers the facts; it also gives *insight* into why things are the way they are.)

As we proceed through the units that follow, try to keep these criteria in mind. When we need to choose between rival grammars, consider which one may cover the data better, which is simpler to think about or easier to use, which suggests new routes to new data, and which seems to yield a better sense of understanding or insight.

---

1. A useful discussion of theory choice is given in chapter 14 of Derry 2002.

Comparing Rules and Theories

Review

1. Grammars are ...

    Scientific theories of part of the knowledge that people have of their language.

2. Like other theories ...

    Grammars must be tested, revised, and extended when compared with the facts.

3.

Testing a grammar	Revising a grammar	Extending a grammar
Checking whether its rules generate some set of expressions.	Changing it so as to avoid generating ill-formed expressions.	Changing it so as to generate additional well-formed expressions.

Comparing Alternative Rules

In building a theory, there will almost always be different ways of proceeding at any given point. In accounting for the facts, we will often have to choose between alternative rules, and sometimes between whole alternative grammars.

Choosing is not merely a practical necessity; it is a theoretical one too. When speakers acquire a language, they presumably learn some definite set of rules. This means that the question "Which rule(s) do they actually know?" is always a factual one. There *is* an answer to it, no matter how hard it may be to discover the answer. It also means that if we have several different candidates for the rule that speakers know, at most one of them can be the right one.

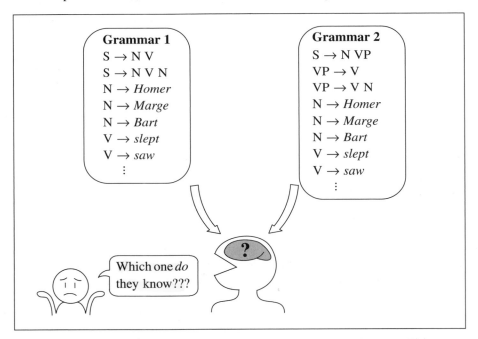

When we're faced with competing rules and theories, how do we tell which one is right? What principles can we use to compare rules and theories?

An Example with Conjunctions

Consider some new examples involving **conjunctions** of sentences from Unit 2, sentences joined using the words *and* and *or*.

Data Set 1 (Sentence conjunctions)

Homer sleeps and Maggie crawls.
Homer sleeps or Maggie crawls.
Bart ran and Homer chased Bart.
Bart ran or Homer chased Bart.
Bart ran and Homer handed Lisa Maggie.
Bart ran or Homer handed Lisa Maggie.
Maggie petted SLH and Bart saw Maggie.
Maggie petted SLH or Bart saw Maggie.
Bart saw Maggie and Homer handed Lisa Maggie.
Bart saw Maggie or Homer handed Lisa Maggie.
Homer handed Lisa Maggie and Marge sent Bart SLH.
Homer handed Lisa Maggie or Marge sent Bart SLH.

? QUESTION   Conjoined sentences are part of the grammar of English. They are something that we will want our theory to cover. What rules should we add to accommodate these sentences?

 **PROPOSAL 1**   Add the following twelve rules to our grammar:

S → N Vi *and* N Vi   S → N Vi *or* N Vi
S → N Vi *and* N V N   S → N Vi *or* N V N
S → N Vi *and* N V N N   S → N Vi *or* N V N N
S → N V N *and* N V N   S → N V N *or* N V N
S → N V N *and* N V N N   S → N V N *or* N V N N
S → N V N N *and* N V N N   S → N V N N *or* N V N N

 **PROPOSAL 2**   Add the following three rules to our grammar:

S → S Conj S   Conj → *and*
                      Conj → *or*

Now answer the following questions to help decide which proposal should be preferred (if either):

? **QUESTIONS**

1. What tree diagram is assigned to *Homer sleeps and Maggie crawls* under Proposal 1?

2. What tree diagram is assigned to *Homer sleeps and Maggie crawls* under Proposal 2?

3. Are there additional conjunctions of sentences that cannot be generated under Proposal 1?

4. Can these same examples be generated under Proposal 2?

5. Which proposal covers the data more adequately?

6. Which proposal yields the better theory?

Different Theories, Different Predictions

Sometimes when we are comparing theories, the theories make different predictions and one theory ends up being **more empirically adequate** than the other; that is, it predicts the facts better. In the case of grammars, this will happen when one set of rules generates a wider class of grammatical sentences and/or fewer ungrammatical sentences than its competitors. Choosing between theories is easy in this case: we prefer the theory that is empirically more adequate.

The choice between Proposal 1 and Proposal 2 is a situation like this. Proposal 1 and Proposal 2 are equal with respect to Data Set 3 in the sense that both generate all the sentences in the set. However, the data set is not complete, by any means. Notice that the following examples are also well-formed conjunctions:

Data Set 2 (Additional sentence conjunctions)

Homer chased Bart and Bart ran.
Homer chased Bart or Bart ran.
Homer handed Lisa Maggie and Bart ran.
Homer handed Lisa Maggie or Bart ran.
Homer handed Lisa Maggie and Bart saw Maggie.
Homer handed Lisa Maggie or Bart saw Maggie.

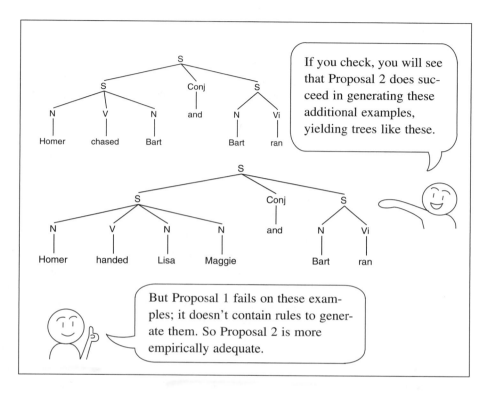

Can This Theory Be Saved?

This comparison of grammars may not seem decisive. Even though Proposal 1 doesn't generate the sentences in Data Set 2, clearly it could be revised to do so. If we add the new rules shown below, the two proposals become equal again with respect to the data; they both generate all the examples in Data Set 2.

S → N V N *and* N Vi   S → N V N *or* N Vi
S → N V N N *and* N V N   S → N V N N *or* N V N

But the problems for Proposal 1 do not end here. There are lots of other conjoined sentences—in fact, infinitely more—that we have to contend with. To see this, just think about the following list:

Homer sleeps and Maggie crawls.
Homer sleeps and Maggie crawls and Homer sleeps.
Homer sleeps and Maggie crawls and Homer sleeps and Maggie crawls.
Homer sleeps and Maggie crawls and Homer sleeps and Maggie crawls and Homer sleeps ...

Note that this list could go on forever. Notice too that all of the sentences in this list, no matter how long it gets, will be well-formed sentences of English. True, as the sentences get longer they become highly repetitive: at each point, all we do is tack a new *Homer sleeps* or *Maggie crawls* onto the end of the previous sentence in the list. But remember that being a well-formed sentence of English is not a matter of being useful or informative or nonrepetitive; it's a matter of grammatical pattern. And, to repeat, all of the examples in this infinite list have a good English grammatical pattern.

Proposal 1 breaks down after the very first item in this list. Proposal 1 handles **binary conjunctions**—conjunctions of two sentences—but it doesn't handle conjunctions of three, four, or more sentences. Furthermore, no simple addition of rules is going to help:

To accommodate these new sentences following the pattern of Proposal 1, we would have to add *an infinite number of new rules*!

S → N Vi *and* N Vi *and* N Vi
S → N Vi *and* N Vi *and* N Vi *and* N Vi
S → N Vi *and* N Vi *and* N Vi *and* N Vi *and* N Vi
S → N Vi *and* N Vi *and* N Vi *and* N Vi *and* N Vi *and* N Vi

. . .

The Problem of Infinite Lists

Having to add an infinite rule list is not simply an inconvenience. It's flat out unacceptable, given what we're trying to do. Remember that in writing a grammar, we are trying to give a theory of what speakers of a language know about their language: we are trying to describe something that they have in their brains. So far as we know, the brain is a finite object with finite storage capabilities. Since an infinite list won't fit into a finite storage device, a speaker's grammar simply cannot contain an infinite list of rules! In other words, Proposal 1 simply cannot be expanded to accommodate all of the data involving conjunctions that our grammar will need to cover. Proposal 1 needs separate rules for conjunctions that are two sentences long, three sentences long, four sentences long, and so on; and the fact is that conjunctions can become arbitrarily long.

How does Proposal 2 fare when faced with an infinite set of conjunctions? Somewhat surprisingly, perhaps, Proposal 2 handles *all* the examples in this list with no problems. If you examine the following tree diagrams generated by Proposal 2, you'll see why:

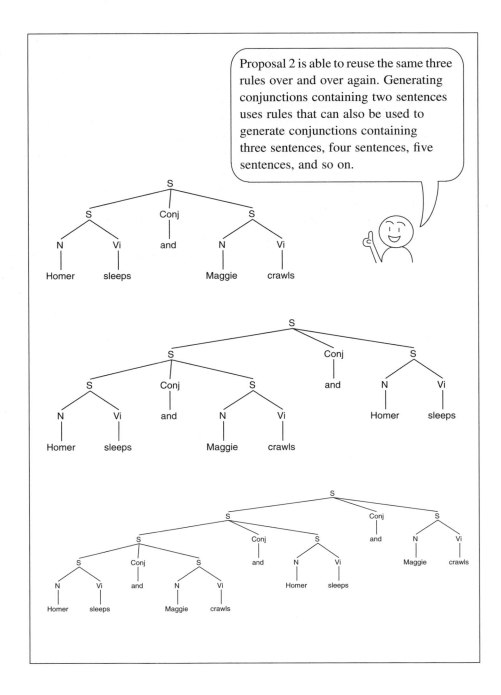

Proposal 2 is able to reuse the same three rules over and over again. Generating conjunctions containing two sentences uses rules that can also be used to generate conjunctions containing three sentences, four sentences, five sentences, and so on.

The Power of Recursive Rules

Proposal 2's rule for conjoining Ss is a very special kind of rule. Its special feature is that the symbol (S) appearing on the left-hand side of the arrow also appears on the right-hand side:

This feature allows the rule to apply to its own output: once we rewrite an S node as S Conj S, we can then choose one of the Ss just introduced and use the very same rule again to rewrite it. This is what gives Proposal 2 the power to generate an infinite list of conjunctions: every use of the S conjunction rule brings with it the option of using that very same rule again. A rule (or set of rules) that can apply to its own output like this is said to be **recursive**.

Recursive rules provide some insight into a property of human language that we noted earlier in comparing the linguistic output of humans with that of a talking doll. Whereas a doll has a finite corpus of utterances, humans can in principle produce an unbounded number of well-formed expressions in their language. Recursive rules show how this is possible, even if the human brain has limited storage capacity: if some of our rules can be used over and over again, unboundedly, then we have the means to produce unbounded collections of sentences. The scholar-linguist Wilhelm von Humboldt noted the unbounded nature of human linguistic ability several centuries ago and regarded it as a fundamental mystery!

> [Language] must therefore make infinite employment of finite means.
> —*On Language*, p. 91

Wilhelm von Humboldt
1767–1835

Recursive rules give us a way of understanding just what this would amount to.

Equivalent Theories

Although competing theories very often differ in their data coverage, it is possible to have different grammars that nonetheless generate exactly the same sentences. That is, we can have different grammars that are still **equivalent** in terms of the sentences they produce.

An Example

The following two grammars contain the same lexical rules, but different structural rules:

Grammar A		Grammar B	
S → N Vi	Vi → *ran*	S → N VP	Vi → *ran*
S → N Vt N	Vi → *sleeps*	VP → Vi	Vi → *sleeps*
S → N Vd N N	Vi → *crawls*	VP → Vt N	Vi → *crawls*
	Vt → *chased*	VP → Vd N N	Vt → *chased*
N → *Homer*	Vt → *saw*		Vt → *saw*
N → *Marge*	Vt → *petted*	N → *Homer*	Vt → *petted*
N → *Lisa*	Vd → *sent*	N → *Marge*	Vd → *sent*
N → *Bart*	Vd → *handed*	N → *Lisa*	Vd → *handed*
N → *Maggie*		N → *Bart*	
N → *SLH*		N → *Maggie*	
		N → *SLH*	

1. What are five sentences generated by Grammar B?
2. What are the tree diagrams for these five sentences under Grammar B?
3. Can these sentences also be generated using Grammar A?
4. What are the tree diagrams for these five sentences under Grammar A?
5. Are there any sentences that can be generated by Grammar A but not by Grammar B, and vice versa?

If you reason correctly, you will observe two important things:

Grammar A and Grammar B generate exactly the same set of sentences.
Grammar A and Grammar B assign different tree diagrams to the sentences they generate.

Two Definitions

 Two theories that generate exactly the same set of sentences are **weakly equivalent theories**.

 Two theories that generate the same set of sentences and assign them exactly the same tree diagrams are **strongly equivalent theories**.

Grammar A and Grammar B are weakly equivalent theories because they generate the same sentences. They are not strongly equivalent theories, however, since they assign the sentences different tree diagrams.

Comparing Equivalent Theories

The issues that arise with competing rules also arise with competing theories. Even if two theories both cover a given set of data equally well, at most one of them can be the grammar that a speaker actually knows. So, as with rules, we must find principles for comparing and evaluating equivalent theories.

Simplicity

One natural criterion for judging among theories is **simplicity**. In our earlier example of sentence conjunctions, the recursive set (Proposal 2) contained only three rules, whereas the nonrecursive set (Proposal 1) contained a dozen rules. The recursive set was therefore simpler in the sense of containing fewer rules.

This notion of simplicity might be justified on grounds of language learning. Children typically learn language quite rapidly. Preferring a grammar with fewer rules seems very natural from this perspective: fewer rules means fewer things to learn—hence, quicker learning.

If we reason like this in connection with Grammars A and B above, then it seems we have reason to prefer Grammar A. Grammar A uses fewer rules than Grammar B in generating sentences. This is because Grammar B contains an additional node VP that must be spelled out in any derivation. We might say that Grammar A looks preferable because it is simpler.

Ease of Extension

Another way of evaluating theories might be to compare how easily they can be extended to cover *new* facts. If they are equivalent with respect to some initial set of data, maybe one or the other will gain an advantage when we consider further data.

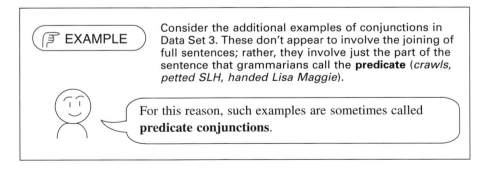

☞ EXAMPLE

Consider the additional examples of conjunctions in Data Set 3. These don't appear to involve the joining of full sentences; rather, they involve just the part of the sentence that grammarians call the **predicate** (*crawls, petted SLH, handed Lisa Maggie*).

For this reason, such examples are sometimes called **predicate conjunctions**.

Data Set 3 (Predicate conjunctions)

Homer sleeps and crawls.
Homer sleeps or crawls.
Lisa petted SLH and saw Maggie.
Lisa petted SLH or saw Maggie.
Bart ran and chased Lisa.
Bart ran or chased Lisa.
Bart ran and handed Lisa Maggie.
Bart ran or handed Lisa Maggie.
Bart saw Maggie and handed Lisa Maggie.
Bart saw Maggie or handed Lisa Maggie.
Homer handed Lisa Maggie and sent Bart SLH.
Homer handed Lisa Maggie or sent Bart SLH.

 QUESTION   What rules should we add to accommodate these new sentences?

 **PROPOSAL A**   Add the following twelve rules to Grammar A:

S → N Vi *and* Vi   S → N Vi *or* Vi
S → N Vt N *and* Vt N   S → N Vt N *or* Vt N
S → N Vi *and* Vt N   S → N Vi *or* Vt N
S → N Vi *and* Vd N N   S → N Vi *or* Vd N N
S → N Vt N *and* Vd N N   S → N Vt N *or* Vd N N
S → N Vd N N *and* Vd N N   S → N Vd N N *or* Vd N N

PROPOSAL B   Add the following three rules to Grammar B:

VP → VP Conj VP
Conj → *and*
Conj → *or*

? QUESTIONS

1. What tree diagram is assigned to *Lisa petted SLH or saw Maggie* under Proposal A?
2. What tree diagram is assigned to *Lisa petted SLH or saw Maggie* under Proposal B?
3. Are there additional conjunctions of this kind that cannot be generated under Proposal A?
4. Can these same examples be generated under Proposal B?
5. Which proposal covers the data more adequately?
6. Which proposal is simpler?
7. Which proposal yields the better theory?
8. What kind of rule are the rules in Proposal B?

This example shows that simplicity isn't simple! Initially, Grammar A appears simpler because it contains fewer rules than Grammar B. But when we move to generating predicate conjunctions, it becomes far easier to extend Grammar B than to extend Grammar A. To cover predicate conjunctions in Grammar B, we add the three rules in Proposal B—that's it! To cover predicate conjunctions in Grammar A, we must add at least the twelve rules in Proposal A, and in fact more than those would be required in the end. So what seems simpler at first does not turn out to be so at last.

Grouping (Constituency)

We saw that Grammar A and Grammar B are weakly equivalent: they generate the same sentences, but not the same trees. For example, Grammar A assigns Tree (1) to *Homer chased Bart*, whereas Grammar B assigns Tree (2):

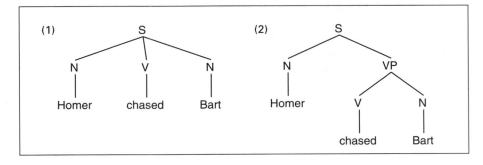

Suppose we had a way to choose between these trees. For example, suppose we could find reasons for saying that although Grammar A successfully generates *Homer chased Bart*, the tree it produces is not the right one, whereas the tree Grammar B produces is much better. Then we would have a way of choosing between grammars. We could prefer Grammar B to Grammar A on the basis of its trees.

Choosing between Trees

Are there grounds for preferring one tree over another for a given sentence? Look at the shape of Trees (1) and (2) for *Homer chased Bart*. Notice that in Tree (1), N, V, and N are equal daughters under the node S. In Tree (2), by contrast, the first N is a daughter of S, whereas V and N are daughters of the intermediate node VP. One way of viewing this difference is as follows:

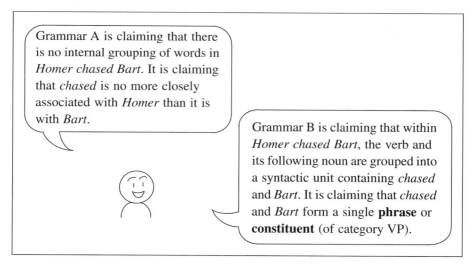

> Grammar A is claiming that there is no internal grouping of words in *Homer chased Bart*. It is claiming that *chased* is no more closely associated with *Homer* than it is with *Bart*.

> Grammar B is claiming that within *Homer chased Bart*, the verb and its following noun are grouped into a syntactic unit containing *chased* and *Bart*. It is claiming that *chased* and *Bart* form a single **phrase** or **constituent** (of category VP).

Some people do seem to feel an internal grouping of the verb and its following noun when they think about where it's most natural to pause in pronouncing the sentence *Homer chased Bart*. It is very natural to say *Homer - chased Bart*, with a pause between the subject and the verb. It seems less natural to say *Homer chased - Bart*, with a pause between the verb and its object. It is attractive to interpret this as evidence for Tree (2), which posits a major break in the internal grouping of the sentence at exactly the point where we prefer to pause.

In the next unit, we will look at better evidence for internal grouping, evidence that yields good reasons for preferring one tree to another.

Constituency and Constituency Tests

Review

1. Grammars, like other scientific theories ...

Must be tested, revised, and extended.

2. There will typically be many ways of building or refining a grammar at any point.

 We must be prepared to compare rules and grammars.

3. Sometimes grammars may simply be compared on the basis of their strings.

One may generate different strings than the other. We can compare on the basis of which one produces the right strings.

4. When grammars are weakly equivalent, we must compare by considering the trees that they generate.

 We need principles for telling us which tree is right.

More on Conjunction

In the last unit, we considered the following two grammars, which are weakly equivalent.

Grammar A

S → N Vi	Vi → *ran*
S → N Vt N	Vi → *sleeps*
S → N Vd N N	Vi → *crawls*
	Vt → *chased*
N → *Homer*	Vt → *saw*
N → *Marge*	Vt → *petted*
N → *Lisa*	Vd → *sent*
N → *Bart*	Vd → *handed*
N → *Maggie*	
N → *SLH*	

Grammar B

S → N VP	Vi → *ran*
VP → Vi	Vi → *sleeps*
VP → Vt N	Vi → *crawls*
VP → Vd N N	Vt → *chased*
	Vt → *saw*
N → *Homer*	Vt → *petted*
N → *Marge*	Vd → *sent*
N → *Lisa*	Vd → *handed*
N → *Bart*	
N → *Maggie*	
N → *SLH*	

We saw that Grammar B extended to handle predicate conjunctions more easily than Grammar A because of the internal grouping, or **constituency**, that it assigns. Grammar B introduces the node VP, containing the verb and its following nouns. Because it does this, we can capture predicate conjunctions by using simple rules.

VP → VP Conj VP

Conj → *and*
Conj → *or*

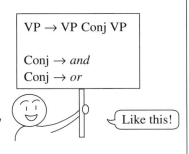

Like this!

Recursive Rules Again

Capturing conjunctions using recursive rules is a very attractive idea, for reasons we have already discussed.

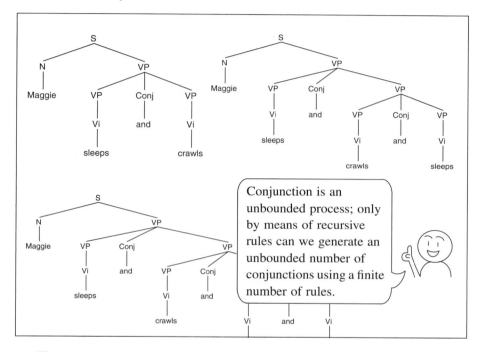

Conjunction is an unbounded process; only by means of recursive rules can we generate an unbounded number of conjunctions using a finite number of rules.

The reason we can appeal to recursive rules for predicate conjunctions is precisely that Grammar B contains a node VP that groups the verb and its following nouns together. Because Grammar B analyzes the shaded strings in the following sentences as constituting groups of the same single category (VP), we can appeal to recursive rules that conjoin these groups. That is:

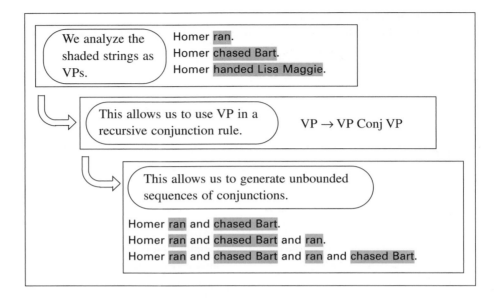

Conjunction as a Constituency Test

It seems reasonable to extend this strategy to *all* conjunctions; that is, it's natural to try to capture all conjunctions by means of recursive rules of this general form:

$$X \rightarrow X \; \text{Conj} \; X$$

Notice that if we make this move, we will be adopting the following broad idea, which we can call Principle 1 (P1):

> **P1**
> If a string of words can be conjoined, then it is a constituent.

Conjunction thus becomes a test for the grouping of words: a **constituency test**. Whenever we find a sentence with a conjunction, we know that the parallel strings joined by the conjunction must be constituents. And whenever we have a sentence and want to know whether a given string in it is a constituent, we can test by constructing another sentence in which the string is conjoined with another one like it. If the constructed sentence is well-formed, the string is a constituent. Let us call this the **conjunction test**.

 QUESTION

According to the conjunction test for constituency, which strings must be constituents in the sentences below?

Homer talked to Marge and to Lisa.
(Ans: *to Marge, to Lisa*)
Homer talked to a woman and a girl.
(Ans: *a woman, a girl*)
Homer chased Bart on Monday and on Tuesday.
(Ans: *on Monday, on Tuesday*)
Homer chased Bart and chased Lisa on Monday.
(Ans: *chased Bart, chased Lisa*)
Homer chased Bart on Monday and chased Lisa on Tuesday.
(Ans: *chased Bart on Monday, chased Lisa on Tuesday*)

 QUESTION

In the sentence *Homer handed Lisa Maggie yesterday*, is the string *handed Lisa Maggie yesterday* a constituent?

 ANSWER

We test by constructing a sentence in which the string in question is conjoined with another one like it:

Homer **handed Lisa Maggie yesterday** and **handed Lisa SLH today**.

This sentence is well-formed. Since the string can be conjoined, we conclude that it is a constituent.

 **QUESTION**   In the sentence *Homer handed Lisa a baby*, is the string *Lisa a* a constituent?

 **ANSWER**   We test by constructing a sentence in which the string is conjoined with another one like it:

*Homer handed **Lisa a** and **Bart a** baby.

This sentence is not well-formed. Since the string cannot be conjoined, it does not seem to be a constituent. (More on this below.)

Other Constituency Tests

The general idea behind the conjunction constituency test is that we have a certain form of rule (X → X Conj X) that we want to use in analyzing conjunctions. Using such a rule requires that words be grouped together in a certain way. So the phenomenon (conjunction) becomes a test for the grouping.

There are a number of other linguistic phenomena besides conjunction that furnish constituency tests of this kind.

Proform Replacement

English (like many other languages) allows a redundant expression to be replaced by what is called a **proform**. For example, (1a) contains two instances of the name *Bart*. In (1b), the pronoun *him* replaces the second, redundant instance of *Bart*. Intuitively, the two sentences (can) have the same meaning.

(1) a. Homer chased Bart, and Marge saw Bart.
     b. Homer chased Bart, and Marge saw **him**.

What rule should we add to introduce *him*? Since *him* replaces *Bart*, it presumably belongs to the same category and is introduced by a rule of the same kind. So we might offer a rule like this:

N → *him*

Now consider the pair of sentences in (2). In (2b), the **pro-predicate** *did so* replaces the redundant string *chased Bart* in (2a) and is understood as having the same meaning:

> (2) a. Homer chased Bart, and Marge chased Bart too.
> b. Homer chased Bart, and Marge **did so** too.

What rule should we add to introduce *did so*? Notice that if we have a grammar like Grammar B above, which analyzes the string *chased Bart* as a constituent and assigns it to the category VP, then we can proceed exactly as above. We can write a lexical rule for *did so* that gives it the same category as the phrase it replaces:

> VP → *did so*

If *chased Bart* is not analyzed as a single constituent, then it is much less clear how we should proceed.

Proform Replacement as a Constituency Test

Just as it seemed reasonable to extend the VP conjunction strategy to all cases of conjunction, so it seems reasonable to extend the N and VP proform strategy to *all* cases of proform replacement, and introduce proforms by simple lexical rules that are of the same category as what they replace:

> X → Proform

If we make this move, we will be adopting Principle 2 (P2):

> **P2**
> If a string of words can be replaced by a proform, then it is a constituent.

Proform replacement thus becomes another constituency test. Whenever we find a sentence with a proform, we know that the string it replaces must be a constituent of the same category. And whenever we have a sentence and want to know whether a given string in it is a constituent, we can test by constructing another sentence in which the string is replaced by an appropriate proform. If the constructed sentence is well-formed, the string is a constituent. Let us call this the **proform replacement test**.

 **QUESTION**   According to the proform replacement test, which strings must be constituents in the sentences below?

> Homer left a tip on the table, but Marge left a tip under **it**.
> (Ans. *the table*)
> I left a tip on the table, but Mr. Burns didn't leave a tip **there**.
> (Ans. *on the table*)
> Bart gets a new radio on his birthdays, but Milhouse always gets a new synchrotron **then**.
> (Ans. *on his birthdays*)
> Homer bought the green deck chair with solar-heated footbath, and Moe bought the blue **one**.
> (Ans. *deck chair with solar-heated footbath*)

 **QUESTION**   In the sentence *Homer handed the cutest little baby to Lisa*, is the string *the cutest little baby* a constituent?

 **ANSWER**   We test by constructing a sentence in which the string in question is replaced by an appropriate proform (in this case, the pronoun *her*):

> Homer handed **her** to Lisa.

This sentence is well-formed. Since the string can be replaced, we conclude that it is a constituent.

Ellipsis

Besides allowing redundant expressions to be replaced by proforms, English allows them to be **elided** or left unpronounced. For example, (3a) contains two instances of *chase Bart*. In (3b), the second instance of *chased Bart* has been elided (left unpronounced). Again, the two sentences have the same meaning.

> (3) a.   Homer could chase Bart, and Marge could chase Bart too.
>   b.   Homer could chase Bart, and Marge could too.

How should we account for ellipsis? One natural idea is to proceed just as we did with proform replacement, but instead of writing a rule that introduces a pronounced form like *did so*, we write a rule that introduces an empty or unpronounced element (symbolized with Ø):

> VP → Ø

> Homer could chase Bart, and Marge could Ø too.
>
> So (3b) really looks like this, with an unpronounced element Ø replacing *chase Bart*.

Ellipsis as a Constituency Test

As with proform replacement, if we adopt this strategy generally and treat *all* cases of ellipsis by means of rules like X → Ø, then we will be implicitly adopting Principle 3 (P3):

> **P3**
> If a string of words can be elided, then it is a constituent.

So whenever we find a sentence with a missing string, we know that the elided material forms a constituent. And whenever we have a sentence and want to know whether some string in it is a constituent, we can test by constructing another sentence in which the string is elided (replaced by Ø). If the constructed sentence is well-formed, the string is a constituent. Let us call this the **ellipsis test**.

 **QUESTION**   According to the ellipsis test, which strings must be constituents in the sentences below?

Homer left a tip on the table, but Marge didn't Ø.

(Ans. *leave a tip on the table*)

Bart gets a new radio on his birthdays, but Milhouse always gets a new synchrotron Ø.

(Ans. *on his birthdays*)

Homer bought the green deck chair with solar-heated footbath, and Moe bought the blue Ø.

(Ans. *deck chair with solar-heated footbath*)

 **QUESTION**   In the sentence *I don't know why Marge plans to visit Waxahachie*, is the string *Marge plans to visit Waxahachie* a constituent?

 **ANSWER**   We test by constructing a sentence in which the string in question is replaced by Ø (and so is unpronounced):

I know that **Marge plans to visit Waxahachie**, but I don't know why Ø.

This sentence is well-formed. Since the string can be elided, we conclude that it is a constituent.

Dislocation

We are all familiar with the fact that many sentences of English have alternative permutations of their words that, roughly speaking, express the same thought. For example, alongside (4a) we find (4b) and (4c), which express the same thought but differ in matters of emphasis:

(4) a. Bart gave Maggie to Lisa.
     b. Maggie, Bart gave to Lisa.
     c. To Lisa, Bart gave Maggie.

In (4b) and (4c), a word or string of words has been preposed, or moved to the front of the sentence (*Maggie*, *to Lisa*). Here are more examples of the same kind:

> (5) a. Homer left the car and the lawn mower in the garage.
> b. The car and the lawn mower, Homer left in the garage.
> c. In the garage, Homer left the car and the lawn mower.

Notice that not every sequence of words in such examples can be preposed or **dislocated** from its basic position. For example, the following sound pretty awful:

> (6) a. *Maggie to Lisa, Bart gave.
> b. *The car and the lawn mower in the garage, Homer left.

What's the principle here? One idea that has been suggested is that the ill-formed examples violate Principle 4 (P4):

> **P4**
> If a string of words can be dislocated, then it is a constituent.

Suppose, for example, that the sentence *Bart gave Maggie to Lisa* has the following tree structure:

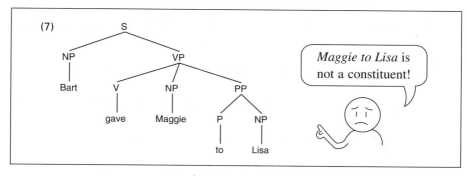

In this tree, *Maggie* is a constituent (NP) and *to Lisa* is a constituent (PP). But *Maggie to Lisa* is not a constituent: there is no node that includes under it just this string of words in the tree. It follows under P4 that although *Maggie* and *to*

Lisa can be dislocated on their own, *Maggie to Lisa* cannot; *Maggie to Lisa* is not a constituent.

Dislocation as a Constituency Test

If this kind of reasoning is accepted (and indeed, the idea of only being able to move groups is very natural), then dislocation provides another constituency test. Whenever we find a sentence in which a string has been dislocated, we know that the dislocated material forms a constituent. And whenever we have a sentence and want to know whether some string in it is a constituent, we can test by constructing another sentence in which the string is moved (for example, preposed). If the constructed sentence is well-formed, the string is a constituent. Let us call this the **dislocation test**.

? QUESTION   According to the dislocation test, which strings must be constituents in the sentence *Homer told Lisa that the earth is flat on Thursday*?

Lisa, Homer told that the earth is flat on Thursday.
(Ans. *Lisa*)
That the earth is flat, Homer told Lisa on Thursday.
(Ans. *that the earth is flat*)
On Thursday, Homer told Lisa that the earth is flat.
(Ans. *on Thursday*)

? QUESTION   In the sentence *Homer told Lisa that the earth is flat on Thursday*, is the string *Lisa that the earth is flat* a constituent?

☞ ANSWER   We test by constructing a sentence in which the string in question is preposed:

*Lisa that the Earth is flat, Homer told on Thursday.

This sentence is not well-formed. Since the string cannot be preposed, it does not appear to be a constituent.

place it in front of the sentence

The dislocation test is a little different from the conjunction, proform replacement, and ellipsis tests. In the latter cases, we had phrase structure rules of a certain form that we wanted to adopt. If we adopted such rules, they had implications about how words and phrases are grouped in sentences. Here it's not a phrase structure rule we're talking about, but another kind of rule: one that moves or dislocates sentence parts. We're saying that such a rule should only move or dislocate constituents. If we accept this, then movement phenomena become tests for constituency. We will talk more about this kind of rule in later units, even though we will appeal to the test now in anticipation of that discussion.

Semantic Ambiguity

We noted earlier that a string of words can have more than one structure under a given grammar. Strings with this property were called **syntactically ambiguous**, and we distinguished syntactic ambiguity from **semantic ambiguity**, in which a string has more than one meaning.

Although syntactic and semantic ambiguity are different, there is a relationship between them in many cases. Consider these sentences:

(8) a. The old dogs and cats were hungry.
 b. Bart saw the man with the telescope.
 c. Lisa studied the whole year.

Each of these examples is semantically ambiguous: it has more than one meaning. Moreover, on reflection, they all seem to be ambiguous in a way that intuitively arises from the way we understand the words to be combining. For instance, (8a) is ambiguous according to what we think *old* applies to. On one reading, *old* applies to just the dogs, so it's the old dogs and all the cats that the speaker declares to be hungry. On the other reading, *old* applies to the dogs and cats together, so it's the old dogs and the old cats that are said to be hungry. Similarly, (8b) is ambiguous according to what we think *with the telescope* combines with. On one reading, it modifies *the man*: the man is understood as having the telescope. On the other reading, it modifies *saw the man*: the seeing of the man is understood as having been accomplished using the telescope. And so on for (8c).

We can capture these facts by assuming that the semantic ambiguity corresponds to a syntactic ambiguity: that the two different readings for these sentences correspond to two different trees for each. For example, suppose our grammar were to assign (8a) both of these trees:

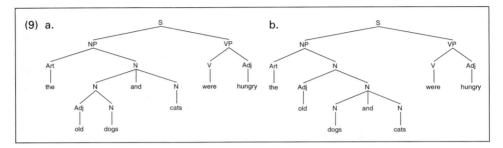

(9) a. ... b. ...

Putting aside details, Tree (9a) would correspond to the reading where it is elderly dogs and all cats that are hungry; *old* applies to *dogs* alone. Tree (9b) would correspond to the reading where both elderly dogs and elderly cats are hungry: *old* applies to the conjunction *dogs and cats*.

A similar analysis can be given for (8b). Trees like these will account for the readings we observe:

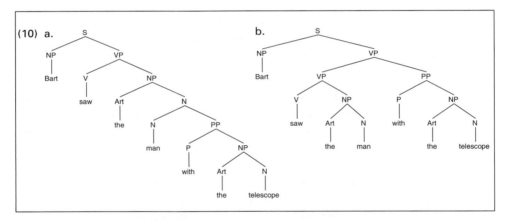

(10) a. ... b. ...

Tree (10a) corresponds to the reading where *with the telescope* modifies *the man*. Tree (10b) corresponds to the reading where it modifies *saw the man*.

Ambiguity thus gives us another indication of constituency relations. It's not a constituency test per se, in the sense that we can't just take a given sentence, construct a counterpart showing ambiguity, and draw conclusions about constituency from the results. Rather, when we find semantic ambiguity in a sentence that cannot be traced to ambiguity in individual words (as in *Bart went to the bank*), it can often be analyzed as arising from an ambiguity in the way those unambiguous words are combined—that is, from the internal constituency of the sentence.

The tests and phenomena reviewed above are useful indicators of constituency, but they are not foolproof. Indeed, the tests can sometimes yield, or appear to yield, conflicting results! Such situations are among the most interesting that linguists encounter in theory building, and we will return to them in Unit 10.

Trees and Tree Relations

Review

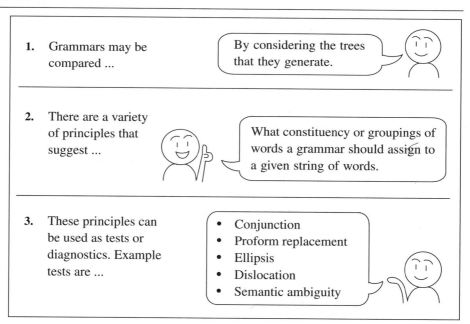

1. Grammars may be compared ...

By considering the trees that they generate.

2. There are a variety of principles that suggest ...

What constituency or groupings of words a grammar should assign to a given string of words.

3. These principles can be used as tests or diagnostics. Example tests are ...

- Conjunction
- Proform replacement
- Ellipsis
- Dislocation
- Semantic ambiguity

More about Trees

We've seen that certain phenomena (conjunction, proform replacement, etc.) show how words in a sentence are organized into groups or phrases. In this unit, we will look at a different kind of evidence for this conclusion—evidence involving what might be called **tree properties**.

Reviewing Terminology

First, let's reconsider terminology for talking about trees. Recall that the points in a tree labeled by categories like S or words like *Homer* are called **nodes**; the lines that connect nodes are **branches**. The single node at the very top of a tree is the **root node**, and the nodes at the ends of the branches are the **leaf nodes** or **terminal nodes**.

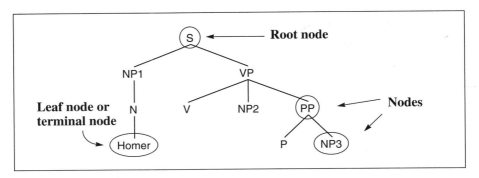

Two Basic Relations

Now, let's look at two basic relations that nodes can bear to each other in a tree. One is **dominance**. Adopting an informal definition, we will say that one node X **dominates** another node Y when it is possible to go from X to Y in the tree by tracing a strictly downward path of branches. For example, in the tree above, the VP node dominates the P node since it is possible to get from VP to P via PP by going *downward* only (see (1)). By contrast, the V node does not dominate the P node since in order to get from V to P, we must first go *up* to VP and then *down* to P (see (2)).

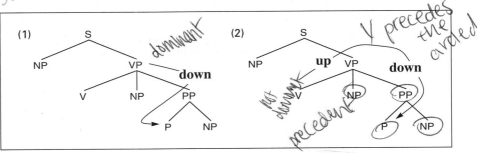

A second basic tree relation is **precedence**. Again, adopting an informal definition, we will say that one node X **precedes** another node Y when X does not dominate Y (or vice versa) and when X is to the left of Y in the tree.[1] In the tree above, then, V precedes P and two instances of NP. Likewise, V precedes PP.

---

1. For this definition to work, we must assume that trees are drawn so that when one node X precedes another node Y, all of the daughters of X precede all of the daughters of Y.

However, VP does not precede PP, since it dominates PP; and likewise, PP does not precede VP.

Structural Prominence: C-Command

Dominance and precedence allow us to define and talk about other tree relations. For example, consider our simple S structure again:

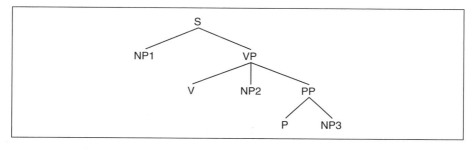

Notice that it is possible to speak informally of some nodes as being higher and hence more structurally prominent than others. For instance, there is a clear sense in which NP1 is higher in S than V or NP2, hence more structurally prominent than either of them. Correlatively, there is also a sense in which NP1 and VP are of equal height, and so equally prominent in S.

 **EXERCISE**   Try to write out an informal definition of the notion of prominence that we are getting at here. (Such a definition might have the following general form: "A node X has prominence over node Y if and only if ... ," where you fill in the "..." part.)

There are a number of possible definitions of structural prominence that would answer to our visual intuitions. Here's one due essentially to the linguist Tanya Reinhart:

Definition   A node X has **prominence** over a node Y iff (= if and only if) neither X nor Y dominates the other, and the first branching node dominating X also dominates Y.

pro...   X over y

To convince yourself that this definition captures prominence appropriately, consider our example tree again:

NP1 has prominence over V and NP2, but V and NP2 do not have prominence over NP1.

Beginning with NP1, V, and NP2, we see that no one of these nodes dominates any of the others. The first branching node dominating NP1 is S, which dominates V and NP2; hence, NP1 has prominence over both V and NP2. On the other hand, the first branching node dominating V and NP2 is VP, and this node fails to dominate NP1; hence, neither V nor NP2 has prominence over NP1. This squares with our visual intuition that NP1 has prominence (asymmetrically) over V and NP2. Now consider NP1 and VP. Again, neither of these two nodes dominates the other. Furthermore, the two nodes have prominence over each other since the first branching node dominating NP1 dominates VP, and vice versa. Again, the explicit definition squares with our visual intuition that NP1 and VP are equally prominent in S.

Henceforth, we will adopt standard technical terminology and rather than saying that a node X has prominence over a node Y, we will say that X **c-commands** Y. So the proper definition looks like this:[2]

Definition   A node X **c-commands** a node Y iff neither X nor Y dominates the other, and the first branching node dominating X also dominates Y.

---

2. The term *c-command* is an abbreviation of *constituent-command*.

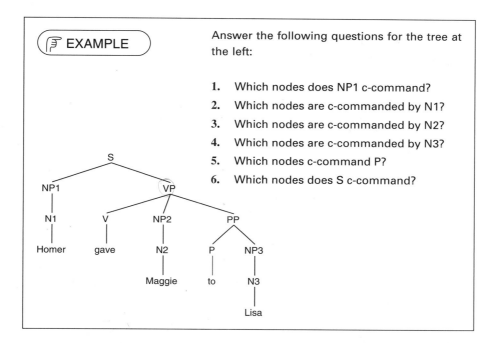

EXAMPLE

Answer the following questions for the tree at the left:

1. Which nodes does NP1 c-command?
2. Which nodes are c-commanded by N1?
3. Which nodes are c-commanded by N2?
4. Which nodes are c-commanded by N3?
5. Which nodes c-command P?
6. Which nodes does S c-command?

Some Distributional Facts

With the definition of c-command in mind, let's now turn to some interesting facts about the distribution of certain English words and phrases. We'll look at three types of forms: negative polarity items, reflexives, and *each … the other* constructions.

Negative Polarity Items

Let's begin with the (rather peculiar) words *ever* and *anyone.* These words are often referred to as **negative polarity items** (or **NPIs** for short). The name arises from the fact that in order for these forms to occur smoothly in a sentence, there has to be a **trigger element**—usually a negative item like *no, not, n't, no one, nothing*—in the same sentence. So contrast (3a) and (4a) with (3b) and (4b):

NPI + trigger element

(3) a.   *John saw anything.
    b.   John did**n't** see anything.
(4) a.   *Someone will ever have pizza again.
    b.   **No one** will ever have pizza again.

Now as it turns out, it isn't enough that an NPI and a negative item occur in the same sentence. The following additional data concerning *any* show that something more is required:

(5) a.   No one saw anything.
    b.   No one gave Maggie to anyone.
    c.   Homer gave nothing to anyone.
    d.   *Anyone saw nothing.
    e.   *Anyone gave Maggie to no one.
    f.   *Homer gave anything to no one.

trigger element comes first, TRIGGERS the NPI

🙂 EXERCISE   Thinking about the tree relations discussed above, state a hypothesis about what additional requirement holds of the relation between a trigger and an NPI.

Reflexive Pronouns

Now let's consider a second class of data. English has a collection of items that grammar books typically call **reflexive pronouns**: forms such as *himself, herself, itself, themselves*. An interesting property of these elements is that although they can occur in positions where other nominals can appear (including other pronouns), they cannot stand alone:

(6) a.   Homer left.
    b.   He / She / They left.
    c.   *Himself / *Herself / *Themselves left.

Instead, reflexives require another nominal in the sentence (one with appropriate person (1st, 2nd, etc.), number (singular or plural), and gender (masculine, feminine, or neuter)) on which to depend:

> (7) a. Homer saw himself.
> b. Homer gave himself to Marge.
> c. Homer gave a present to himself.
> d. Homer showed the girl to herself (in the mirror).

[handwritten annotation: antecedent then reflexive]

We call the item on which the reflexive depends the **antecedent** of the reflexive. So *Homer* is the antecedent of *himself* in (7a–c), and *the girl* is the antecedent of *herself* in (7d).

Now notice that—similarly to NPIs—it is not enough that a reflexive and a potential antecedent simply occur in the same sentence. Again, something more is required:

> (8) a. *Himself saw Homer.
> b. *Himself gave Homer to Marge.
> c. *Himself gave a present to Homer.
> d. *Homer showed herself to the girl.

 **EXERCISE**   What more is required of the relation between an antecedent and its dependent reflexive? State a hypothesis.

Each ... the Other

Finally, consider the following paradigm involving the words *each* and *the other*:

> (9) a. Each man saw the other.
> b. Homer introduced each girl to the other.

Sentence (9a) says that each member of some pair of men saw the remaining member of the pair. Sentence (9b) says that Homer introduced each member of some pair of girls to the remaining member of the pair. Evidently, *each ... the other* establishes a pairwise relation between members of some set.

each comes first

To get the desired reading, it is (yet again) insufficient that a phrase of the form *each N* and one of the form *the other* occur in the same sentence:

(10) a.   *The other saw each man.
     b.   *Homer introduced the other to each girl.

Neither of these examples seems well-formed under the desired "pairwise" reading.

☺ EXERCISE   These facts are strongly reminiscent of the facts about NPIs and reflexives. Some particular relation must hold between the *each*-phrase and the *the other*-phrase. What relation?

C-Command Again

What the questions in the last three sections are angling for is the idea that in order for certain kinds of dependent elements (NPIs, reflexives, etc.) to be properly sanctioned, they must stand in a particular **structural relation** to the items upon which they depend (trigger, antecedent, etc.). Specifically, if we think about tree relations, the general situation seems to be this:

Hypothesis A   A phrase X can be dependent on a phrase Y in a tree Z only if Y c-commands X in Z.

Y has to co-command X

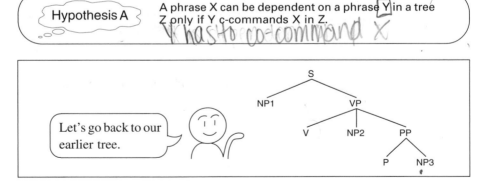

Let's go back to our earlier tree.

Since the subject (NP1) c-commands the direct object (NP2), we predict under Hypothesis A that a sentence with an NPI in direct object position and its trigger in subject position should be well-formed, but a sentence with the reverse structure should not. This is indeed what we found earlier (recall *No one saw anything* versus **Anyone saw nothing*). Likewise, since the direct object (NP2) c-commands the indirect object (NP3), we predict under Hypothesis A that a sentence with an NPI in indirect object position and its trigger in direct object position should be well-formed, but a sentence with the reverse structure should not. Again, this is what we found (recall *Homer gave nothing to anyone* versus **Homer gave anything to no one*). The same predictions hold for reflexives and *each ... the other* constructions.

An Alternative Hypothesis

If Hypothesis A is right, it provides strong additional evidence for the idea that sentences have internal, treelike constituent structure. If the best explanation for where NPIs and reflexives may occur appeals to c-command, a notion defined in terms of trees, then clearly the best theory is the one that assumes that there are in fact trees.

But is this generalization really the best account of the facts? Consider an alternative proposal—one that may have already occurred to you in thinking about these data, and one that makes no appeal to the tree notion c-command:

Hypothesis B	A phrase X can be dependent on a phrase Y in a tree Z only if Y precedes X in the terminal string of Z.

Under Hypothesis B, the starred examples that we've encountered are ruled out because the dependent item precedes the item on which it is supposed to depend: the NPI precedes its trigger, the reflexive precedes its antecedent, or the *the other*-phrase precedes the *each*-phrase. Tree structure would have nothing to do with it.

Hypotheses A and B are both compatible with the limited set of facts discussed above. To choose between them, we must therefore try to find data about which they make different predictions. Consider the following additional facts:

(independent)   (dependent)

Y has to precede X

(has to not dominate & be to the left)

(11) a. *A picture of Homer fell on himself.

b. *The painting that Homer treasures most doesn't belong to himself.

c. *A picture of no one fell on anyone.

d. *Something that Homer didn't think of occurred to anyone else.

e. *A picture of each man fell on the other's head.

f. *The friend that each man recommended spoke to the other.

These data appear to support one of our two hypotheses and to contradict the other. Which is which?

The new data all exhibit the following structural relationship between the dependent element, X, and the item that it is trying to depend upon, Y.

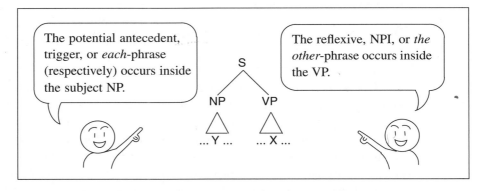

The potential antecedent, trigger, or *each*-phrase (respectively) occurs inside the subject NP.

The reflexive, NPI, or *the other*-phrase occurs inside the VP.

For example, here is a plausible tree for (11a):

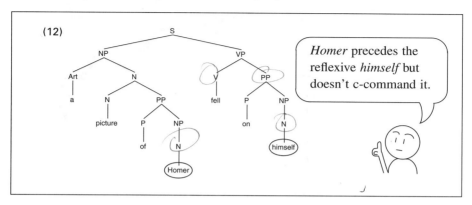

Under Hypothesis A, which ties dependency to tree structure, we predict the new examples will be ill-formed since the dependent item (reflexive, NPI, or *the other-*phrase) is not c-commanded appropriately. By contrast, under Hypothesis B, which ties dependency to linear order in the terminal string, the new examples are predicted to be well-formed since in each case the dependent item (reflexive, NPI, or *the other*-phrase) is preceded by an appropriate phrase on which it could depend. In fact, however, these sentences are ill-formed. So these data constitute evidence in favor of Hypothesis A and against Hypothesis B.

C-Command Phenomena as Constituency Tests

Assuming that c-command gives the right account for our sentences involving NPIs, reflexives, and *each ... the other* constructions, these items give us new probes for testing the constituency and branching structure of a tree. In particular, we can check the relative heights of two items in a tree by simply inserting a dependent item and a potential licenser and seeing whether the resulting sentence is well-formed. If it is, then we know that the dependent item is in a position from which it is c-commanded by the licensing phrase. If it is not, then (barring other sources of ungrammaticality) it is likely that the dependent item is in a position from which it is not c-commanded by the licensing phrase. This allows us to evaluate competing proposals about sentence structure.

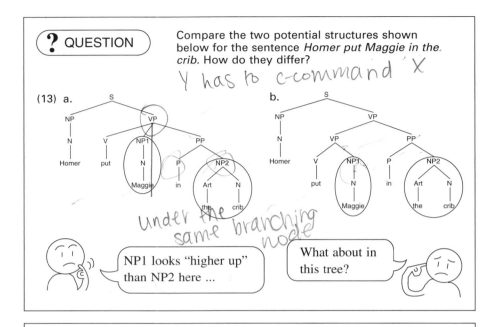

? QUESTION

Compare the two potential structures shown below for the sentence *Homer put Maggie in the. crib*. How do they differ?

Y has to c-command X

(13) a.

NP1 looks "higher up" than NP2 here ...

What about in this tree?

under the same branching node

≋ ANSWER

One difference between the two structures is the relative position of the direct object (NP1) and the object of the preposition (NP2). In Tree (13a), NP1 c-commands NP2. In Tree (13b), NP1 does not c-command NP2.

Given this difference, we can test which tree is right by placing an NPI like *anything* in the NP2 position and a suitable trigger like *no one* in the NP1 position. If NP1 c-commands NP2, as in Tree (13a), the resulting sentence should be good. If NP1 doesn't c-command NP2, as in Tree (13b), the resulting sentence should be bad. Here is the relevant sentence:

(14) Homer put no one in anything.

This sentence seems just fine. If you concur with this judgment, then NPIs, a c-command-dependent phenomenon, provide evidence we can use in choosing between the two structures.

Determining Category

Review

1. For a given set of sentences ... There will be different grammars that generate that set.

2. Given this, an important aspect of linguistic theorizing lies in ... Discovering which grammar is right and finding empirical evidence for it.

3. Finding the right grammar means ... Finding one that assigns the right structures.

Determining Category

Deciding on the structure of a sentence or other expression means answering at least two questions:

- What is the constituency of the expression? (How do its parts group together?)
- What are the categories of its words and phrases?

We've found ways of determining constituency using diagnostics like the conjunction or dislocation test. It's natural to ask whether similar tests exist for determining category.

The Category of Words

Earlier, we referred to the category of a word as its **part of speech**. This notion was introduced by the Greek philosopher/grammarian Dionysius Thrax, who proposed eight different parts of speech, based on his native language, Greek:

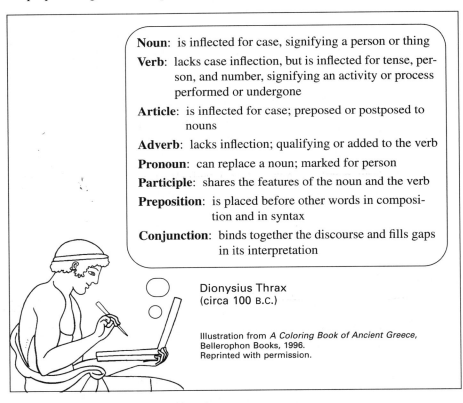

Noun: is inflected for case, signifying a person or thing

Verb: lacks case inflection, but is inflected for tense, person, and number, signifying an activity or process performed or undergone

Article: is inflected for case; preposed or postposed to nouns

Adverb: lacks inflection; qualifying or added to the verb

Pronoun: can replace a noun; marked for person

Participle: shares the features of the noun and the verb

Preposition: is placed before other words in composition and in syntax

Conjunction: binds together the discourse and fills gaps in its interpretation

Dionysius Thrax
(circa 100 B.C.)

Illustration from *A Coloring Book of Ancient Greece*, Bellerophon Books, 1996.
Reprinted with permission.

Notice that these category definitions employ three different criteria.

Inflection

One criterion is **inflection**—systematic variation in word form. In Greek (and many other languages), nouns are marked differently according to whether they occur as subjects, direct objects, indirect objects, and so on. These markings are called **case inflections**. For example, in Japanese the subject is marked with *-ga* (nominative case), the direct object is marked with *-o* (accusative case), and the indirect object is marked with *-ni* (dative case).

☞ **EXAMPLE**

Taroo-ga   Hanako-ni   Pochi-o   ageta.
Taroo-NOM Hanako-DAT Pochi-ACC gave
'Taroo gave Pochi to Hanako.'

If nouns alone can be marked with case inflection, as Thrax proposed, then case inflection can be used as a test for nounhood.

Modern English, unlike Old English, Japanese, and Greek, does not show case inflection (except in pronouns). However, nouns (Ns) in English *do* generally inflect for **number** (singular or plural):

 → case inflection (N)

```
book - books     man - men        knife - knives
dog - dogs       woman - women    wolf - wolves
judge - judges   wreath - wreaths (sheep - sheep)
```

Similarly, members of the category verb (V) generally inflect for **tense** (present or past):

→ tense inflection (V)

```
look - looked    think - thought   go - went
gaze - gazed     see - saw         eat - ate
bet - betted     lose - lost
```

Members of the category adjective (A) typically inflect for **degree** (positive, comparative (*-er* or *more*), or superlative (*-est* or *most*)): → degree inflection (A)

```
tall - taller - tallest
quick - quicker - quickest
soft - softer - softest
red - redder - reddest
happy - happier - happiest
old - older - oldest
tough - tougher - toughest
(astute - more astute - most astute)
```

But: former - ?? - ??

Finally, members of the category adverb (Adv) formed from adjectives are commonly marked with *-ly*:

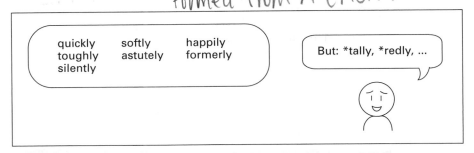

formed from A (Adv)

quickly	softly	happily	
toughly	astutely	formerly	But: *tally, *redly, ...
silently			

These inflectional patterns can often be used to identify nouns, verbs, adjectives, and adverbs, respectively.

Position

A second criterion Thrax used is **position**. Certain classes of words seem to favor specific locations in the sentence. For example, English articles and determiner elements nearly always cooccur with a noun; they don't usually combine with other elements:

articles + determiner + noun

> the man - a man   no fish - every fish - most fish
> *the say - *a looked   *no tall - *every in - *most likes

Similarly, English prepositions (*to, from, under, over, after, before, during*, etc.) very typically cooccur with a noun phrase:

preposition + NP

> to [the doctor], from [a friend], under [my chair], over [the rainbow], ...

Accordingly, if we find a word occurring in the same positions as other words whose category we know, a natural move is to classify the word as belonging to that category.

Meaning/Function

A third criterion Thrax appealed to is **sense** or **function**. Certain categories of words seem to have a conventional meaning or use. For example, referring to concrete objects or individual persons is typically the job of nouns. Prepositions often denote relations, for example, relations of time (*before, after, while, during*), space (*at*, *in*, *on*, *under*), cause or purpose (*because-of*). Verbs often describe actions (*hit*) or states (*like*, *know*). Adjectives usually pick out properties that can be attributed to an object (*tall*, *big*, *black*, *gray*, *smart*, *fast*, *hard*, *ductile*). Many determiners are counting words (*every*, *no*, *some*, *most*, *two*, *both*). Conjunctions are typically used to bind sentences together. And so on.

    These three criteria are simply **heuristics**—useful guides to the classification of words, but not decisive tests. In all cases, there are exceptions: items of a category that don't show the usual inflection, or that occur out of the normal position, or that don't have the expected use or meaning. In these cases, we usually decide on category based on what the majority of criteria suggest.

The Category of Phrases

Determining the category of phrases is somewhat more systematic. Here, there are at least two commonly suggested tests.

Substitution

One plausible indicator of category is what we might call "substitution potential." If one phrase can replace another in a sentence (or other expression) without changing the function of the original, then a reasonable idea is that the two phrases belong to the same category. This point can be made into a test as follows:

> **Substitution test**
> If a phrase whose category we are unsure about (X) can, without change of function, replace another phrase (Y) whose category we know, then we can conclude that X belongs to the same category as Y.

☞ EXAMPLE   Consider the boldfaced words in these examples:

Homer chased Bart **in the park**.
Homer chased Bart **there**.

both are PP

Suppose we've already determined that *in the park* is a PP. Then the fact that the proform *there* can replace *in the park* without change of function suggests that it too is a PP.

We might capture this by means of a rule like PP → *there*.

EXAMPLE   Consider the boldfaced words in these examples:

Homer and Marge **ran away together**.
Homer and Marge **eloped**. $\} \; VP$

Suppose we've already determined that *ran away together* is a VP. Then the fact that the single verb *eloped* can replace *ran away together* without change of function suggests that it too is a VP.

We might capture this by means of two rules: VP → V, V → *eloped*. This classifies *eloped* as a V that can also stand alone as a VP.

EXAMPLE   Consider the boldfaced words in these examples:

Homer left **the room**. NP
Homer left **quickly**. Adv

Suppose we've already determined that *the room* is an NP. Does the fact that the adverb *quickly* can replace *the room* imply that it too is an NP? If not, why not?

On reflection, the substitution test is quite familiar: it was an important part of our strategy for capturing syntactic patterns in the first place. We assigned words to general categories (N, V, etc.) and then used those categories to state patterns. How did we determine how to assign words to categories in the first place? By substitution! We assigned words to categories by seeing what other words they can substitute freely for. Two or more forms that substitute freely were analyzed as belonging to the same part of speech.

Conjunction
Conjunction also provides a test for category membership. Recall that our conjunction rules have this general form:

X → X Conj X

Note that conjunction doesn't simply join constituents—it joins constituents of the same category. This observation can be made into a test as follows:

combine the same elements

> **Conjunction test**
> If a phrase whose category we are unsure about (X) can be conjoined with another phrase (Y) whose category we know, then we can generally conclude that X belongs to the same category as Y.

☞ EXAMPLE   Consider the boldfaced words in these examples:

Homer and Marge **ran away together**.
Homer and Marge **quarreled**.
Homer and Marge **quarreled and ran away together**.

Suppose we've already determined that *ran away together* is a VP. Then the fact that the single verb *quarreled* can conjoin with *ran away together* suggests that it too is a VP.

Again, we capture this by means of two rules: VP → V, V → *quarreled*. This classifies *quarreled* as a V that can constitute its own VP.

Revising, Refining, and Reconsidering

Review

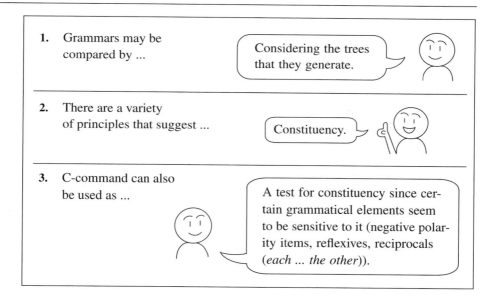

1. Grammars may be compared by ...

   Considering the trees that they generate.

2. There are a variety of principles that suggest ...

   Constituency.

3. C-command can also be used as ...

   A test for constituency since certain grammatical elements seem to be sensitive to it (negative polarity items, reflexives, reciprocals (*each ... the other*)).

Interpreting Test Results

In the simplest situation, when you are testing some hypothesis, you get unequivocal results: the test outcomes all point to the same conclusion. For example, suppose you are testing for the presence of some chemical XYZ and have a number of methods for detecting it. You apply these methods to a particular sample and they all point to the same conclusion: XYZ is present in the sample.

Similarly, suppose you are testing the English sentence *Homer chased Bart* for the presence of a constituent that groups the verb and its object together (what we earlier labeled a "VP"). Thus:

You apply the conjunction test and find that the verb and its object can be conjoined. ⇨ Homer [chased Bart] and [chased Lisa].

You apply the ellipsis test and find that the verb and its object can be deleted. ⇨ Homer chased Bart, but Marge didn't Ø.

You apply the proform replacement test and find that the verb and its object can be replaced by the proform *do so*. ⇨ Homer chased Bart, but Marge didn't **do so**.

You apply the dislocation test and find that the verb and its object can be fronted as a group. ⇨ (Homer said he would chase Bart and) [Chase Bart], Homer did.

In this case, our tests all point to the same conclusion: the verb and the object form a constituent.

External Factors

As you might suspect, the situations we face are rarely so simple. The interpretation of results can be complicated in various ways. One familiar kind of complication is *the intrusion of external factors*.

To illustrate, suppose that in testing whether verb and object form a constituent, we had considered the sentence *Homer knew Bart* instead of *Homer chased Bart*. The conjunction and ellipsis tests apply as before, indicating that *knew* and its object *do* form a group:

> (1) a. Homer [knew Bart] and [knew Lisa].
> b. Homer knew Bart, but Marge didn't Ø.

However, when we try proform replacement with *do so*, the outcome is unacceptable:

> (2) *Homer knew Bart, but Marge didn't **do so**.

It might seem tempting to conclude at this point that perhaps *knew Bart* isn't a constituent after all. But on further exploration, an alternative explanation for the ill-formedness might occur to you. Notice that the proform *do so* does not replace just any predicate; rather, it replaces predicates that contain a verb that *describes an action that someone does (like chasing)*. It does not replace predicates that express states that hold, or situations that someone may be in (like knowing).

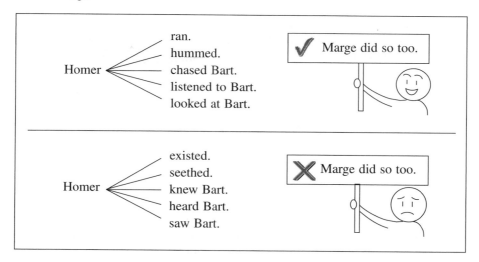

This suggests that what blocks proform replacement with *knew Bart* has nothing to do with constituency. Rather, it has to do with more fine-grained properties of the predicate: the fact that *know* doesn't describe an action.

Test results therefore cannot always be taken at face value. The fact that *knew Bart* cannot be replaced with the predicate proform *do so* does not automatically imply that *knew Bart* is not a constituent. Lack of agreement with expected results can occur because of other intruding factors that are irrelevant to what we're testing for. As we will see in later units, there are usually many factors to consider when applying any principle.

Some Logic

These remarks raise an important point about applying our tests. Principles like P2 from Unit 7 have the form of "*if-then* statements"—or **conditionals**, as they are called:

> **P2**
>
> *If* a string of words can be replaced with a proform, *then* it is a constituent.

According to logic, a true conditional can never have a true *if*-part (the **antecedent of the conditional**) and a false *then*-part (the **consequent of the conditional**). The truth of the antecedent requires the truth of the consequent. So if P2 is true, then whenever you find a string of words in a sentence that can be replaced by a proform, that string must be a constituent.

Saying that the truth of the antecedent requires the truth of the consequent is different from saying that the truth of the consequent requires the truth of the antecedent. According to logic, P2 is *not* equivalent to Principle 2' (P2'):

> **P2'**
>
> *If* a string of words is a constituent, *then* it can be replaced with a proform.

This means that it is perfectly compatible with P2 that a string be a constituent and not be replaceable with a proform. This is just the situation that seems to hold with *knew Bart*. Our conjunction and ellipsis tests both imply that *knew Bart* is a constituent. However, *knew Bart* cannot be replaced by the proform *do so*. Logic says that this situation is compatible with the truth of P2, and does not contradict it. All we know according to P2 is that if a string *is* replaceable, it is a constituent. P2 doesn't allow us to conclude anything in the situation where a string is *not* replaceable.

These points are general ones holding for all of our constituency test principles. A principle of the form P (where the blank is filled in by *be conjoined, be elided, be replaced by a proform*, etc.) is not equivalent to one of the form P′ (where "⇎" is read "is not equivalent to").

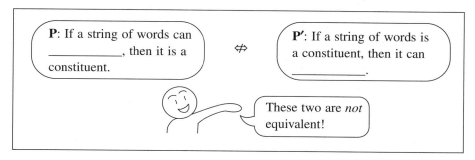

So, the truth of P1 (given in Unit 7) doesn't imply that any constituent can be conjoined. The truth of P3 doesn't imply that any constituent can be elided. The truth of P4 doesn't imply that any constituent can be dislocated. And so on.

Using the Reversed, Negative Form of a Conditional

Logic tells us another useful point about conditionals: any conditional statement is equivalent to another conditional statement in which its two parts (antecedent and consequent) are negated and their order is reversed. So the following is true (where "⇔" is read "is equivalent to"):

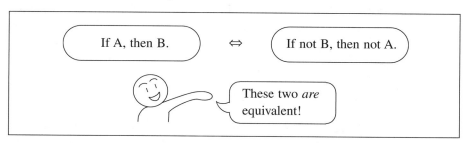

This means that each of our principles will have an alternative negative form that is equivalent to it. For example:

P: If a string of words can be replaced with a proform, then it is a constituent.   ⟺   **P′**: If a string of words isn't a constituent, then it cannot be replaced with a proform.

It is sometimes easier to use the negative forms in applying our constituency test principles. For example, suppose you are told that a particular string is not a constituent. Then the negative form of P2 tells you that the string cannot be replaced by a proform. You can now perform the replacement to see if it can be made.

More on Revising Grammars

Problematic test results cannot always be explained by appeal to external intruding factors. Sometimes our principles may truly give conflicting results. When this happens, it is a sign that our theory is in need of genuine revision. What must we do now?

Data, Structures, and Principles

Our discussions of constituency bring together three basic components. First, there are the data that we are accounting for. To this point, the data have consisted mostly of grammaticality judgments. Second, there is the tree structure that we propose for the data. Third, there are the principles that we use to relate the data and the structure.

For example, in considering the constituency of a verb and its object, we had the fact that *Homer ran and chased Bart* is a well-formed sentence of English. We proposed a structure in which *ran* and *chased Bart* are both constituents (in our grammar, constituents of category VP). And we had a principle (P1) that brought the fact and the structure together:

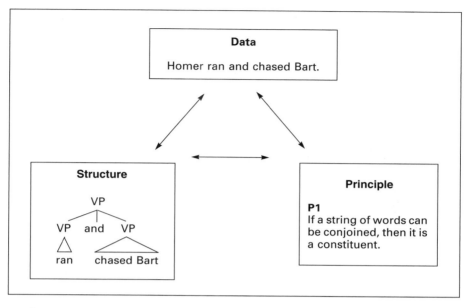

So when a problem or contradiction arises in our results, we must take another look at one (or more) of these three basic elements. We must revise the structure, or refine the principles, or reconsider the data. Let's look at some concrete cases.

Revising the Structure: Possessive NPs

English contains what are often called **possessive NPs**. Some examples are given below. A question that arises for syntax is, What is the structure of a possessive NP like *Bart's father*?

(3) a.   **Bart's father** chased Lisa.
     b.   Homer gave Marge **Lisa's report card**.
     c.   **Lisa's picture of Bart** fell on Homer.

Under P1, the following data imply that in (3a) the strings *Bart's father* and *Bart* are constituents. (Question: Why?)

(4) a.   Bart's father and Maggie's mother chased Lisa.
     b.   Bart and Maggie's father chased Lisa.

A possible structure for possessive NPs is shown below, together with the trees it assigns to *Bart's father* and *Lisa's picture of Bart*:

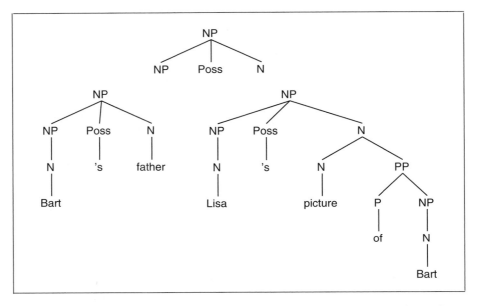

This proposal has two advantages. First, it allows us to generate the conjunctions *Bart's father and Maggie's mother* and *Bart and Maggie's father* in a straightforward way.

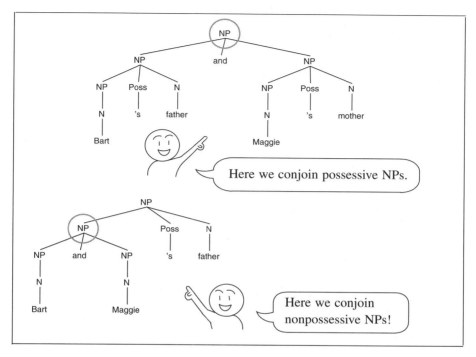

Second, the proposal accommodates the recursive character of possessive NPs, observed in sequences like (5a–c). (Question: How?)

> (5) a. **Bart's father** chased Lisa.
>   b. **Bart's father's mother** chased Lisa.
>   c. **Bart's father's mother's father** chased Lisa.

Nonetheless, the structure encounters problems with another piece of conjunction data. Consider this sentence:

> (6) **Bart's and Maggie's mother** chased Lisa.

Note that this example is fully well-formed, but it involves neither a conjunction of possessive NPs nor a conjunction of nonpossessive NPs. Rather, it contains a conjunction of possessors (NP + Poss). This is problematic for our structure, which does not group NP + Poss into a single constituent:

Because of this, our structure creates a conflict between the new conjunction data and P1:

> **P1**
> If a string of words can be conjoined, then it is a constituent.

Trying New Trees

A natural move at this point is to try to revise the structure for possessives so that the new conjunction facts are accounted for. For example, suppose we revise our tree to contain an element PossP, which includes just the possessor NP and the *'s* element:

Our example NPs *Bart's father* and *Lisa's picture of Bart* now look like this:

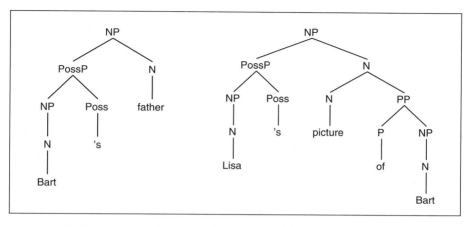

All of the conjunction examples generated by the old structure can be generated by our new one as well:

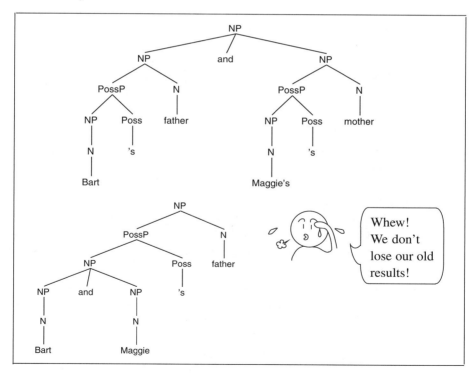

The new structure is also recursive, producing the "nested possession examples" in (5), repeated here. (Do you see how?)

(5)   a.   **Bart's father** chased Lisa.
      b.   **Bart's father's mother** chased Lisa.
      c.   **Bart's father's mother's father** chased Lisa.

However, the new structure has an additional advantage. It is able to generate the conjunction-of-possessors examples that were problematic under the old proposal:

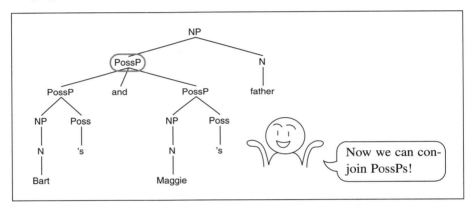

So revising the structure allows us to bring our data and principles back into alignment.

Refining the Principles: Reflexives and Negative Polarity Items

In Unit 8, we encountered reflexives and negative polarity items (NPIs). These are dependent items requiring an antecedent or a trigger (respectively) that stands in a particular structural relation to them in the tree. We considered two hypotheses for this relation:

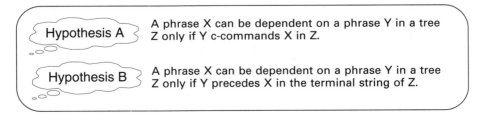

Hypothesis A   A phrase X can be dependent on a phrase Y in a tree Z only if Y c-commands X in Z.

Hypothesis B   A phrase X can be dependent on a phrase Y in a tree Z only if Y precedes X in the terminal string of Z.

We found evidence in favor of Hypothesis A. The evidence included (7a–d), which exhibit the structural relationship shown in (7e) between a dependent element X and an item Y that it is trying to depend on:

(7) a.   *A picture of Homer fell on himself.
     b.   *The painting that Homer treasures most doesn't belong to himself.
     c.   *A picture of no one fell on anyone.
     d.   *Something that Homer didn't think of occurred to anyone else.
     e.

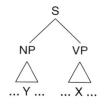

The reflexive or NPI occurs inside the VP, and the potential antecedent or trigger (respectively) occurs inside the subject NP. In this circumstance, Hypothesis A correctly predicted that X should not be able to depend on Y, whereas Hypothesis B incorrectly predicted that X should be able to depend on Y.

Evidence for Precedence

Now consider sentences involving the verbs *show* and *give*, and two object NPs. A plausible idea for the structure of such sentences is that the two objects are equal daughters under VP:

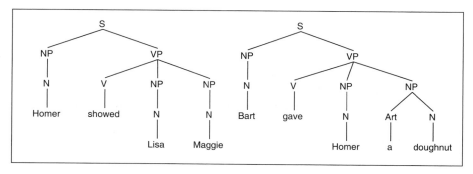

However, consider the following examples combining *show*, *give*, reflexives, and NPIs:

(8) a.   Homer showed Maggie herself.
     b.   Homer showed herself Maggie.
     c.   Bart gave no one anything.
     d.   Bart gave anyone nothing.

? QUESTIONS

1.   What does Hypothesis A predict about the well-formedness of (8a–d)? Which ones should be well-formed according to the hypothesis?

2.   What does Hypothesis B predict about the well-formedness of (8a–d)? Which ones should be well-formed according to the hypothesis?

3.   Which sentences actually *are* well-formed? Therefore, which hypothesis, A or B, fits these data better?

Many English speakers judge (8a,c) to be fine, but find (8b,d) ungrammatical. Here are the sentences again, with judgments added:

(8) a.   Homer showed Maggie herself.
     b.   *Homer showed herself Maggie.
     c.   Bart gave no one anything.
     d.   *Bart gave anyone nothing.

On careful reflection, Hypothesis A does not predict this result. Hypothesis A incorrectly predicts that all four examples should be fine since the two NPs c-command each other. By contrast, Hypothesis B correctly predicts the judgments just given, since only in (8a,c) does the dependent item follow the phrase it depends upon.

Hypothesis A or Hypothesis B or Both?

We thus face an apparent conflict. There now seems to be evidence for *each* of our two hypotheses over its rival. That is:

- There are structures and data favoring Hypothesis A over Hypothesis B.

- There are structures and data favoring Hypothesis B over Hypothesis A.

How do we resolve this situation? Which hypothesis is right and, whichever we choose, what do we say about the evidence that seems to argue against it and in favor of its opposite?

One way of looking at our situation is that both Hypothesis A and Hypothesis B appear to capture something right about the distribution of dependent items like reflexives and NPIs. If that idea is correct, then the right move is not to try to dispense with one of Hypothesis A or Hypothesis B; rather, we should combine them so that the insights behind *both* are retained. How might Hypotheses A and B be combined into a single hypothesis that fits all of the facts considered so far? One simple possibility is this, where we write both c-command and precedence into the dependence relation:

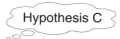 Hypothesis C   A phrase X can be dependent on a phrase Y in a tree Z only if Y c-commands and precedes X in Z.

Hypothesis C predicts the facts in (7a–d). These examples display precedence but not c-command, and Hypothesis C requires both. Hypothesis C also predicts the facts in (8a–d). Sentences (8b,d) display c-command, but not precedence. Only (8a,c) exhibit both c-command and precedence, and here exactly the examples are well-formed.

If this line of reasoning is correct, this is a case where we revise our principles in response to a conflict. Here we have revised the principle governing dependent items and the structural relations governing their dependence.

Reconsidering the Data: Center Embedding

English allows sentences that contain other sentences. In cases like (9a,b), a sentence appears as the subject of another sentence:

(9) a. [That Bart saw Homer] surprised us.
      b. [That Lisa admires Bart] is doubtful.

In both of these examples, the bracketed phrase contains a sentence, and this sentence functions as the subject of the bigger sentence.

One way of incorporating such **sentential subjects** might be to add a rule like this:

NP → *that* S

This yields the following trees for *That Bart saw Homer surprised us* and *That Lisa admires Bart is doubtful*:

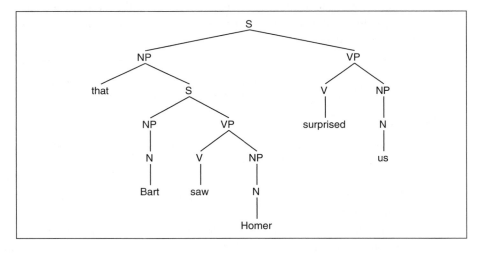

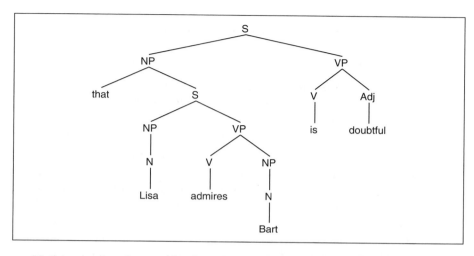

Notice now that the combination of S → NP VP and our new rule NP → *that* S is recursive. These rules can be applied to their own output:

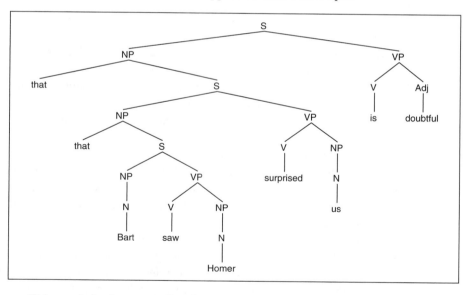

This result looks correct insofar as *That that Bart saw Homer surprised us is doubtful* is comprehensible, even if very complicated. In short order, however, further iterations become highly unacceptable:

(10) a. That that that Bart saw Homer surprised us is doubtful puzzled Lisa.
      b. That that that that Bart saw Homer surprised us is doubtful puzzled Lisa pleased Marge.
      c. That that that that that Bart saw Homer surprised us is doubtful puzzled Lisa pleased Marge annoyed Maggie.
          ...

One conclusion we might draw from this result is that the rule NP → *that* S and the structures it generates for sentential subjects are simply wrong. But, if they are wrong, it is hard to see what should replace them. After all, it seems that almost any sentence can be made the subject of another sentence in the frame ... *is obvious* or ... *surprised us* or ... *is doubtful*. But if that's true, then we would expect the result could itself become the subject of a sentence and that this result could become the subject of still another sentence, and so on. In other words, the whole process looks like it should be recursive, just as our rule NP → *that* S predicts.

Remember: Unacceptable ≠ Ungrammatical!

One way to deal with this conflict might be to **reconsider the basic data** and ask whether they are really ungrammatical at all. Surely (10a–c) are unacceptable. We could not say them and expect to be understood, nor could we understand them readily if they were spoken to us. But recall that this is a different thing from saying that they are ungrammatical: that their sentence structure doesn't conform to the proper patterns of English.

In fact, it has been proposed that examples like (10a–c) are not really ungrammatical but instead **grammatical and simply very hard to process**. The source of the difficulty (the suggestion goes) lies in the way they are built up. Notice that each embedded sentence in, for example, *That that that Bart saw Homer surprised us is doubtful puzzled Lisa* is flanked on both sides by a *that* and a VP from the sentence that contains it. To figure out which sentence the first *that* is associated with, you must wait until you get to the final VP, *puzzled Lisa*. In waiting for that sentence piece, you encounter another *that* that you must wait to associate with its VP, *is doubtful*. And in waiting for that sentence piece, you encounter yet another *that* that you must wait to associate with its VP, *surprised us*. Graphically:

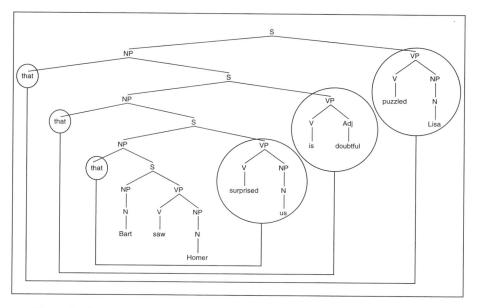

The point is clear. Processing such sentences, in which one constituent is embedded in the middle of another, plausibly involves an operation in which you mentally "store" a certain element (*that*) while waiting to associate it in the clause. If, in the process of doing this, you encounter the very same kind of element that you must also hold in memory and draw out at the appropriate time, it is quite reasonable to think that comprehension difficulties would arise.

Under this line of thinking, when we encounter difficulties with our rule NP → *that* S and the sentences it generates, our strategy is not to abandon the rule—rather, it is to **reconsider the data**. We accept that a large—in fact, infinite—portion of the sentences this rule generates are unacceptable, and useless for communication. But, we suggest, the example sentences themselves are not ungrammatical per se.

EXERCISES

1. Here are two grammars for a small part of English:

   Grammar 1

   S → NP V PP
   PP → P NP
   PP → P NP Conj P NP
   NP → Art CN
   NP → N

   V → spilled
   N → Marge
   N → beer

   CN → sofa
   CN → carpet
   Art → the
   P → on
   P → near
   P → onto
   Conj → and

   Grammar 2

   S → NP V PP
   PP → P NP
   PP → PP Conj PP
   NP → Art CN
   NP → N

   V → spilled
   N → Marge
   N → beer

   CN → sofa
   CN → carpet
   Art → the
   P → on
   P → near
   P→ onto
   Conj → and

   A. Both Grammar 1 and Grammar 2 generate trees for the sentence *Beer spilled on the sofa and near Marge*. Give the two trees.

   B. For each statement, say whether it is true or false.

      a. The rule PP → P NP Conj P NP is recursive.

      b. The rule PP → PP Conj PP is recursive.

   C. Although they are similar, Grammar 1 and Grammar 2 are *not* equal in their generative power. In particular, Grammar 2 can generate well-formed sentences that Grammar 1 cannot generate.

a.   Give an example of a well-formed sentence that *can* be generated by Grammar 2 but *cannot* be generated by Grammar 1.

b.   Give the tree that Grammar 2 generates for the example you just wrote.

2. Here are two grammars for a small part of English:

Grammar 1

S → NP V AP   V → *arrived*

AP → A   N → *Homer*

AP → A PP   CN → *plane*

AP → AP Conj AP   CN → *trip*

PP → P NP   A → *hungry*

NP → Art CN   A → *tired*

NP → N   Art → *the*

                     P → *from*

                     Conj → *and*

Grammar 2

S → NP V AP   V → *arrived*

AP → A   N → *Homer*

AP → A PP   CN → *plane*

AP → A Conj A PP   CN → *trip*

PP → P NP   A → *hungry*

NP → Art CN   A → *tired*

NP → N   Art → *the*

                     P → *from*

                     Conj → *and*

A.   Both Grammar 1 and Grammar 2 generate trees for the sentence *Homer arrived hungry and tired from the trip*. Give the two trees.

B.   For each statement, say whether it is true or false.

a.   The rule AP → AP Conj AP is recursive.

b.   The rule AP → A Conj A PP is recursive.

C.   Although they are similar, Grammar 1 and Grammar 2 are *not* equal in their generative power. In particular, Grammar 1 can generate well-formed sentences that Grammar 2 cannot generate.

a.   Give an example of a well-formed sentence that *can* be generated by Grammar 1 but *cannot* be generated by Grammar 2.

b.   Give the tree that Grammar 1 generates for the example you just wrote.

3. Sentence (1) contains an intransitive verb + an adverb. (2a,b) are two potential trees for this sentence:

(1)   Maggie crawled slowly.

(2)   a.   b.

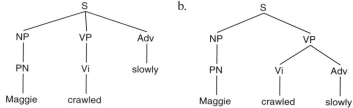

A.   What set of phrase structure rules generates (2a)? (Call this set *Grammar 1*.)

B.   What set of phrase structure rules rules generates (2b)? (Call this set *Grammar 2*.)

C.   For each statement, say whether it is true or false.

   a.   *Crawled* and *slowly* form a constituent in (2a).

   b.   *Crawled* and *slowly* form a constituent in (2b).

D.   Consider sentence (3):

(3)   Maggie crawled slowly and slept soundly.

   a.   What structural rule would you add to Grammar 1 to accommodate (3)? (Call the new grammar *Grammar 1′*.)

   b.   What structural rule would you add to Grammar 2 to accommodate (3)? (Call the new grammar *Grammar 2′*.)

E.   Consider sentence (4) and then answer the questions that follow:

(4)   Maggie crawled slowly and ate heartily and slept soundly.

   a.   Can Grammar 1′ generate (4) without additional structural rules? Answer "yes" or "no." If "yes," give the tree for (4) under Grammar 1′.

   b.   Can Grammar 2′ generate (4) without additional structural rules? Answer "yes" or "no." If "yes," give the tree for (4) under Grammar 2′.

4. Consider the following two grammars:

Grammar 1

S → N Vi	N → *man*
S → N Vt N	N → *woman*
S → N Vt Art N	N → *girl*
S → Art N Vi	N → *boy*
S → Art N Vt N	Art → *a*
S → Art N Vt Art N	Art → *the*
	Vi → *ran*
N → *Homer*	Vi → *slept*
N → *Marge*	Vi → *crawled*
N → *Lisa*	Vt → *chased*
N → *Bart*	Vt → *saw*
N → *Maggie*	Vt → *knew*

Grammar 2

S → N Vi	N → *man*
S → NP Vt NP	N → *woman*
NP → N	N → *girl*
NP → Art N	N → *boy*
	Art → *a*
N → *Homer*	Art → *the*
N → *Marge*	Vi → *ran*
N → *Lisa*	Vi → *slept*
N → *Bart*	Vi → *crawled*
N → *Maggie*	Vt → *chased*
	Vt → *saw*
	Vt → *knew*

Understanding the differences

A. Here is a list of sentences:

(1) a. Homer slept.

    b. The man slept.

    c. The girl saw Homer.

    d. Marge knew the boy.

    e. The girl chased the woman.

Both Grammar 1 (G1) and Grammar 2 (G2) generate these sentences, but they assign different trees in doing so.

    a.   Give the trees assigned by G1 to each of the sentences in (1). Give the trees assigned by G2 to each of the sentences in (1).

    b.   What, in general terms, is the difference in shape between the respective trees?

Revising the grammars

B.   Here is another list of sentences:

(2) a.   *The Marge slept.

    b.   *Man slept.

    c.   *The Marge saw man.

    d.   *Woman knew the Bart.

    e.   *The Lisa chased woman.

G1 and G2 both generate the ungrammatical sentences in (2).

    a.   Revise G1 and G2 so that they no longer produce the ungrammatical sentences. Give the revised grammars. (Call them *G1′* and *G2′*.)

    b.   Which grammar was easier to revise? Why was it easier to revise?

Choosing between the grammars

C.   Here is a final list of sentences:

(3) a.   Marge and Lisa slept.

    b.   Marge and the girl slept.

    c.   Marge and Lisa saw Homer.

    d.   Marge saw Homer and Bart.

    e.   Marge and the girl saw the boy and Homer.

Neither G1′ nor G2′ generates the new sentences in (3).

    a.   How would you revise G1′ to accommodate these new examples? (Call your new grammar *G1″*.)

    b.   How would you revise G2′ to accommodate these new examples? (Call your new grammar *G2″*.)

    c.   Are there examples that *are* generated by G2″ and that *are not* generated by G1″?

    d.   Which grammar (G1 or G2) appears to be the better, more adequate one?

5. So far we have been concerned strictly with grammars for English. In this exercise, we will construct a grammar for a small fragment of Korean.

Part I: Basic Korean sentences

Observe the following data. (Note: In all examples, *TOP* stands for *topic marker* and *OBJ* stands for *object marker*.)

(1) Chelsu ga   uletta.
     Chelsu TOP cried
     'Chelsu cried.'

(2) Chelsu ga   gu sagwa lul   boatta.
     Chelsu TOP that apple   OBJ saw
     'Chelsu saw that apple.'

(3) Chelsu ga   Sunhee lul   jonkyunghanda.
     Chelsu TOP Sunhee OBJ respect
     'Chelsu respects Sunhee.'

(4) Chelsu ga   gu gemun gae lul   joahanda.
     Chelsu TOP that black   dog OBJ like
     'Chelsu likes that black dog.'

(5) Chelsu ga   hakgyo e gatta.
     Chelsu TOP school to went
     'Chelsu went to school.'

(6) Chelsu ga   Sunhee ege chaek lul   juetta.
     Chelsu TOP Sunhee to   book OBJ gave
     'Chelsu gave a book to Sunhee.'

Now do the following:

A.   Give a grammar that generates these Korean data.

B.   Check to see whether your grammar generates any of the ungrammatical examples in (7):

(7) a.   *Chelsu lul uletta.

     b.   *Sunhee ga Chelsu lul uletta.

     c.   *Chelsu ga boatta.   (Korean speakers: For the purposes of this exercise, consider this example to be ungrammatical.)

     d.   *Chelsu ga Sunhee lul chaek lul juetta.

C.   If your grammar does generate any of these, revise it so that they will be correctly excluded. Give the new set of rules.

D.   Give the phrase markers (tree diagrams) that your grammar above assigns to sentences (1)–(6).

Part II: Incorporating conjunction

Consider the following additional Korean facts:

(8) Chelsu ga   Sunhee ege i   chaek lul   guligo gu   pen lul   juetta.
     Chelsu TOP Sunhee to   this book OBJ and   that pen OBJ gave
     'Chelsu gave this book and that pen to Sunhee.'

(9) Chelsu ga   Sunhee ege guligo Jae ege chaekdul lul   juetta.
     Chelsu TOP Sunhee to   and   Jae to   books   OBJ gave
     'Chelsu gave books to Sunhee and Jae.'

(10) Chelsu ga   gu   chaek lul   Sunhee ege guligo i   pen lul
     Chelsu TOP that book OBJ Sunhee to   and   this pen OBJ
     Jae ege juetta.
     Jae to   gave
     'Chelsu gave that book to Sunhee and this pen to Jae.'

Now do the following:

E.   State what rules you must add to your grammar in order to generate the conjunctions in (8) and (9).

F.   Give the phrase marker your rules assign to (8).

G.   Do your rules also generate (10)? If they do, give the phrase marker that they assign. If they do not, explain why they do not.

Part III: Reflecting on what you've done

H.   On the basis of your results for Parts I and II, compare the structure of Korean with that of English. Discuss any similarities and differences you can see in their syntactic patterning and/or their phrase structure rules. Be precise and explicit.

6. Along with simple PPs like *under the sofa*, English contains more complex PPs like those in *Bart jumped **out from under the sofa*** and *Lisa came **in out of the rain***. Three potential structures for the PP *out from under the sofa* are shown in (I), (II), and (III):

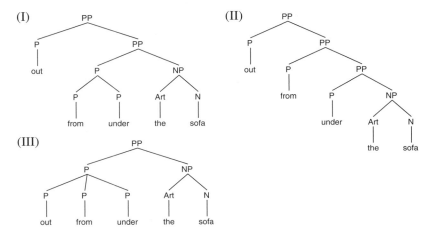

Now consider the following well-formed sentences:

(1) Bart jumped out from under the sofa and out from behind the chair.

(2) Bart jumped out from under the sofa and from behind the chair.

(3) Bart jumped out from under the sofa and behind the chair.

(4) Bart jumped out from under the sofa and Lisa jumped out from there too.

(5) Bart jumped out from under the sofa and Lisa jumped out from under it too.

(6) From under the sofa, Bart jumped out.

(7) Out from under the sofa, Bart jumped.

(8) Bart jumped out from under the sofa and the chair.

(Note: (2), (3), and (8) are to be understood as meaning the same as (1).)

A. Look at each box in the table below.

    a. Put a check (√) in the box if the tree structure *does* predict the sentence to be grammatical.

    b. Put a cross (×) in the box if the tree structure *does not* predict the sentence to be grammatical.

SENTENCE	(1)	(2)	(3)	(4)	(5)	(6)	(7)	(8)
I								
TREE II								
III								

B. Given your results in Question A, which tree diagram—I, II, or III—seems to give the best account of the structure of *out from under the sofa*? Explain your reasoning.

C. What problem does the following well-formed example raise for the results so far?

(9)   Kids jumped out from under and out from behind the sofa.

7. Consider the VP in (1) and the three possible structures for it in (I), (II), and (III) (where a triangle △ indicates that we are ignoring the internal structure of the node in question):

(1)   meet Bart at USB

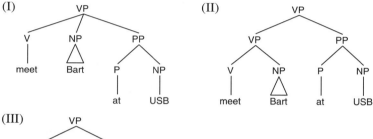

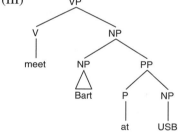

Assume that *at 3:00*, *in the Student Center*, and *near the Information Booth* are all PPs. Which of the structures in (I), (II), (III) (if any) can account for the following additional VPs?

(2)   a.   meet Bart at USB at 3:00

b.   meet Bart at USB at 3:00 in the Student Center

c.   meet Bart at USB at 3:00 in the Student Center near the Information Booth

Explain your answer carefully.

8. Consider the VP in (1) and the two possible structures for it shown in (I) and (II):

(1)   showed the boys pictures of Maggie
(as in *Homer showed the boys pictures of Maggie*)

(I)

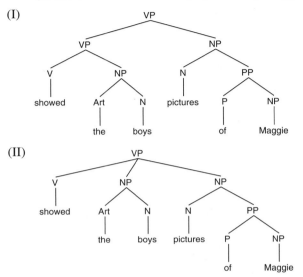

(II)

Which of these structures (if either) can handle the following additional data?

(2)   showed the boys pictures of themselves
(as in *Homer showed the boys pictures of themselves*)

Explain your answer carefully.

9. Consider the structure of possessive nominals like *Bart's mother* proposed in the text, where *Bart's* makes up a PossP.

   A.   What challenges do the following data present for this structure?

   (1)   a.   Bart's picture of himself (turned out well).

   b.   Bart and Lisa's pictures of each other (turned out well).

   c.   No one's pictures of anyone (turned out well).

   Explain your answer carefully.

   B.   Can you suggest a revision for the structure of possessives that will answer the challenge posed by (1a–c)?

PART IV Arguing for a Theory

Human activities differ in whether they are public or private. For some people, religious worship is a public thing: a matter of coming together as a congregation to express gratitude for existence, to ask forgiveness for one's failings, and to celebrate or mourn important transitions, like birth and death. For others, religion is an essentially private matter: a personal relationship between an individual and his or her creator. The views and beliefs of others are not pertinent.

Science is an essentially public enterprise. Scientists are part of a *community of researchers* who explore and investigate, and who communicate their findings and ideas with each other.

[Science] is to a large extent a common enterprise in which students are expected to come up with new ideas, to question and often undermine what they read and are taught, and to somehow pick up, by experience and cooperative inquiry, the trick ... of discerning important problems and possible solutions to them.
—"Rationality/Science," p. 91

Communicating one's findings and ideas requires framing them in an illuminating way. We need to be able to explain clearly

- The facts we are concerned with,
- The ideas we have about them,
- The assumptions lying behind our thinking, and
- The conclusions that our investigations have led us to.

Ideally, if we have gotten the facts right, if our ideas about the facts are sound, and if our background assumptions and reasoning are not mistaken, others in the community of researchers will be persuaded by our results and will follow our lead. Scientists usually derive great personal satisfaction in seeing others build upon their results and carry them forward. But this can only happen if those results are presented clearly and effectively in the first place. The task of presenting our investigations so as to lead others to the same conclusions we will call **arguing for those conclusions**.

The power of effective argument is one that has been appreciated since ancient days. In the early Greek democracies, where citizens debated public policy in open assembly, the ability to frame arguments effectively and persuasively meant the ability to get one's fellow citizens to do what one wanted. Noble families retained in-house teachers to school their children in argumentation skills (what was called **rhetoric**). Middle-class families hired private tutors (the so-called Sophists) for the same purpose. Ancient Rome also understood the power of argumentation, but usually as a threat to government authority. As a result, a succession of Roman governments discouraged the teaching of argumentation and from time to time even expelled teachers of rhetoric from the city.[1]

In Units 11 and 12, we will concentrate on developing the practical skill of arguing for linguistic analyses, working our way through a range of different cases. Although the focus will be on linguistic argumentation, the general four-part form presented here has wider application. Arguments in many different domains can be framed in this way. Try to get a feel for the general structure of a successful argument. Proceeding this way will help you to separate the various components of analysis more clearly in your mind, whether you are constructing an argument yourself or evaluating someone else's.

---

1. For an interesting discussion of the importance of rhetoric in ancient Greece and Rome, see Chapter 4 of Stone 1980.

Constructing Arguments I

Review

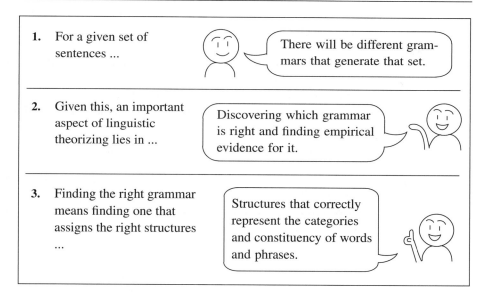

1. For a given set of sentences ...

   There will be different grammars that generate that set.

2. Given this, an important aspect of linguistic theorizing lies in ...

   Discovering which grammar is right and finding empirical evidence for it.

3. Finding the right grammar means finding one that assigns the right structures ...

   Structures that correctly represent the categories and constituency of words and phrases.

Giving an Argument

After we have done some investigation, we will want to set down our results, and our reasons for the structures we have settled on. That is, we will want to give **arguments** for our analysis.

What ingredients go into a sound argument for a structure? Let's look at a sample case where the language is English, and where we're arguing for the existence of a constituent that groups the verb, its object, and a following PP.

 EXAMPLE

Claim
Sentences of English containing the sequence NP V NP PP can have the structure in (i):

(i)
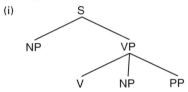

Argument

1. In (i), the verb and the phrases that follow it form a constituent (VP).

2. Consider the following data:

    (ii)   Homer gave Maggie to Lisa and sent SLH to Bart.

    Sentence (ii) shows *gave Maggie to Lisa* being conjoined with *sent SLH to Bart*.
    The example is well-formed.

3. By the conjunction test, only constituents can be conjoined. (Principle P1)

4. *Conclusion:* These data support structure (i) since it correctly analyzes *gave Maggie to Lisa* as forming a constituent.

Four Steps of an Argument and Their Relations

The sample argument given above contains *four essential steps*:

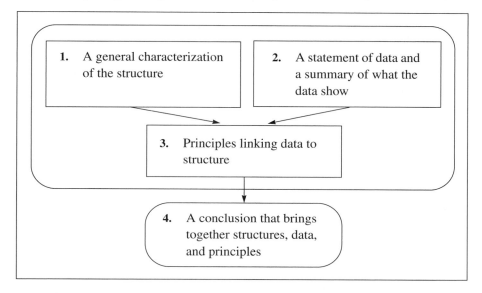

Let's examine some features of these steps more closely.

Characterization of the Structure

First, notice that the general characterization of the structure (Step 1) *is formulated in a way that is relevant to the principle(s) that we will later draw upon* (Step 3). Since the principle in Step 3 of our sample argument talks about constituency, the characterization of the structure in Step 1 is also given in terms of constituency. If the relevant principle used c-command instead, then we would characterize the structure in terms of c-command.

Data Statement and Summary

Second, observe that in introducing the data, we do more than simply list expressions or sentences; we summarize what the data show. We do this because *a given set of expressions might show a number of different things*; hence, it's necessary to say what particular point about the data we are interested in.

Furthermore, the data are introduced *in terms that don't presuppose what we are trying to show*. Notice that our data summary in Step 2 does not mention constituency. All we talk about there is what is conjoined and what is well-formed. Consider the following alternative version of the data summary: "Sentence (ii) shows that *gave Maggie to Lisa* forms a constituent with *sent SLH to Bart*. The example is well-formed." Here, we have already introduced constituency in the way we talk about the data. In effect, we have already assumed the conclusion that we are going to draw in Step 4. This is what is called **circular reasoning**. Since the constituency of these expressions is what we are arguing for, the data should not be characterized in these terms.

Principle and Conclusion

Finally, Step 3 is just a straightforward statement of what principle we are using. But—to repeat—what principle we are using determines how we characterize the structure we are arguing for in Step 1, and what phenomena are relevant in the data we are using in Step 2.

The conclusion states that the data support the constituency claimed by the structure, given the principle.

Convergent Evidence

The argument given above is a simple one using a single piece of data and a single principle. It is easy to see how we could enrich it to include several pieces of data involving several principles:

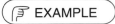 **EXAMPLE**

Argument

1. In the tree in (i), above, the verb and the phrases that follow it form a constituent (VP).
2. Consider the following data:
    (ii) a. Homer gave Maggie to Lisa and sent SLH to Bart.
         b. Homer gave Maggie to Lisa and Marge did too.
         c. (Homer said he would give Maggie to Lisa and)
           Give Maggie to Lisa, he did.

    Sentence (iia) shows *gave Maggie to Lisa* being conjoined with *sent SLH to Bart*.
    Sentence (iib) shows *gave Maggie to Lisa* being deleted.
    Sentence (iic) shows *gave Maggie to Lisa* being dislocated to sentence-initial position.
    All of these examples are well-formed.
3. By the conjunction test, only constituents can be conjoined. (Principle P1)
    By the ellipsis test, only constituents can be deleted. (Principle P3)
    By the dislocation test, only constituents can be dislocated. (Principle P4)
4. *Conclusion:* These data support structure (i) since it correctly analyzes *gave Maggie to Lisa* as forming a constituent.

Now the argument draws on several different kinds of phenomena (conjunction, ellipsis, dislocation) that all point to the same conclusion. Clearly, being able to appeal to **convergent evidence** strengthens our argument considerably. As in all sciences, being able to cite independent lines of evidence all leading to the same result inspires confidence that we're on the right track. A proposal that can explain a variety of facts is a powerful one, and to be as powerful, a competing analysis would have to do at least as well. So the general point is this:

 **POINT 1** | Try to give a number of lines of evidence in arguing for a position. The more phenomena your hypothesis explains, the stronger it is.

Nonconvergent Evidence

Of course, the data do not always converge, or converge fully. Recall our example sentence *Homer knew Bart*. Although conjunction and ellipsis give evidence for the constituency of the verb plus object in this case, proform replacement with *do so* does not (**Homer knows Bart, and Smithers does so too*). We hypothesized that this result follows from an additional constraint on *do so*, namely, that it is only allowed to replace predicates containing an action verb.

This case teaches two lessons. First, when we are collecting data, we should look at a range of examples. If we had started with *Homer knew Bart*, noted the problem with *do so* replacement, and looked no further, we would have missed other data supporting the idea that in a transitive sentence, the verb and the object form a constituent.

Second, when we do find data that fail to support our hypothesis, we should look for alternative lines of explanation. If we can account for a range of data under our hypothesis *and* we can give a plausible explanation for the recalcitrant facts, then the account gains depth and breadth. Here is an example of how we might draw the facts about *do so* with *know* into the argument given earlier.

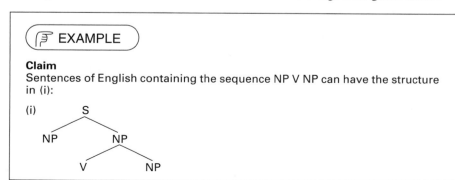

EXAMPLE

Claim
Sentences of English containing the sequence NP V NP can have the structure in (i):

(i)

Argument

1. In (i) above the verb and the noun phrase that follows it form a constituent (VP).

2. Consider the following data:

   (i)   a.   Homer chased Bart and tripped Mr. Burns.

         b.   Homer burped Maggie and Marge did so too.

         c.   Homer must know Lisa and Marge must too.

         d.   (Homer said he would find Bart and) Find Bart, he did.

   Sentence (ia) shows *chased Bart* being conjoined with *tripped Mr. Burns*.
   Sentence (ib) shows *burped Maggie* being replaced with the proform *do so*.
   Sentence (ic) shows *know Lisa* being deleted.
   Sentence (id) shows *find Bart* being dislocated to sentence-initial position.
   All of these examples are well-formed.

3. By the conjunction test, only constituents can be conjoined. (Principle P1)
   By the proform replacement test, only constituents can be replaced by a proform. (Principle P2)
   By the ellipsis test, only constituents can be deleted. (Principle P3)
   By the dislocation test, only constituents can be dislocated. (Principle P4)

4. *Conclusion:* These data support structure (i) since it correctly analyzes all the relevant phrases as forming constituents.

   Note: Proform replacement by *do so* appears to fail for certain predicates, including predicates of the verb-object form. Consider:

   (ii)   a.   *Homer   calmed.   Marge did so too.

          b.   seethed.

          c.   knew Lisa.

          d.   heard Bart.

          e.   saw Bart.

   The ill-formedness of (iia, b) shows that this restriction has nothing to do with verb-object constituency. A shared property of examples where *do so* replacement succeeds is that V describes an action or event. A shared property of the examples in (ii) is that V fails to describe such an action. Hence we hypothesize that *do so* obeys an additional constraint permitting it to replace only action predicates.

The general lessons are these:

POINT 2   Examine a range of data, not simply a couple of examples. Check that your results are representative.

POINT 3   Consider not only data that support the conclusion, but also data that don't; try to account for the latter by alternative means.

Coming Up With the Parts of an Argument

Putting together an argument requires assembling all the pieces—characterization of structure, data, principles, and so on—and arranging them appropriately. You might wonder: where do we get the pieces in the first place?

In general, you can't construct an argument without something specific to argue for. In our case, we're arguing for structures (trees). So this is where we start. Once we have the structure we want to argue for, the usual move is to go collect facts that might support it. Since facts support structures through principles, this means collecting facts that are relevant to our principles.

For instance, suppose you have the sentence in (i) below containing the **auxiliary** (or **"helping"**) **verbs** *could*, *have*, and *be*, which pattern like verbs in some ways and like an independent category in others. You're interested in how these elements attach in the tree, and, fiddling about, you've come up with the candidate structure in (ii). In this tree, the strings *chasing Bart*, *been chasing Bart*, and *have been chasing Bart* are all represented as constituents. In evaluating this structure, your strategy would be to look for data that would test whether all these strings are constituents after all.

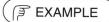 EXAMPLE

Claim

The structure of the example with auxiliary verbs in (i) is as shown in (ii):

(i)   Homer could have been chasing Bart.

(ii)

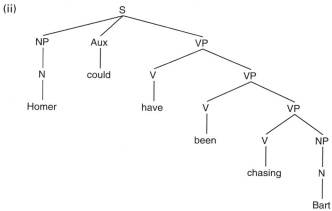

Argument

1.   In (ii), the strings *chasing Bart*, *been chasing Bart*, and *have been chasing Bart* are all constituents.

2.   Consider the following data:

...

If you don't already have the tree—for example, if all you have are sentence strings and no definite structures yet—then you are not yet in a position to construct an argument. At this point, you might try to brainstorm a bit, writing down a variety of trees. Alternatively, you might try constructing examples involving phenomena like conjunction, ellipsis, proform replacement, and negative polarity items, and see where they lead you. The results of the test should suggest ways of constructing a tree.

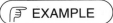 **EXAMPLE**   Suppose you have the sentence *Homer could have been chasing Bart*, with **auxiliary** (or **helping**) **verbs** *could, have, be*. You might try constructing data that involve ellipsis applied to *Homer could have been chasing Bart*. For example:

(i)   a.   Homer could have been chasing Bart and Marge could too.
    b.   Homer could have been chasing Bart and Marge could have too.
    c.   Homer could have been chasing Bart and Marge could have been too.

At this point, by P1, you already know something about constituency, so you can make an educated guess about the shape of the tree you want to argue for.

Keep in mind that in the course of constructing an argument, you may encounter data that cause you to change your mind about the structure you want to argue for. For example, suppose you are following out the argument given a couple of paragraphs back. You have sentence (i) and structure (ii), and you are in the process of collecting conjunction data to support the structure. Your plan is to use P1 to argue for the constituency shown in the tree.

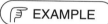 **EXAMPLE**

Claim

The structure of the example with auxiliary verbs in (i) is as shown in (ii):

(i)   Homer could have been chasing Bart.

(ii)

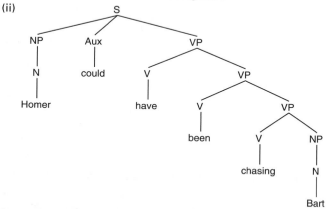

Argument

1.   In (ii), the strings *chasing Bart, been chasing Bart*, and *have been chasing Bart* are all constituents.

2.   Consider the following data:

(iii)   a.   Homer chased Bart and chased Lisa (too).

        b.   Homer was chasing Bart and was chasing Lisa (too).

        c.   Homer has been chasing Bart and has been chasing Lisa (too).

However, at this point you notice that along with the examples in (iiia–c), the following example is also well-formed:

d.   Homer could have been chasing Lisa and could have been chasing Lisa (too).

This fact is not correctly predicted by the tree in (ii).

At this point, you might decide to go back, amend the tree you began with, and argue for a new structure like this:

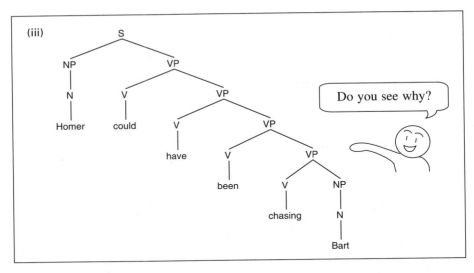

So a new proposal may emerge in the process of constructing an argument, leading us to a different point from the one where we started. This example also shows the importance of collecting a range of facts and of not being too narrow or too focused on the idea we begin with. We need to be constantly on the lookout for additional facts that may modify the picture.

Constructing Arguments II

Review

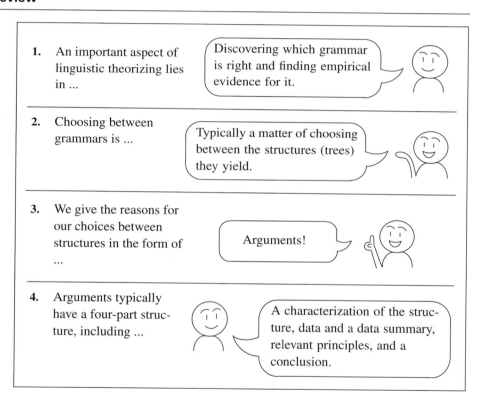

1. An important aspect of linguistic theorizing lies in ...

   Discovering which grammar is right and finding empirical evidence for it.

2. Choosing between grammars is ...

   Typically a matter of choosing between the structures (trees) they yield.

3. We give the reasons for our choices between structures in the form of ...

   Arguments!

4. Arguments typically have a four-part structure, including ...

   A characterization of the structure, data and a data summary, relevant principles, and a conclusion.

Choosing between Alternative Structures

In the last unit, we examined arguments for the structure of a single tree. Similar points apply to arguments that choose between two or more alternative structures.

Here is a sample case from English, where we argue in favor of trees that contain a verb phrase (VP) and against ones that don't.

Claim:
The structure of (i) is better represented by (iia) than by (iib):

(i)   Bart sent SLH to Maggie.

(ii)   a. 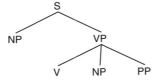   b.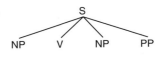

Argument

1. Structures (iia,b) differ in the following way: in (iia), the verb and the phrases that follow it form a constituent (VP); in (iib), they don't.

2. Consider the following data:

      (iii)   a.   Bart sent SLH to Maggie and handed Maggie to Marge.

             b.   Bart sent SLH to Maggie and Homer did too.

      Sentence (iiia) shows *sent SLH to Maggie* being conjoined with *handed Maggie to Marge*.
      Sentence (iiib) shows *sent SLH to Maggie* being elided.
      Both of these sentences are well-formed.

3. By the conjunction test, only constituents can be conjoined. (Principle P1)
    By the ellipsis test, only constituents can be elided. (Principle P3)

4. *Conclusion:* These data favor (iia) over (iib) since (iia) correctly analyzes *sent SLH to Maggie* as forming a constituent.

The four parts of an argument that we noted in the last unit are present here too.

In the following pages, we will consider similar arguments that are "missing" various steps or elements. Try to supply the missing parts before reading the discussion section that follows.

Missing Principle

Here, you're given all the parts of an argument except the principle in Step 3. What principle should be entered there?

Claim

The structure of (i) is better represented by (iia) than by (iib):

(i) Bart sent SLH to Maggie.

(ii) a.
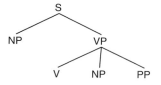

b.
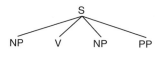

Argument

1. Structures (iia,b) differ in the following way: in (iia), the verb and the phrases that follow it form a constituent (VP); in (iib), they don't.

2. Consider the following data:

(iii) a. Bart sent SLH to Maggie and Homer did so too.

b. (Bart said he would send SLH to Maggie and) send SLH to Maggie, Bart did.

Sentence (iiia) shows *sent SLH to Maggie* being replaced by *do so*. Sentence (iiib) shows *sent SLH to Maggie* being dislocated to sentence-initial position.

3.

4. *Conclusion:* These data favor structure (iia) over (iib) since (iia) correctly analyzes *sent SLH to Maggie* as forming a constituent.

Discussion

Since the argument concerns constituency and since the data involve proforms and dislocation, what we need for Step 3 are principles that relate occurrence of proforms and dislocation to constituency. That is, we need P2 and P4:

3. By the proform replacement test, only constituents can be replaced with a proform. (Principle P2)
    By the dislocation test, only constituents can be dislocated. (Principle P4)

Principles P2 and P4!

This completes the argument.

Missing Data Summary and Principle

In the following example, summarize the data in Step 2 and state what principle should be entered in Step 3.

Claim
The structure of (i) is better represented by (iib) than by (iia):

(i)   Bart talked to Homer.

(ii) a. 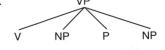   b.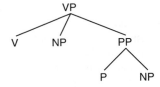

Argument

1. Structures (iia,b) differ in the following way: in (iib), the phrases following the verb form a constituent (PP); in (iia), they don't.

2. Consider the following data:
    (iii) a. Bart talked to Homer.
           b. Lisa walked toward Maggie.
           c. Bart lives in Springfield.
           d. To Homer, Bart talked.
           e. Toward Maggie, Lisa walked.
           f. In Springfield, Bart lives.

3.

4. *Conclusion:* These data favor structure (iib) over (iia) since (iib) correctly analyzes *to Homer, toward Maggie,* and *in Springfield* as forming a constituent.

Discussion

The data involve dislocation: moving various parts of the sentence to the front. Therefore, our data summary should be stated in terms of dislocation:

---

2. Consider the following data:

   (iii) a. Bart talked to Homer.

          b. Lisa walked toward Maggie.

          c. Bart lives in Springfield.

          d. To Homer, Bart talked.

          e. Toward Maggie, Lisa walked.

          f. In Springfield, Bart lives.

> Sentence (iiid) shows *to Homer* being dislocated to sentence-initial position.
> Sentence (iiie) shows *toward Maggie* being dislocated to sentence-initial position.
> Sentence (iiif) shows *in Springfield* being dislocated to sentence-initial position.
> All of these sentences are well-formed.

Since the argument concerns constituency, and since the data involve dislocation, what we need for Step 3 is a principle that relates occurrence of dislocation to constituency.

---

3. By the dislocation test, only constituents can be dislocated. (Principle P4)

Principle P4!

This completes the argument.

Missing Data Summary, Principle, and Conclusion I

In the following example, summarize the data in Step 2, state the relevant principle in Step 3, and give a conclusion that draws all these results together.

Claim
The structure of (i) is better represented by (iia) than by (iib):

(i) Bart talked to Homer.

(ii) a.

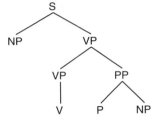

b.

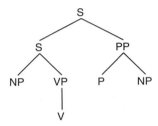

Argument

1. Structures (iia,b) differ in the following way: in (iia), the subject c-commands the PP object; in (iib), the subject fails to c-command the PP object.

2. Consider the following data:

    (iii) a. Bart talked to himself.

         b. No one talked to anyone.

         c. Each man talked to the other.

         d. They talked to themselves.

         e. No woman talked to any man.

         f. Each woman spoke to the other.

3.

4. *Conclusion:* These data favor structure (iia) over (iib) because ...

Discussion

The data involve reflexives, negative polarity items (NPIs), and *the other*-phrases; these are elements whose well-formedness depends on relative position with respect to an antecedent, trigger, or *each*-phrase (respectively). Therefore, our data summary should be stated in terms of these elements and their relative position:

2. Consider the following data:

   (iii) a. Bart talked to himself.

          b. No one talked to anyone.

          c. Each man talked to the other.

          d. They talked to themselves.

          e. No woman talked to any man.

          f. Each woman spoke to the other.

> Sentences (iiia,d) show that a phrase in subject position can serve as an antecedent for a reflexive in PP object position.
> Sentences (iiib,e) show that a negative phrase in subject position can serve as trigger for an NPI in PP object position.
> Sentences (iiic,f) show that an *each*-phrase in subject position can license a *the other*-phrase in PP object position.
> All of these sentences are well-formed.

Since the argument concerns relative position, and since the data involve reflexives, NPIs, and *the other*-phrases, we need a principle for Step 3 that relates reflexives, NPIs, and *the other*-phrases to position. Such a principle is Hypothesis C from Unit 10:

3. A phrase X can be dependent on a phrase Y in a tree Z only if Y c-commands and precedes X in Z. (Hypothesis C)

Hypothesis C!

The conclusion must pull all these various points together: structures, data, and principle:

4. *Conclusion:* These data favor structure (iia) over (iib) because although both structures analyze the subject as preceding the PP object position, only structure (iia) analyzes the subject position as both preceding and c-commanding the PP object position. Since c-command is required for licensing reflexives, NPIs, and *the other*-phrases, (iia) is favored over (iib).

This completes the argument.

Missing Data Summary, Principle, and Conclusion II

In this last example, only the tree is given. You must come up with relevant data, choose a principle, and give the appropriate conclusion.

Claim
The verb phrase in (ia) has a different structure than the verb phrase in (ib):

(i) a. Homer ran up a hill.

   b. Homer ran up a bill.

Specifically, the structure of (ia) is (iia); the structure of (ib) is (iib):

(ii) a.   b.

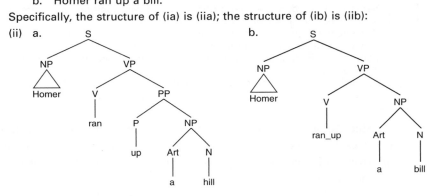

Argument

1. Structures (iia,b) differ in the following way:

2. Consider the following data:

3.

4. *Conclusion:*

Discussion

Notice that here we are not choosing between trees. Rather, we are arguing that two superficially similar sentences should have two different tree structures. Looking at these phrase markers, we see that in (iia), *up a hill* forms a constituent, whereas *ran up* does not. By contrast, in (iib), *ran up* forms a constituent, whereas *up a bill* does not.

Given this basic difference, we might construct an argument using evidence that bears on the constituency of *up a hill* in (iia) versus *up a bill* in (iib). For this, we can use any of our usual tests: conjunction, proform replacement, ellipsis, dislocation. For example, think about dislocation. To argue for the constituency of *up a hill* using dislocation, we would look for examples in which *up a hill* moves as a single unit. Correspondingly, if *up a bill* is not a constituent, we wouldn't expect it to be able to move. Data of this kind are not hard to come up with. Consider (iiia,b):

(iii) a.   Up a hill, Homer ran.
       b.   *Up a bill, Homer ran.

If we make use of these facts, the relevant principle to invoke will be P4.

Similarly, to argue for the constituency of *up a hill* using conjunction, we would look for examples in which *up a hill* is conjoined with a similar phrase. Correspondingly, if *up a bill* is not a constituent, we wouldn't expect it to be able to conjoin. Again, data of this kind are not hard to come up with:

> (iii)   c.   Homer ran up a hill and up a mountain.
>   d.   *Homer ran up a bill and up a debt.

In this case, the relevant principle would be P1.

Let's now use these data to construct a full-fledged argument:

Argument

1. Structures (iia,b) differ in the following way: in (iia), the verb and the following preposition do not form a constituent, whereas the preposition and the following NP do; in (iib), the verb and the following preposition do form a constituent, whereas the preposition and the following NP do not.

2. Consider the following data:
    (iii)   a.   Up a hill, Homer ran.
            b.   *Up a bill, Homer ran.
            c.   Homer ran up a hill and up a mountain.
            d.   *Homer ran up a bill and up a debt.
    Sentence (iiia) shows *up a hill* being dislocated.
    Sentence (iiic) shows *up a hill* being conjoined with *up a mountain*.
    Sentence (iiib) shows that *up a bill* cannot be dislocated.
    Sentence (iiid) shows that *up a bill* cannot be conjoined.

3. By the dislocation test, only constituents can be dislocated.
    (Principle P4)
    By the conjunction test, only constituents can be conjoined.
    (Principle P1)

4. *Conclusion:* These data support the differences in structures (iia) and (iib). (iia) analyzes *up a hill* as forming a constituent, and indeed this phrase can be dislocated and conjoined. (iib) analyzes *up a bill* as not forming a constituent, and indeed this phrase can be neither dislocated nor conjoined. This result is consistent with the view that *up a bill* is not a constituent, as in (iib).

Note carefully that in the conclusion above, we are not claiming that our principles *prove* nonconstituency, only that they *are consistent with* it. As we observed earlier, our principles (P1, P2, etc.) are conditionals, whose general form says that if a sentence substring manifests a certain behavior, then that substring is a constituent. The principles do *not* say that if a string fails to manifest a certain behavior, it cannot be a constituent; there might be other reasons for the behavior (recall our results with *do so*). Nonetheless, the failure of *up a bill* to manifest constituent behavior in *Homer ran up a bill* under *any* of our tests gives us confidence in analyzing it as a nonconstituent. Although we might expect a true constituent to fail one or another of our tests for special reasons, we do not expect it to fail them all.

EXERCISES

1. Below are two possible structures for the adjective phrase (AP) *very happy with Bart* (where a triangle indicates that we are ignoring the internal structure of the phrase in question):

   (1) Homer is [very happy with Bart].

   (2) a.

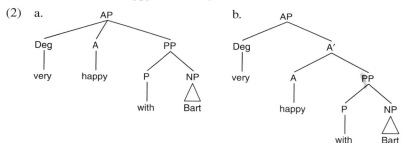

   Construct a formal argument for the structure in (2b) based on the following data:

   (3) a. Homer is very happy with Bart and fond of Lisa.

   b. *Lisa:* Mom, is Dad happy with Bart?

   Marge: Very.

   c. Homer said he was very happy with Bart, and happy with Bart he is.

   Use the four-part argument form discussed in Units 11 and 12, separating characterization of the structures, data and data summary, principle, and conclusion.

   ## Claim

   The structure of *very happy with Bart* in (1) is represented better by (2b) than by (2a).

   ## Argument

   ...

2. In (1) and (2) below, the bracketed APs are understood as modifying different NPs in the sentence. In (1), *tired* is understood as modifying the subject *Bart* (it is Bart who is tired). In (2), *raw* is understood as modifying the object *the fish* (it is the fish that is raw).

(1)   Bart left the party [$_{AP}$ tired].

(2)   Lisa ate the fish [$_{AP}$ raw].

One plausible suggestion is that this difference in what is modified by AP is matched by a difference in where AP attaches in the tree. Specifically, APs modifying the subject are sisters to the VP (3a), whereas APs modifying the object are sisters to the V (3b):

(3)   a.   b.

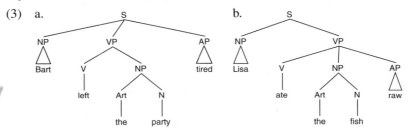

In this exercise, we will explore evidence suggesting that this proposal is correct.

First, consider sentence (4). Notice that it is ambiguous between a reading where *angry at someone else* modifies *Homer* (Homer is angry) and a reading where *angry at someone else* modifies *Marge* (Marge is angry):

(4)   Homer left Marge [$_{AP}$ angry at someone else].

"Homer left Marge with Homer being in a state of being mad at someone else."

"Homer left Marge with Marge being in a state of being mad at someone else."

Next, consider sentence (5). Like (4), this example is ambiguous. The AP can modify either the subject or the object:

(5)   No one left Marge [$_{AP}$ angry at **anyone** else].

"No one left Marge with that person being in a state of being mad at someone else."

"No one left Marge with Marge being in a state of being mad at someone else."

Finally, consider sentence (6). Unlike (4) and (5), this example appears to have only one reading—it is unambiguous. It only seems to be possible to understand the AP as modifying the object *no one* (# indicates an unavailable reading):

(6)   Homer left no one [$_{AP}$ angry at **anyone** else].

> #"Homer left no one with Homer being in a state of being mad at someone else."

> "Homer left no one with that person being in a state of being mad at someone else."

In Unit 8, we learned the following principle about negative polarity items like *anyone*:

(7)   A negative polarity item must be c-commanded by its trigger.

On the basis of this principle, explain how the structures in (3a) and (3b) predict the data in (4), (5), and (6). Specifically, show how the principle and the structures predict the range of readings we find. Explain your reasoning fully and step by step. (Hint: Recall the point made in the text that semantic ambiguity often indicates syntactic ambiguity.)

PART V   Searching for Explanation

As noted at the outset, science is a search for *understanding*. It tries to grasp not merely what exists and how it works, but also *why* it exists and *why* it works that way. And why this way, and not some other?

Our results so far show that the elements of a sentence—its words—are not simply strung together like beads on a chain, despite being spoken and perceived sequentially:

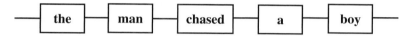

Rather, they form a **structure**. Words divide into categories like Art, N, and V; and categories group together into phrases such as NP, VP, and S:

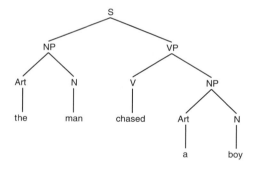

This structure accounts for important properties of a sentence, such as which parts can be conjoined, deleted, moved, or replaced with a proform, and also the positions available to reflexives and negative polarity items in relation to the elements they depend on. We have learned to construct formal arguments for structure based on data of these kinds.

Nonetheless, discovering and arguing for sentence structure is not the same thing as *explaining* it. Suppose we are asked, "*Why* does *The man chased a boy* have the structure that it has?" Right now, we can only point to our PS rules and say, "It has that structure because our rules *assign* that structure." But is that really all there is to say?

Looking at our tree diagram, we might wonder whether the presence of two noun phrases isn't related to the presence of a verb like *chase*, whose meaning relates two participants, a "chaser" and a "chasee." We might also wonder whether the presence of the articles *the* and *a* isn't linked to the fact that we are dealing with common nouns like *man* and *boy*, versus proper nouns like *Homer* and *Bart*. More generally, we might suspect that various aspects of the sentence structure actually follow from properties of the words it contains.

Structural Formulas

An analogy from chemistry is useful here. In the nineteenth century, chemists hit on the idea of representing the molecules of organic compounds by means of "structural formulas." The formula for methane, for example, looks like this:

$$H - \underset{\displaystyle H}{\overset{\displaystyle H}{C}} - H$$

Methane

This diagram captures important properties of the substance, such as its atomic constituents (hydrogen and carbon) and their relative proportions (four parts hydrogen to one part carbon in each part of methane).

Structural formulas can also capture a kind of "recursion" occurring in organic molecules built from methane—the fact that you can form new molecules by adding successive carbon-plus-two-hydrogen units, yielding longer and longer chains:

Methane   Ethane   Propane

Chemical diagrams can even express what we might call "structural ambiguities" among molecules. For instance, ethyl alcohol and dimethyl ether contain exactly the same elements in exactly the same proportions (C_2H_6O). Nonetheless, the two substances diverge sharply in their chemical properties and behavior. How is this possible? According to chemists, it results from a difference in "constituency"—from different arrangements of the same atomic parts. Whereas ethyl alcohol has its oxygen atom near one end, dimethyl ether has its oxygen in the middle:[1]

$$
\begin{array}{ccccc}
 & H & & H & \\
 & | & & | & \\
H - & C & - C & - O & - H \\
 & | & & | & \\
 & H & & H &
\end{array}
\qquad
\begin{array}{ccccc}
 & H & & H & \\
 & | & & | & \\
H - & C & - O & - C & - H \\
 & | & & | & \\
 & H & & H &
\end{array}
$$

Ethyl alcohol   Dimethyl ether

Now when chemists are asked, "Why do these substances have the structures that they do?," they have an interesting answer. Molecular structures are understood by chemists as arising from specific properties of their atomic parts, together with certain general principles governing the combination of those parts. Individual atoms are analyzed as having a certain **valence** that determines the number of other atoms they can combine with. Carbon atoms have a valence of 4; hydrogen atoms a valence of 1; oxygen atoms a valence of 2; and so on. Combinations occur in the form of (covalent) **bonds** between individual atoms (indicated by lines in the diagrams). A "well-formed molecule" is one that respects the valence of its constituent atoms together with general bonding principles.

Explaining Phrase Markers?

This analogy suggests a potential route forward toward a deeper understanding of syntactic structure. We might look more closely into the properties of lexical items (words), with an eye to seeing what properties of syntactic structure might be traced to them.

Just as the structural formulas of molecules are, in a sense, projected from the valence of their constituent atoms, so we might hope to understand the constituent structure of a tree as reflecting the "valence requirements" of individual words, perhaps in the presence of more general combining principles that

---

1. Different substances having the same elements in the same proportions are called **isomers**. For a useful introduction to these concepts, see Asimov 1965.

assemble those words together. If we proceed in this way, phrase structure rules might be seen as a kind of artifact—a reflection of something more basic:

The phrase structure component ... [could] be regarded as a kind of "projection" of lexical properties.
—*Knowledge of Language*, p. 81

As we will see in this part and the next, this strategy can indeed carry us a long way. It promises not only an attractive answer to the question of why sentences have the structures that they do, but also a deeper understanding of how children are able to acquire language as quickly as they do.

Introducing the Lexicon

Review

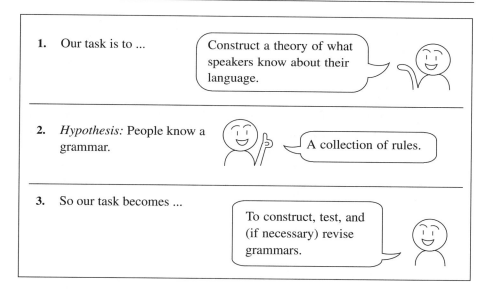

1. Our task is to ...

   Construct a theory of what speakers know about their language.

2. *Hypothesis:* People know a grammar.

   A collection of rules.

3. So our task becomes ...

   To construct, test, and (if necessary) revise grammars.

Categories and Subcategories

Our treatment of lexical items is very simple at this point. Lexical items are entered in the tree by lexical rules such as N → *Homer* or Vt → *saw*. We will now look at certain problems with this kind of treatment. As we will see, solving these problems leads us toward restructuring the grammar in an important way.

Capturing Cooccurrence Restrictions with Categories

In Unit 5, we looked at this little grammar:

S → N V	N → *Homer*	V → *ran*
S → N V N	N → *Marge*	V → *sleeps*
S → N V N N	N → *Lisa*	V → *crawls*
	N → *Bart*	V → *chased*
	N → *Maggie*	V → *saw*
	N → *Santa's Little Helper*	V → *petted*
		V → *sent*
		V → *handed*

We noticed that it generated ungrammatical sentences like *Bart sent*, *Homer crawls Maggie*, and *Homer saw Lisa Marge*. The problem was that verbs may require other elements to occur or not occur with them. That is, verbs appear to enforce certain **cooccurrence restrictions**.

Our solution to this problem was to separate categories. We distinguished what grammarians call intransitive, transitive, and ditransitive verbs and assigned them to different categories. We then adjusted our structural rules to use the new categories in the right places:

S → N Vi	N → *Homer*	Vi → *ran*
S → N Vt N	N → *Marge*	Vi → *sleeps*
S → N Vd N N	N → *Lisa*	Vi → *crawls*
	N → *Bart*	Vt → *chased*
	N → *Maggie*	Vt → *saw*
	N → *Santa's Little Helper*	Vt → *petted*
		Vd → *sent*
		Vd → *handed*

Later, when we introduced the VP node, we retained the division of verb types in our structural rules for VP:

S → NP VP	N → *Homer*	Vi → *ran*
VP → Vi	N → *Marge*	Vi → *sleeps*
VP → Vt NP	N → *Lisa*	Vi → *crawls*
VP → Vd NP NP	N → *Bart*	Vt → *chased*
	N → *Maggie*	Vt → *saw*
	N → *Santa's Little Helper*	Vt → *petted*
		Vd → *sent*
		Vd → *handed*

This move correctly blocks the ungrammatical sentences. For example, it ensures that *crawls* occurs with no object (*crawls* __), that *chased* occurs with one object (*chased* **Bart**), and that *handed* occurs with two objects (*handed* **Lisa Maggie**).

A Lost Connection?

This solution is attractively simple. But it also has an important negative consequence of breaking the connection among *crawl*, *chase*, and *hand*. In particular, it loses the intuitive idea that these three words are all members of the same part of speech: verb.

This claim might seem puzzling at first. After all, we use "Vi" as the category for intransitive verbs, "Vt" as the category for transitive verbs, and "Vd" as the category for ditransitive verbs. All of these involve a "V," which we intend to mean "verb." Isn't this enough to connect them? In fact, the impression of connection here is really an illusion. From the standpoint of the rules and how they operate, "Vi" and "Vt" are actually treated as completely separate categories. The grammar treats "Vi" and "Vt" as no more closely related than "Vi" and "N."

To see this clearly, simply notice that we could reformulate our grammar so as to get rid of any resemblance among the category symbols for intransitive, transitive, and ditransitive:

S → NP VP	N → *Homer*	X → *ran*
VP → X	N → *Marge*	X → *sleeps*
VP → Y NP	N → *Lisa*	X → *crawls*
VP → Z NP NP	N → *Bart*	Y → *chased*
	N → *Maggie*	Y → *saw*
	N → *Santa's Little Helper*	Y → *petted*
		Z → *sent*
		Z → *handed*

This revised grammar will generate all the same sentences as before. It will also assign trees with the same shape. But here there is no relation at all among the categories (or the category symbols) for *crawl*, *chase*, and *hand*. This shows that the visual similarity among "Vi," "Vt," and "Vd" is not used in any way by the grammar. We can replace these symbols with others that don't resemble each other, and nothing bad will happen. All the two grammars really require is that the categories for *crawl*, *chase*, and *hand* be different.

A Missed Generalization!

At this point, we might say to ourselves, "Okay, so what?" After all, maybe lumping words like *crawl*, *chase*, and *hand* together as verbs was a mistake in the first place—just an idea inherited from grammatical tradition.

But actually, on further reflection, words like *crawl*, *chase*, and *hand* do have important properties in common. For example, these words show a common pattern of syntactic marking (or **inflection**) for person, for tense, and in their participial forms.

Person marking	I crawl you crawl he/she/it crawls we crawl you crawl they crawl	I chase you chase he/she/it chases we chase you chase they chase	I hand you hand he/she/it hands we hand you hand they hand
Tense	she crawls she crawled she will crawl	he chases he chased he will chase	he hands he handed he will hand
Participial forms	he was crawl**ing** he has crawl**ed**	he was chas**ing** he has chas**ed**	he was hand**ing** he has hand**ed**

This marking is not found with words that we've assigned to the category N or the category A (**boyed*, **boying*, **happied*, **happying*).

So the point is that there *are* properties that words like *crawl*, *chase*, and *hand* share and that we would like to capture by grouping them into a single category. We would like to be able to state generalizations like this:

Verbs are inflected for person and tense, and have participial forms.

But using categories to capture cooccurrence restrictions prevents us from doing this because there is no category Verb to which all these words belong. In using different categories, we've therefore **missed a generalization**.

From Bad to Worse

The problem with using categories to capture cooccurrence restrictions is bad enough with forms (*crawl*, *chase*, and *hand*) that occur in different sentence patterns but that we'd like to assign to the same category (V). However, it arises in an even worse way with forms that occur in different sentence patterns and that we'd like to call *the same word*. *Give* is such a case. *Give* occurs in a pattern with two object NPs and in a pattern with an NP and a PP containing *to*:

(1) a.   Homer gave Bart a present.   **NP - NP**
     b.   Homer gave a present to Bart.   **NP - *to* - NP**

Not all verbs occurring in the NP-NP frame occur in the NP-*to*-NP frame. Consider *spare* and *donate*. *Spare* shows the NP-NP pattern, but not NP-*to*-NP. And *donate* shows the NP-*to*-NP pattern, but not NP-NP:

(2) a.   The judge spared [Homer] [his life].   **NP - NP**
     b.   *The judge spared [his life] [to Homer].   **NP - *to* - NP**
(3) a.   *Marge donated [the charity] [old clothes].   **NP - NP**
     b.   Marge donated [old clothes] [to the charity]. **NP - *to* - NP**

With our current tools, we have no choice but to assign verbs occurring in the two frames to two different categories:

This seems very odd. Most people would take the *give* appearing in *Homer gave Bart a present* to be the very same word as the *give* appearing in *Homer gave a present to Bart*. But that isn't true according to our rules. There are two *gives* that are not even members of the same part of speech! One is a Vd and the other is a Vto. So using rules this way not only cuts across the natural category of verbs, it even cuts across individual words.

Subcategorial Differences

Our current tools for building grammars allow us to capture differences of category between words—for example, the fact that *Bart* and *ran* belong to different parts of speech. But they don't seem to allow us to capture more "fine-grained" differences, differences that we think of as somehow "below" the part-of-speech level. They do not allow us to capture **subcategorial** differences.

This is an important respect in which the classifications made by our rules differ from those of a standard dictionary. Dictionaries classify *crawl*, *chase*, and *hand* equally as verbs. Furthermore, they classify *give* as a single word, even though it occurs in different syntactic frames. Examine the following entry for *give* from *Webster's Ninth New Collegiate Dictionary*:

---

¹**give** \'giv\ vb **gave** \'gāv\; **giv-en** \'giv-ən\; **giv-ing**
[ME *given*, of Scand origin; akin to OSw *giva* to give; akin to OE *giefan*, *gifan* to give, L *habēre* to have, hold] *vt* (13c)

1: to make a present of ⟨*give* a doll to a child⟩

2a: to grant or bestow by formal action ⟨the law *gives* citizens the right to vote⟩

  b: to accord or yield to another ⟨*gave* him her confidence⟩

Give is classified as a *vt* (meaning that it is a verb that takes an object). Notice further that the different syntactic frames for *give* are collected and treated in subentries for this single word. For example, the NP-*to*-NP pattern for *give* is noted in Subentry 1 (and an example of this pattern is given). The NP-NP pattern is noted in Subentry 2.

So a dictionary doesn't treat differences of syntactic frame as differences of category. It treats them as differences *within* a category. It treats them as **subcategory features** of the word.

The Lexicon

These results suggest that it might be useful to think about reorganizing the grammar, replacing lexical rules with something like dictionary entries, in which cooccurrence restrictions are captured as subcategory features.

Subcategory Features

To treat subcategory features in this way, we'll need some method of indicating subcategory features. Basically, what we want these features to do is to show the syntactic frame that a given form can appear in. For this purpose, we'll adopt the following notation:

[+ __ X Y Z]

We'll understand this notation as saying that you can insert the word only where it would be followed by X followed by Y followed by Z:

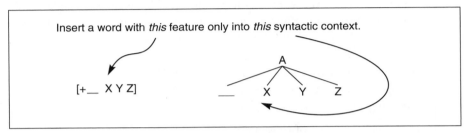

Insert a word with *this* feature only into *this* syntactic context.

[+__ X Y Z]

Here are some example features and their interpretations:

Feature	Interpretation
[+ __]	"Insert me into a frame where nothing follows."
[+ __ NP]	"Insert me into a frame where a single NP follows."
[+ __ NP NP]	"Insert me into a frame where a pair of NPs follow."
[+ __ NP PP]	"Insert me into a frame where an NP and a PP follow."

Lexical Entries

With features like this, we can now dispense with lexical rules in favor of lexical entries that use general categories and subcategory features. That is:

- We categorize an item in the general part of speech in which it belongs.
- We express cooccurrence restrictions using subcategory features.

Our notation for lexical entries will give the word, its category, and its subcategory features, which allow for a word to be inserted into any appropriate frame:

word, CAT, [+ __ ...], [+ __ ...], ...

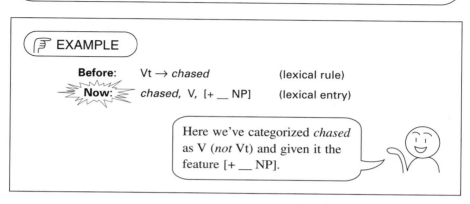

Of course, once we do this, we must also go back and reformulate our structural rules so that they mention only the general category V:

Generalizing this to the whole grammar, lexical rules go away, and structural rules with fine-grained categories like "Vi" and "Vt" are simplified.

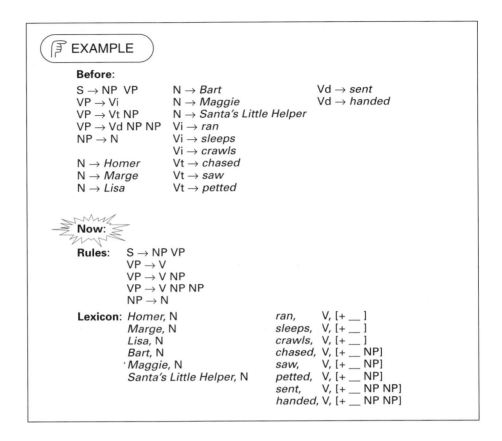

Multiple Features

The use of entries and subcategories doesn't just permit us to keep words (like *crawl*, *chase*, and *hand*) in the same part of speech. It also permits us to hold words together. Recall the earlier situation with *give*, *donate*, and *spare*. *Donate* shows the NP - PP pattern, but not the NP - NP pattern. *Spare* shows the NP - NP pattern, but not the NP - PP pattern. And *give* shows both:

(4) a.   Marge donated old clothes to the charity.

  b.   *Marge donated the charity old clothes.

(5) a.   The judge spared Homer his life.

  b.   *The judge spared his life to Homer.

(6) a.   Marge gave Maggie to Homer.

  b.   Marge gave Homer Maggie.

We can capture this behavior by assigning *donate* and *spare* one subcategory feature each in their lexical entries and by assigning *give* two:

(7) a. *donate*, V, [+ __ NP PP]

  b. *spare*, V, [+ __ NP NP]

  c. *give*,   V, [+ __ NP PP], [+ __ NP NP]

These entries allow *donate* and *spare* to occur in their separate frames and *give* to occur in either one.

More Features

The general notion of features suggests a way of capturing many other aspects of cooccurrence restrictions beyond category. For example, consider *put* and *give*. Both occur in the NP - PP frame, but the range of prepositions is quite different in the two cases. *Put* requires a preposition expressing spatial location (a **locative preposition**), but is quite liberal about which spatial prepositions it accepts. *Give*, on the other hand, requires PPs containing the specific preposition *to*. Nothing else is acceptable:

(8) a. Bart put the box on / in / under / near / in-front-of / in-back-of / behind Lisa.

  b. Bart gave the box to Homer.

  c. *Bart gave the box on / in / under / near / in-front-of / in-back-of / behind Homer.

We might capture this distribution, too, by using features. Suppose we label PPs containing locative prepositions [+loc] and prepositions containing the **dative preposition** *to* [+dat] (for the term *dative* from traditional grammar). The entries for *put* and *give* will then be as follows:

(9) a. *give*, V, [+ __ NP   PP], [+ __ NP NP]
                    [+dat]

  b. *put*, V, [+ __ NP   PP]
                  [+loc]

These features will allow *give* to be inserted only into an NP - PP frame whose PP contains the specific preposition *to*:

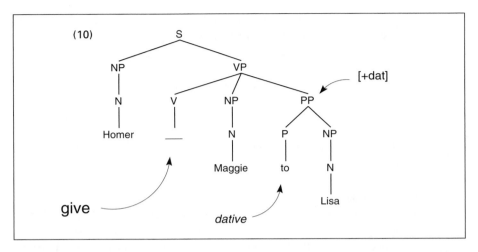

Likewise, *put* can only be inserted into an NP - PP frame whose PP contains a locative PP:

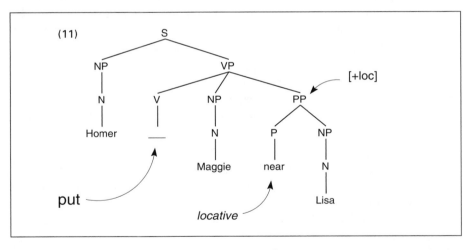

So features can be used to further fine-tune the statement of syntactic patterns.

Features, Heads, and Phrases

Review

1. Lexical rules capture differences in cooccurrence restrictions ...

   By dividing words into different categories.

2. But cooccurrence restrictions appear to be subcategorial ("below the level of the category").

   Hence, lexical rules miss important generalizations.

3. Traditional dictionaries state cooccurrence restrictions ...

   In subentries of a single lexical entry.

4. This suggests our grammars should contain ...

   Lexical entries in place of lexical rules.

Expanding Our Feature Set

In Unit 13, we classified the verb *put* as requiring an object and a prepositional phrase (PP) of a particular kind: one expressing spatial location (1a,b). Nonspatial PPs—for example, ones expressing temporal relations—cannot occur with *put* (1c):

> (1) a.   Marge put the carrots [PP in the sink].
>   b.   Marge put the carrots [PP on the counter].
>   c.   *Marge put the carrots [PP during the afternoon].

We expressed the locational requirement of *put* in terms of a feature [+loc] in its subcategorization frame. That is, we used the feature [+loc] to restrict the class of PPs available to *put*:

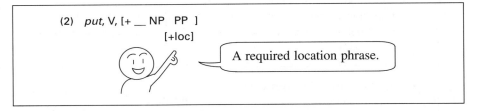

> (2) *put*, V, [+ ___ NP   PP]
>   [+loc]
>
> A required location phrase.

Proceeding in the same way, by looking at the cooccurrence restrictions of verbs, we can motivate a variety of features in addition to [+loc].

[+Dir]

Consider the verb *dash*, which can mean 'to move with sudden speed'. This verb is standardly accompanied by a PP expressing direction of motion (3a–d). When PPs that can express both location and direction are placed after *dash*, they are invariably understood with a directional sense (4a,b). And when the directional PP is missing, or an unambiguously nondirectional PP is positioned after *dash*, the sentence is either ungrammatical or must be understood as containing an implicit directional phrase (5a–c). (The double question marks indicate strong unacceptability.)

(3) a.   Bart dashed **into the house**.
    b.   Lisa dashed **out the door**.
    c.   Marge dashed **through the rain**.
    d.   Homer dashed **to the window**.
(4) a.   The cat dashed **at Bart**. (= 'toward Bart')
    b.   Bart dashed **in the house**. (= 'into the house')
(5) a.   ??Homer dashed.
    b.   ??Homer dashed during the game.
    c.   I must dash. (= 'must dash somewhere')

These results may be taken to motivate a feature [+dir] and the following lexical entry for *dash*:

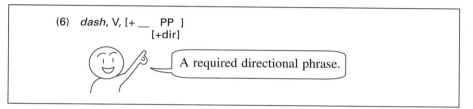

(6)   *dash*, V, [+ __ PP]
          [+dir]

A required directional phrase.

[+Dur]

Consider the verb *last*, on its meaning 'to continue in time', and the verb *spend*, on its meaning 'to cause or permit to elapse'. Both verbs require a complement expressing a duration of time (and *spend* requires an additional location phrase):

(7) a.   The party lasted **for two hours** / **the whole day**.
    b.   Marge spent **last week** / **the whole day** at the beach.

When phrases that can express both point in time and duration are placed after *last* and *spend*, they are invariably understood with their durational sense (8a,b). And when the duration phrase is missing, or an unambiguously nondurational phrase appears, the sentence is either out or must be understood as containing an implicit duration phrase (9a–c).

(8) a. i. Homer spent **yesterday** in the hospital.
      (= 'Homer spent all of yesterday in the hospital.')

   ii. Marge arrived yesterday.
      (= 'Marge arrived at some point during yesterday.')

   b. i. The party lasted **after midnight**.
      (= 'The party lasted until after midnight.')

   ii. Marge arrived after midnight.
      (= 'Marge arrived at some point after midnight.')

(9) a. *Homer spent in the hospital.

   b. *The party lasted at 3:00 p.m.

   c. The party lasted. (= 'The party lasted a long time.')

These results may be taken to motivate a feature [+dur] and the following lexical entries for *last* and *spend*:

(10) *last*, V, [+ __ NP], [+ __ PP]
         [+dur]   [+dur]

Required duration phrases.

(11) *spend*, V, [+ __ NP   PP]
          [+dur] [+loc]

Required duration *and* location phrases!

[+Man]

The verbs *word* and *phrase* both seem to require a complement expressing the way or manner in which something is written (12a,b). Similarly, the verb *behave* requires a phrase describing manner of action (13):

(12) a. Burns worded the memo **carefully / that way**.

   b. Smithers phrased his response **in a very tactful fashion**.

(13) Bart behaved **politely / considerately / that way**.

Similarly to the phrases discussed above, these complements of manner either cannot be absent at all, or else can be absent only when a manner phrase is implicitly understood:

(14) a.   *Burns worded the memo.
      b.   *Smithers phrased his response.
      c.   Bart wouldn't behave. (= 'Bart wouldn't behave well / properly.')

These results may be taken to motivate a feature [+man] and the following lexical entries:

(15) *word*, V, [+ __ NP   PP   ], [+ __ NP AdvP], [+ __ NP   NP   ]
                          [+man]   [+man]   [+man]

(16) *phrase*, V, [+ __ NP   PP   ], [+ __ NP AdvP], [+ __ NP   NP   ]
                             [+man]   [+man]   [+man]

(17) *behave*, V, [+ __   PP   ], [+ __ AdvP], [+ __   NP   ]
                             [+man]   [+man]   [+man]

Required manner phrases.

[+Dat]

As a last example, consider the verb *give*. We have observed that *give*, in one of its subcategorization frames, requires a PP. In this respect, *give* is like *put*:

(18) a.   Homer gave a present **to Lisa**.
      b.   [+ __ NP PP]
(19) a.   Marge put the carrots in the sink.
      b.   [+ __ NP PP]
                        [+loc]

However, the constraints on *give*'s PP are much sharper than on *put*'s. Whereas *put* allows a broad range of locational PPs (recall (1a,b)), *give* permits only PPs containing the specific preposition *to*. No other Ps are allowed:

(20) a.   *Homer gave a present on Lisa.   ([+loc])
      b.   *Homer gave a present in Lisa.   ([+dir] or [+man])
      c.   *Homer gave a present during Lisa. ([+dur])

Again we can use a feature to mark the kind of PP we need—for example, [+dat] to stand for *dative*, the traditional term for this kind of phrase:

> (21) *give*, V, [+ __ NP PP]
>   [+dat]
>
> A required dative PP.

Notice that the feature [+dat] is rather different in nature from [+loc], [+dir], [+dur], and [+man]. The latter serve to mark a *semantic* property shared by some set of words. The features express a dimension of meaning that the words have in common (location, direction, duration, etc.). By contrast, the feature [+dat] doesn't serve to pick out a class of prepositions; rather, [+dat] serves only to mark a *particular lexical item*: the word *to*.

Where Does a Phrase Get Its Features?

Having motivated some features on prepositional phrases, let's ask a very basic question: what determines the status of a given PP as [+loc], [+dur], [+dat], and so on? For example, what makes the PPs in (22) [+loc]?

> (22) a. in the sink / that trash can / the refrigerator
>   b. on the counter / the table / a cutting board
>   c. under the counter / the table / a cutting board
>   d. with the other vegetables / the mushrooms
>   e. near the counter / the table / a cutting board
>   f. between the mushrooms and the broccoli
>
> [+loc]

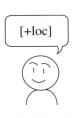

Intuitively, the answer seems clear: a PP is locative in virtue of the preposition it contains. A PP is [+loc] only if it contains a locative P, one like *in, on, under, with*.

The same conclusion follows with directional and durative PPs. Intuitively, a PP is [+dir] in virtue of containing a directional P (23). Likewise, a PP is [+dur] in virtue of containing a durative P (24):

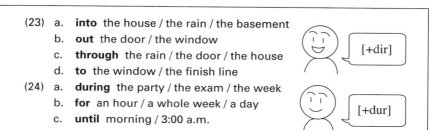

(23) a. **into** the house / the rain / the basement
     b. **out** the door / the window
     c. **through** the rain / the door / the house
     d. **to** the window / the finish line
     [+dir]

(24) a. **during** the party / the exam / the week
     b. **for** an hour / a whole week / a day
     c. **until** morning / 3:00 a.m.
     [+dur]

Feature Inheritance in PP

One way of making this idea explicit is to think of the feature marking on PP as arising from the P inside it and migrating upward. On this view, the [+loc] feature of *on the beach* starts out on the P and migrates up. Similarly, [+dir] and [+dur] PPs inherit features from their respective Ps:

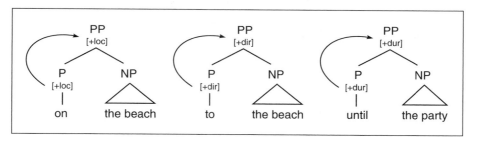

To implement this idea, we would enrich our lexical entries for Ps to contain featural information of this kind:

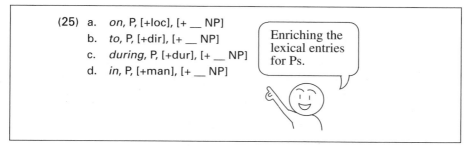

(25) a. *on*, P, [+loc], [+ __ NP]
     b. *to*, P, [+dir], [+ __ NP]
     c. *during*, P, [+dur], [+ __ NP]
     d. *in*, P, [+man], [+ __ NP]

Enriching the lexical entries for Ps.

In addition, we would need a general principle about feature inheritance to the effect that PP inherits its features from P:

Extending to Other Phrases

We can extend these ideas beyond PP. In discussing the verbs *word*, *phrase*, and *behave*, we saw that these words cooccur with phrases describing a manner of action or behavior.

> (26) a.   Burns worded the letter **in that fashion**.
>
> b.   Smithers phrased his response **very carefully**.
>
> c.   Bart often behaves **that way**.

To accommodate these facts, we introduced the feature [+man] and gave lexical entries like this:

> (15) *word*, V, [+ __ NP   PP   ], [+ __ NP AdvP], [+ __ NP   NP]
>   [+man]   [+man]   [+man]
>
> (16) *phrase*, V, [+ __ NP   PP   ], [+ __ NP AdvP], [+ __ NP   NP]
>   [+man]   [+man]   [+man]
>
> (17) *behave*, V, [+ __   PP   ], [+ __   AdvP], [+ __   NP]
>   [+man]   [+man]   [+man]

Notice that the same basic question arising with manner PPs arises with manner AdvPs and NPs as well. Just as we can ask, "What determines whether a PP is [+man]?," we can also ask, "What determines whether an AdvP is [+man]?" and "What determines whether an NP is [+man]?"

In the case of PP, we saw that the preposition was responsible. A similar conclusion seems justified with AdvP and NP. The AdvPs that can occur after *word*, *phrase*, or *behave* are precisely those containing an adverb of manner. Time adverbs like *recently*, for example, won't work (27a). Similarly, the NPs that can occur after *word*, *phrase*, or *behave* are exactly those containing a noun of manner; other kinds of nouns won't do (27b):

(27) a. Smithers phrased his response **very carefully** / ***recently**.

    b. Bart often behaves **that way** / ***that house**.

Once again, a natural idea is to see the [+man] feature as originating on the Adv or N and migrating upward to the larger phrase:[1]

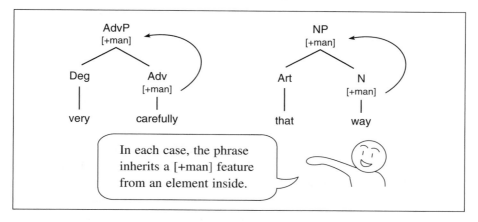

In each case, the phrase inherits a [+man] feature from an element inside.

As with prepositions, we can implement this idea by adding featural information to our lexical entries for adverbs (28) and nouns (29):

(28) a. *carefully*, Adv, [+man], [+ __]

    b. *well*, Adv, [+man], [+ __]

    c. *recently*, Adv, [–man], [+ __]

(29) a. *way*, N, [+man], [+ __]

    b. *house*, N, [–man], [+ __]

We must also adopt the corresponding general principle that AdvP inherits its features from Adv, and NP inherits its features from N:

[+F] on Adv and N migrates upward.

---

1. With the PP *in that manner*, we take [+man] to originate in P, as shown in (25).

Heads and Phrases

The feature inheritance we have observed with PP, AdvP, and NP clearly follows a pattern. Look at the three configurations below. In each case, the larger phrase XP inherits its features from the smaller X within it (circled):

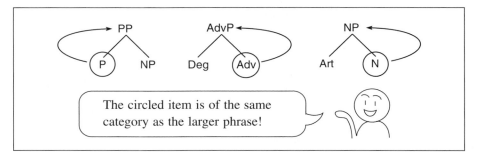

Let's adopt some terminology to describe this pattern. With phrases of the general form [$_{XP}$ ... X ...], call the element X the **head** of XP. Conversely, call XP the phrase **projected** by X. Our results suggest a simple principle relating feature inheritance and headedness. We will call it **Principle F** (*F* for *feature*):

> **Principle F**
> Features pass from a head to the phrase that it projects.

In other words, feature inheritance follows headedness.[2]

Diagnosing Category with Principle F

Principle F (assuming it's correct) provides a useful tool for determining category in certain cases where we are unsure. Suppose we observe a lexical item X selecting for a certain feature [+F] on a following phrase. We are uncertain about the category of this phrase (**?**), but it dominates two elements Y and Z whose categories we *do* know:

---

2. In fact, we will assume here that features of a phrase are inherited *only* from the head of that phrase. See below for what might happen with "exocentric" phrases: ones having no head at all.

Notice that if we can identify one of Y or Z as the source of [+F], then we are in a position to identify **?**. If [+F] comes from Y, then **?** must be YP, since Principle F requires features to pass from head to phrase. By contrast, if [+F] comes from Z, then **?** must be ZP, for the same reason.

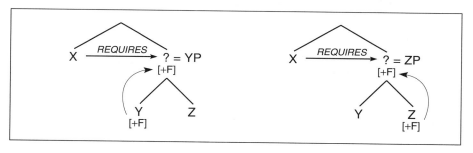

NP or DP?

Using Principle F as a category probe can be tricky when the source of features is unclear. Consider the boldfaced expressions in (30a–d):

(30)   a. **This man** laughs.   c. **That man** laughs.
       b. **These men** laugh.   d. **Those men** laugh.

Our view so far has been that these items are NPs—phrases projected from their nouns. The status of these phrases as singular or plural would seem to support this view. *Man* in (30a) is singular, and so is the larger phrase *this man* (as shown by the verb form *laughs*). Correspondingly, *men* in (30b) is plural, and so is the larger phrase *these men* (as shown by the verb form *laugh*). Similarly for (30c,d). These results follow if N is the head of the phrase and number marking passes upward, following Principle F:

There is another possible analysis, however. Notice that the **demonstrative determiners** in (30) also show number marking (*this~these, that~those*). An alternative idea would be to say that Det(erminer) (sometimes just D) is the true source of number marking in (30), and that these phrases are actually DPs! Here is the basic proposal:

The "DP analysis"

DP → D NP   NP → N

this, D, [+sing], [+ __ NP]   *that*, D, [+sing], [+ __ NP]
                  [+sing]   [+sing]

these, D, [–sing], [+ __ NP]   *those*, D, [–sing], [+ __ NP]
                  [–sing]   [–sing]

The lexical entry for *this* identifies it as a singular D requiring a singular NP; the entry for *these* identifies it as a plural (i.e., nonsingular) D requiring a plural NP. These entries force *this* and *these* to agree in number with their following nominal. Accordingly when a noun is [+sing], its larger containing phrase will always be [+sing] too, but not because the phrase inherits this feature from the noun directly. Rather, it is the number marking on D that passes upward to the higher node. The noun simply agrees with the D:

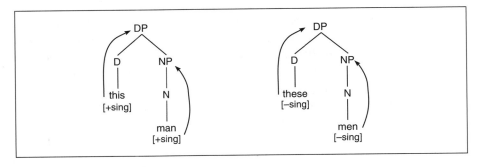

We won't attempt to argue further for the DP analysis here, and we will stick with the NP analysis. We will, however, adopt Det as the general category for prenominal elements like demonstratives (*this, that*), articles (*a, the*), and quantifier words (*every, each, some, most, few, no, any*). In any case, the main point to notice is how different views of feature inheritance for a phrase can yield different views of its category under Principle F.

Exocentric Phrases

Phrases that contain a head are called **endocentric**, and nearly all of the phrases we have considered so far are endocentric. Thus, VP contains V, PP contains P, NP contains N, and so on. However, one of our mother-daughter configurations lacks this property; it is **exocentric**, to use the technical term. S is a possible example of an exocentric phrase, since the sentence node is not clearly a projection of either NP or VP:

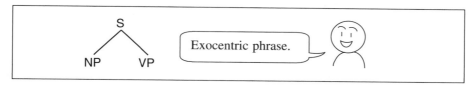

One way of understanding the headless status of a phrase is that such a phrase inherits features from *none* of its children. On this view, features in S get as high as NP and VP, but no higher. An alternative understanding is that headless phrases inherit features from *all* of their children. On this view, S would lack a head only in the sense of not containing any *unique* constituent element that determines its features.

Viewing the headlessness of S in the second way would allow for a simple account of number agreement. In English, as in many languages, subjects must agree with their verbs in number (31a,b). Failure to agree yields an ungrammatical sentence (31c,d):

(31) a.   The man likes Lisa.
      b.   The men like Lisa.
      c.   *The man like Lisa.
      d.   *The men likes Lisa.

Suppose that number is expressed as a feature [sing] in the entries of both nouns and verbs; *man* and *likes* are marked as [+sing], *men* and *like* are marked as [−sing], and so on. Given that features are passed from heads to phrases, NP and VP will inherit [–sing] from their constituent N and V, respectively. Now suppose that NP and VP both pass their features to S. The following trees represent cases where the same number feature is inherited from NP and from VP, yielding a consistent value for S:

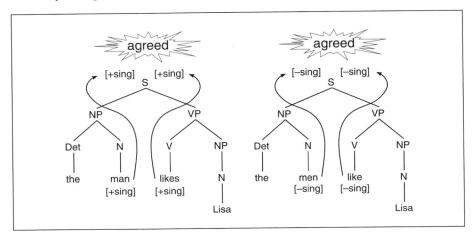

By contrast, these trees represent cases where conflicting number features are inherited from NP and VP, resulting in contradictory values for S:

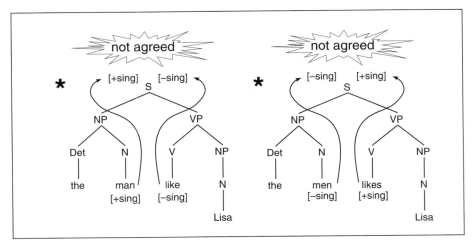

Permitting multiple headedness thus provides us with one means of analyzing number agreement.

In Unit 20, we will explore a surprising alternative to the notion that the sentence is exocentric. For right now, however, we will leave the idea on the table as an interesting possibility.

Verbal Complements and Adjuncts

Review

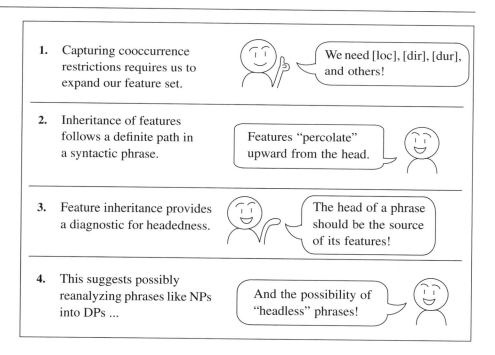

1. Capturing cooccurrence restrictions requires us to expand our feature set.

   We need [loc], [dir], [dur], and others!

2. Inheritance of features follows a definite path in a syntactic phrase.

   Features "percolate" upward from the head.

3. Feature inheritance provides a diagnostic for headedness.

   The head of a phrase should be the source of its features!

4. This suggests possibly reanalyzing phrases like NPs into DPs ...

   And the possibility of "headless" phrases!

Complements

We have seen that in order to occur smoothly, verbs may require or forbid other cooccurring words or phrases. For example, whereas all verbs seem to require a subject, the verb *chase* also requires a following NP to make a well-formed sentence (1); the verb *put* requires a following NP and locative PP (2); and the verb *crawl* rejects a following NP altogether (3):

---

(1) a. *Homer chased.

b.   Homer chased Bart.

(2) a. *Marge put.

b. *Marge put the car.

c.   Marge put the car in the garage.

(3) a.   Maggie crawled.

b. *Maggie crawled Lisa.

The items required by a verb (other than its subject) are called **complements**. The relation between a verb and its complements is referred to as **selection**. Thus, *chase* may be described as selecting a single complement; *put* selects two complements; and *crawl* selects no complements at all.

"Completing the Description"

When we think about selection by verbs, we notice a close connection to their meanings. Intuitively, *chase* describes an action or event that involves two basic participants: a "chaser" (sometimes called the **agent** of the action) and a "chasee" (the so-called **theme** or **patient** of the action). Without both of these participants, it doesn't seem that one can have a chasing. The problem with (1a) is that it is incomplete. It leaves one of the two crucial participants unspecified: the theme.

The situation with *put* is similar. Intuitively, any action of "putting" involves three core participants: an agent (the "putter"), a theme (the "puttee"), and a **location** (where the theme comes to be at the end of the putting). Unless all of these elements are present, we don't have a complete description of a putting event. This seems to be what is wrong with (2a,b): one or more of the two core participants is left out.

Finally, consider the verb *crawl*. Crawling is an action that involves a single participant: the agent of the action. A person, insect, or animal crawls. Specifying this one participant completes the description of the action; nothing more is required. Sticking another participant into the situation would leave that person, insect, or animal with nothing to do as far as the crawling goes, and this seems to be what is wrong with (3b). Since crawling involves one participant, the additional NP *Lisa* is left without a clear role to play in the description of the action.

Thematic Roles (θ-Roles)

These remarks suggest that verbs somewhat resemble the script of a stage play (an analogy borrowed from Haegeman 1994). A script establishes certain basic parts or roles that must be played by individual actors. For a complete and successful performance, all of the established roles in the script must be filled by actors—none can be left unfilled. Furthermore, no actors are permitted on-stage who are not playing an established role in the performance—only cast members are allowed. The verbs *crawl*, *chase*, and *put* establish one, two, and three roles, respectively. So in order to have a successful performance of crawling, chasing, or putting, exactly one, two, or three other phrases must be present to fill these roles.

Note from the previous paragraphs that the roles played by participants in various "verb scripts" may recur to some extent. For example, the "chaser," the "putter," and the "crawler" were all described as the agent of the action. Similarly, the "chasee" and the "puttee" were described as themes. Such recurring parts are sometimes called **participant roles** or **thematic roles** (or **θ-roles** for short). Thematic roles are the basic parts that can be played in actions or events or states. Here is a list of thematic roles with informal descriptions adapted from Haegeman 1994:

Role	Description
Agent	Volitional initiator of action
Patient	Object or individual undergoing action
Theme	Object or individual moved by action
Goal	Individual toward which action is directed
Source	Object or individual from which something is moved by the action, or from which the action originates
Experiencer	Individual experiencing some event or state
Beneficiary	Object or individual that benefits from some action or event
Location	Place at which an individual, event, or state is situated
Instrument	Secondary cause of event; an object or individual causing some event through the action of an agent

Given this list, we can talk about the roles that are **assigned** by various verbs. Thus, we can classify the verb *crawl* as assigning one thematic role (agent), the verb *chase* as assigning two thematic roles (agent and theme), and the verb *put* as assigning three thematic roles (agent, theme, and location).

Roles and Subcategory Features

There is a close connection between the thematic role assignments of a verb and the subcategory features that it possesses:

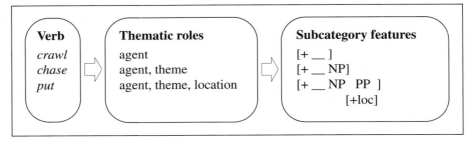

For a given verb, one of its thematic roles will always be assigned to the subject of the clause in which it occurs. The remaining thematic roles will be assigned to the complements:

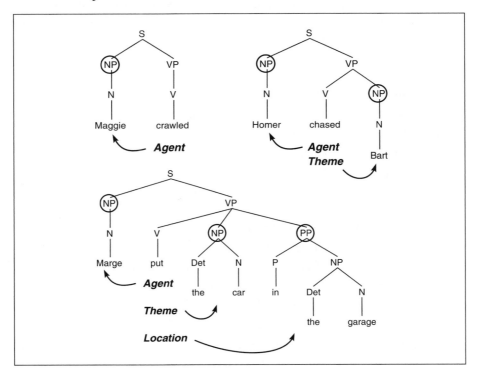

This means that the number of phrases appearing as complements of the verb will always be one less than its total number of thematic roles. The remaining role always goes to the subject.

When there are more complements than (nonsubject) thematic roles to assign, one or more of these complements will be left without a role. And when there are fewer complements than (nonsubject) roles to assign, one or more of these roles will be left unassigned:

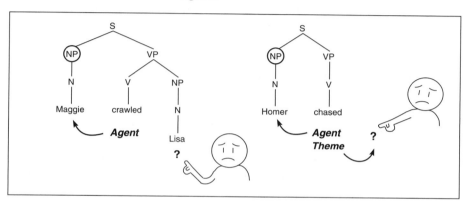

This yields ungrammaticality.

Adjuncts

The claim that *crawl* permits no following phrase, that *chase* requires exactly one following phrase, and that *put* requires two following phrases might seem incorrect given examples like (4)–(6). *Crawl* can be followed by other expressions, and similarly for *chase* and *put*:

(4) a. Maggie crawled **around quietly**.
    b. Maggie crawled **under the sofa**.
    c. Maggie crawled **quickly**.
(5) a. Homer chased Bart **yesterday**.
    b. Homer chased Bart **angrily**.
    c. Homer chased Bart **out of the front door**
(6) a. Marge put the car in the garage **at 2:00 p.m.**
    b. Marge put the car in the garage **carefully**.
    c. Marge put the car in the garage **because it was threatening to rain**.

Expressions like those in boldface are usually distinguished from the kinds of phrases that we have called complements. Words like *around* and *quickly*, and phrases like *under the sofa* and *because it was threatening to rain*, are termed **adjuncts** (or **modifiers**). Their relation to the verb is not selection but **modification**. Thus, *chase* selects a single complement, but it also allows a number of adjunct modifiers, for example, temporal modifiers like *yesterday* and adverbs of manner like *angrily*. Similarly, *put* and *crawl* admit adjunct modifiers in addition to whatever complements they take or do not take. Adjunct modifiers do not depend on the presence of a particular verb. Any action can be done quietly, quickly, under the sofa, and so on.

Fleshing Out the Description

The difference between selection and modification can be understood by returning to our metaphor of a stage play. Recall that the verb functions something like a script: it establishes the basic roles that must be filled for any successful performance of the play.

Any stage play of course has many components that are not specified by the script, and hence are left open to the actors' or director's interpretation. For example, a script may leave a play's exact setting unspecified, including when precisely a scene takes place and in what physical setting. You may have seen performances in which a play, ballet, or opera traditionally set in the Middle Ages is set in modern times, with actors in modern dress and modern living quarters. Because the script leaves the exact setting open, the director is free to manipulate it in odd and interesting ways.

Other unspecified components may include the exact way in which actions are performed. For example, if a play calls for an actor to walk across a room, often it will leave unspecified exactly how this action is to be carried out. Does the actor walk quickly or slowly? Does he or she show visible emotion, and hence walk confidently, timidly, or angrily?

In setting the action at a particular time and place, or in instructing the actors to perform actions in a particular way, the director is not deviating from the script, but fleshing out the actions that it lays down in skeletal form. And generally speaking, of course, it is necessary to do this. After all, any action has to occur at *some* time and in *some* place. And actions have to be done in *some* manner, and for *some* reason, even if the script doesn't stipulate what these manners and reasons are.

Adjunct modifiers in a sentence can be seen as adding information equivalent to that of background setting and performance details in a play. Modifiers flesh out an action or state whose skeletal elements are specified by the verb. The verb determines a basic action (crawling, chasing, putting, etc.) and establishes the core participants in this action (agent, theme, goal, etc.). This typically leaves many dimensions of the state or action unspecified, such as the time and place at which it occurs (*around 10:00 p.m., in the park*), the way in which the actions are carried out (*quietly, angrily*), or the reason why those actions are performed (*because it was threatening to rain*). Modifiers supply such information and in so doing flesh out the action. However, modifier information is not part of the core specified in the "verb script."

The Variety of Adjunct Modifiers

The view of adjunct modifiers as fleshing out an action or state suggests that they should come in a broad range of semantic types. We expect modifiers corresponding to the various ways in which a basic situation could be filled in. And indeed we find such a range, including adjuncts of **manner**, **frequency**, **duration**, **location**, **time**, **reason**, and **purpose**. Furthermore, adjuncts occur in a variety of different categories including NP, PP, AdvP, and even clause (CP):

(7)   a.   Maggie crawled [$_{AdvP}$ quickly].   ***Manner***
      b.   Maggie crawled [$_{NP}$ that way].
      c.   Maggie crawled [$_{PP}$ in this way].

(8)   a.   Maggie crawled [$_{AdvP}$ frequently].   ***Frequency***
      b.   Maggie crawled [$_{NP}$ that often].
      c.   Maggie crawled [$_{PP}$ on two occasions].

(9)   a.   Maggie crawled [$_{NP}$ that long].   ***Duration***
      b.   Maggie crawled [$_{PP}$ for two hours].

(10) a.   Maggie crawled [$_{NP}$ there].   ***Location***
      b.   Maggie crawled [$_{PP}$ under the sofa].
      c.   Homer buys beer [$_{AdvP}$ locally].

(11) a.   Maggie crawled [$_{AdvP}$ recently].   ***Time***
      b.   Maggie crawled [$_{NP}$ that day].
      c.   Maggie crawled [$_{PP}$ after Homer picked her up].
      d.   Maggie crawled [$_{CP}$ when Homer put her down].

(12) a.   Maggie crawled [$_{PP}$ for that reason].   ***Reason***
      b.   Maggie crawled [$_{PP}$ because Homer picked her up].

(13) a.   Maggie crawled [$_{PP}$ in order to find Marge].   ***Purpose***
      b.   Maggie crawled [$_{CP}$ to find Lisa].

Adjuncts come in a variety of different categories ...

... and in a broad range of semantic types!

And this is by no means the end of the list. Think, for example, of conditional sentences (*Maggie will crawl if Homer leaves*), or phrases expressing path of motion (*Maggie crawled along the pathway*) or direction of motion (*Maggie crawled to Homer*).

In principle, all of the ways that we can fill out the description of an action or state can be expressed by adjuncts.

Distinguishing Complements and Adjuncts

Review

1. The phrases that cooccur with a given word may be its complements.

    Alternatively, they may be adjunct modifiers.

2. Complements specify the core participants in an action or state.

    Complements are assigned thematic roles by the words that select them.

3. Adjuncts simply contribute additional information.

    They flesh out the description.

Complement or Adjunct?

Our intuitive characterization of complements versus adjunct modifiers draws a fairly clear line between the two. Nonetheless, in practice there are many subtleties in telling the two apart. For example, notice that one cannot identify all locational phrases as adjunct modifiers once and for all. Although the locative PP *near the sofa* is an adjunct modifier when it occurs with *chase* (1a), we have seen that it is a complement when it occurs with *put* after the NP object (1b):

(1) a. Homer chased Bart [PP near the sofa].   (Adjunct)
     b. Homer put Bart [PP near the sofa].   (Complement)

Similarly, consider the durative PP *for an hour*. This phrase is surely an adjunct when it occurs with *crawl* (2a), but it's arguably a complement when it occurs with the verb *last* (2b):

> (2) a. Maggie crawled [PP for an hour].   (Adjunct)
>   b. The party lasted [PP for an hour].   (Complement)

It is often quite difficult to tell when an expression is supplying a core participant in the verb script, and when it is merely filling in additional informa-tion. Consider the phrases following *sell* in (3):

> (3) Homer sold [NP the car] [PP to Barney] [PP for $100].

In asking which of these phrases is a complement, we are asking these questions: Which ones specify core components of a selling event? Can there be a selling event without someone selling something? And what about the goal phrase [PP *to Barney*] and the *for*-phrase [PP *for $100*]? Must selling always involve a person to whom we sell and a sum that is transferred in the sale?

The fuzziness of our intuitions in these and many similar cases suggests the value of developing specific tests and diagnostics to separate complements from adjuncts.

Three Diagnostics

Complements and adjuncts differ in several properties that have traditionally been used to distinguish them.

Iterability

First of all, adjuncts are typically repeatable or **iterable**, whereas complements are not. Example (4) (from Bresnan 1982, p. 164) shows that a sentence can have a variety of adjuncts of manner, time, and location:

> (4) Fred *deftly* [MANNER] handed a toy to the baby
>   *by reaching behind his back* [MANNER] *over lunch* [TEMP]
>   *at noon* [TEMP] *in a restaurant* [LOC] *last Sunday* [TEMP]
>   *in Back Bay* [LOC] *without interrupting the discussion* [MANNER].

In contrast, (5) shows that adding extra nominal or PP complements yields ungrammaticality:

(5) a.   *Maggie crawled Lisa.
     b.   *Homer saw Bart that building.
     c.   *Marge gave Maggie to Lisa to Homer.

This behavior is expected under our characterization of complements versus adjuncts. Like a script, a verb establishes a definite number of thematic roles in the action it describes. Once these roles are filled by complement phrases, the cast is complete, and no more complements can be added. By contrast, adjuncts simply flesh out the action, filling in pieces of information that have been left unspecified: the exact time, the exact place, the precise manner in which something was done, and so on:

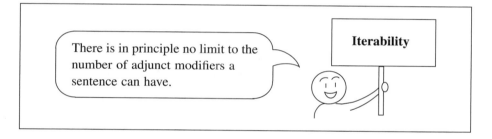

Optionality

A second property distinguishing complements and adjuncts is **optionality**. Whereas complements are obligatory (6), adjuncts can usually be omitted without ill-formedness (7):

(6) a.   *Homer chased.

     b.   *Marge put Lisa.

     c.   *Lisa handed Maggie.

(7) a.   Maggie crawled (quickly) (along the carpet) (to the refrigerator).

     b.   Homer chased Bart (out of the house) (around the block) (after dinner).

     c.   Marge handed Lisa Maggie (carefully) (without losing her balance).

Again, this behavior is expected under our intuitive picture of complements and adjuncts. Since complements fill the core roles in the verb script, they are necessary for a successful performance. Unless they are all present, the cast is not complete. With adjuncts, the situation is different.

> **Optionality**
>
> Since they serve only to provide additional information, adjuncts can be left out. If they are absent, the performance can still be complete.

The optionality test may seem straightforward: if a type of phrase can be added or dropped freely, it is an adjunct; otherwise, it is a complement. In practice, however, the test is complicated by at least two factors:

- Some predicates seem to have different senses, which determine different numbers of complements.
- Some complements might be unpronounced.

Predicate Alternations

A simple case of the first point is the verb *run*. Viewed superficially, the pair in (8a,b) might suggest that *run* allows an optional following NP. Hence, this NP might be diagnosed as an adjunct under the optionality test:

> (8)　a.　Bart ran.
> 　　　b.　Bart ran the meeting.

More careful reflection shows that this reasoning is flawed, however. Notice that two very different senses of *run* are in play here. In (8a), *run* refers to a form of bodily motion: to propel oneself by rapid motion of the legs. In (8b), *run* does not refer to bodily motion; rather, it means something like 'lead' or 'conduct', as in *Bart conducted the meeting*. So this isn't an example of a single verb with an omissible complement. Rather, it is a case of two different verbs, with different selectional requirements, that happen to sound the same. One *run* (8a) is intransitive. The other *run* (8b) is transitive, and its following NP is a complement.

A more subtle example of this point is the verb *write*. *Write* occurs with no trailing phrases (9a), with a trailing NP (9b), with a trailing NP - PP pair (9c), or with a trailing NP - NP pair (9d). The optionality of the NPs and PP might therefore seem to suggest adjunct status:

> (9)　a.　I'm writing.
> 　　　b.　I'm writing a novel.
> 　　　c.　I'm writing a letter to Marge.
> 　　　d.　I'm writing Marge a letter.

Here again, however, we can detect a meaning difference. Example (9a) seems to involve a sense of *write* where it means (roughly) 'to draw letters or characters'. Suppose we come upon a small child who is practicing making letters. We ask, "What are you doing?"; the child answers (9a). On this usage, the verb involves only one participant: an agent.

Example (9b) involves a sense of *write* where the verb means 'to create a document by drawing letters or characters'. In this sense, one doesn't simply write; rather, one writes *something*: a book, a poem, a memo, or the like. Here the verb involves two participants: an agent and a theme.

Finally, (9c,d) involve a sense of *write* where the verb means 'to communicate by means of a written document'—a document created by drawing letters or characters. In this sense, one doesn't simply write, nor does one simply write something. One writes something *to someone*, be it a memo, letter, message, or note. In this last case, the verb involves three participants: an agent, a theme, and a goal.

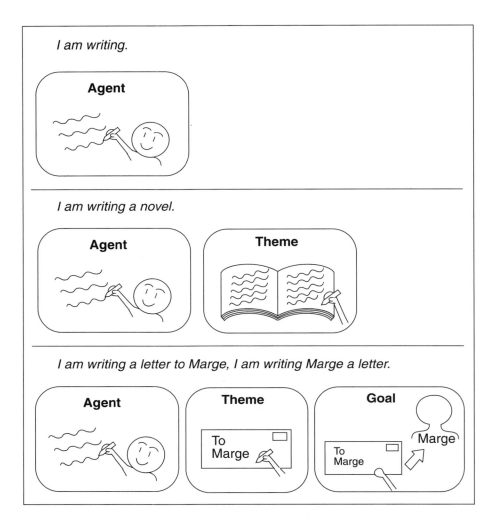

If these intuitions are correct, then we seem justified in speaking about a different sense of *write* in each of the three cases. Hence, we might claim, as with *run*, that we are dealing with complements in all of these cases. Notice however that the situation is more complicated than with *run*, because of the constant element of meaning that is involved: the drawing of letters or characters. This makes it much less clear that we are dealing with several different verbs.

A natural compromise here is to propose that we are dealing with multiple subentries of a single word, as we encountered with *give*.[1] That is, we might claim that *write* bears a variety of subcategory features:[2]

> *write*, V, [+ __], [+ __ NP], [+ __ NP PP], [+ __ NP NP]

Following our earlier discussion, we might understand these features as being associated with subentries for the single verb *write*:

> *write*, V,
> (i)   [+ __], to draw letters or characters (e.g., *Maggie was writing*)
> (ii) [+ __ NP], to create a document by drawing letters or characters (e.g., *Lisa wrote a novel*)
> (iii) [+ __ NP PP], [+ __ NP NP], to communicate by means of a written document (e.g., *Marge wrote a letter to Homer*)

On this view, the phrases following *write* would all be complements. But whereas with *run* we encounter *different verbs* that happen to sound the same, with *write* we encounter *different senses of the same verb*.

Unpronounced Complements?

Another complicating factor in applying the optionality test is the potential for unpronounced complements. Consider:

> (10) a.   Homer ate.
>   b.   Homer ate a doughnut.

Evidently, *eat* can take a following NP or not. But it doesn't seem that *a doughnut* should be analyzed as an adjunct in (10b) since, intuitively, an eating event always involves two things: an eater and a thing eaten. The problem is therefore (10a). If *eat* always assigns two thematic roles, what has happened to the object in this case?

---

1. Recall that *give* shows both a [+ __ NP PP] and a [+ __ NP NP] pattern.
2. The frame [+ __ NP NP] is present in virtue of examples like *Marge wrote Homer a letter*.

One idea might be to appeal to different senses of *eat*, just as we appealed to different senses of *write*:

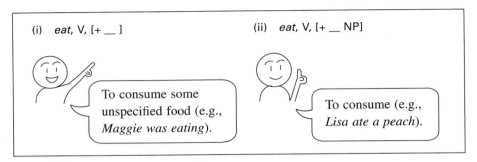

(i)   *eat*, V, [+ __]

To consume some unspecified food (e.g., *Maggie was eating*).

(ii)   *eat*, V, [+ __ NP]

To consume (e.g., *Lisa ate a peach*).

On this view, *eat* would have a sense equivalent to *dine*, where it would assign just one thematic role. But it would also have a sense equivalent to *consume* or *devour*, where it would assign two thematic roles.

There is another possibility, however. Notice that even in entry (i) we still analyze *eat* as 'eating something'. An alternative idea would be to propose an unpronounced object in the tree—an NP equivalent to *SOMETHING-EDIBLE*—that is simply not pronounced:

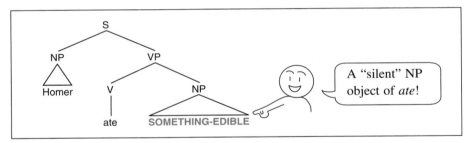

A "silent" NP object of *ate*!

If we take this view, then the lexical entry for *eat* can be made simpler:

eat, V, [+ __ NP], to consume   (e.g., *Lisa ate a peach*)

That is, we would be claiming that *eat* really is transitive in all of its occurrences. Examples like (10a) would not be counterexamples to this claim since they too would contain an object—simply an object that we are unable to hear.

This kind of analysis could be applied to many cases beyond *eat*. Consider *give* and *write*:

> (11) a. Marge gave Ø to charity.
>   b. Marge wrote Ø to Homer.
>   c. Marge wrote Homer Ø.

Despite the missing complements in these cases (marked by "Ø"), we still understand the actions as involving three participants. Thus, (11a) would be typically understood as 'Marge gave MONEY to charity'. Likewise, (11b) and (11c) would be understood as 'Marge wrote SOME-MESSAGE to Homer', whether by means of a letter, a memo, or the like.

Again, given that we understand the element as being present, it is tempting to think that it really *is* present, but in unpronounced form:

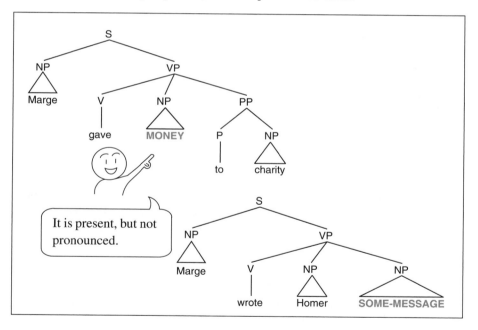

We won't try to settle which of the two approaches we should adopt:

- Simple trees without unpronounced items + more complicated lexical entries.
- More complicated trees with unpronounced items + simpler lexical entries.

Notice, however, that if we adopt the unpronounced-items approach, we have the important responsibility of constraining when and where ghostly phrases like *SOMETHING-EDIBLE*, *MONEY*, and *SOME-MESSAGE* can appear. For example, notice that we cannot use the sentence *Homer dropped* to mean 'Homer dropped something edible' or 'Homer dropped money'. But in order to block this result, we must somehow make sure that our ghostly NPs don't show up as complements to verbs like *drop*:

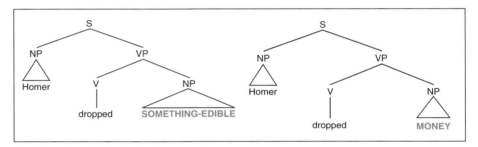

Lexical Sensitivity

A third test for complement versus adjunct status is the presence of **lexical sensitivities** of various kinds. For instance, we noted earlier that when *give* has a following PP, this PP should contain the specific preposition *to* (12a). This contrasts with the case of *ran* in (12b):

> (12) a. Marge gave Maggie to / *from / *on / *toward Homer.
>   b. Maggie ran to / from / on / toward / after / with / because-of Homer.

The presence of special requirements strongly implies that the *to*-phrase has a complement relation with *give*: in order for the verb to satisfy its cooccurrence requirements, a specific form is required. By contrast, *run* doesn't seem to care what kind of preposition follows it. This supports our diagnosis of PPs following *run* as adjuncts.

> Generally speaking, when we can find particular lexical sensitivities, it is a good indication that we are in the presence of the complement relation.

Lexical sensitivity

Attaching Complements

Review

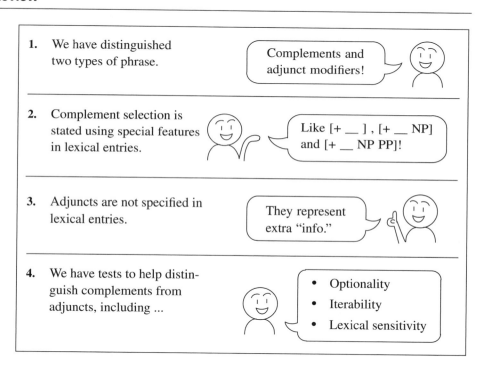

1. We have distinguished two types of phrase.

    Complements and adjunct modifiers!

2. Complement selection is stated using special features in lexical entries.

    Like [+ __] , [+ __ NP] and [+ __ NP PP]!

3. Adjuncts are not specified in lexical entries.

    They represent extra "info."

4. We have tests to help distinguish complements from adjuncts, including ...

    • Optionality
    • Iterability
    • Lexical sensitivity

Complements and Constituency

Up to this point, we have distinguished complements and adjuncts solely by their relation to verb meaning. A verbal complement "completes" the meaning of the verb, whereas a verbal adjunct does not. However, the complement/adjunct difference also seems to be reflected in syntax: the two types of phrase seem to attach in different ways. In this unit, we will consider attachment of complements; in the next unit, we will turn to adjuncts.

The Verb *Chase*

We saw earlier that the verb *chase* selects an object, requiring a following NP in order to form a complete sentence:

(1) a.   *Homer chased.
     b.   Homer chased Bart.

Notice that, by itself, the requirement of a following NP could be met by any number of different structures. For instance, in all three of the trees given below, *chased* is followed by an NP, as required:

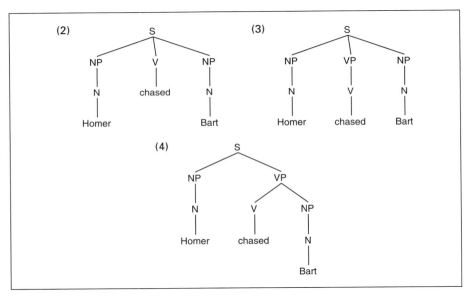

Nonetheless, using constituency tests, we have argued that only one of these trees is correct, namely, (4). Facts like those in (5) suggest this:

(5) a.   Homer chased Bart and caught Bart.
     b.   Homer chased Bart and Marge did so too.

Sentence (5a) shows the sequence *chased Bart* being conjoined. Sentence (5b) shows the sequence *chased Bart* being replaced by the proform *do so*. Our principles P1 and P2 state the following:

> **P1**
> If a string of words can be conjoined, then it is a constituent.
> **P2**
> If a string of words can be replaced by a proform, then it is a constituent.

Accordingly, the sequence *chased Bart* must be a constituent. This result argues for Tree (4) over Trees (2) and (3), since only in (4) is *chased Bart* a constituent.

 **QUESTION**   Given the result that (4) is the correct tree, what do you observe about the relation between the verb *chase* and its complement NP? Where must the latter be located in relation to the former?

The Verb *Put*

As a second example, consider the verb *put*. Earlier, we saw that *put* selects an object NP and a location phrase (usually a PP). Both of these elements must be present for a complete sentence:

> (6) a.   *Homer put.
>   b.   *Homer put the car.
>   c.   *Homer put in the garage.
>   d.   Homer put the car in the garage.

Notice again that the requirement of a following NP and PP could be met by a range of different tree structures:

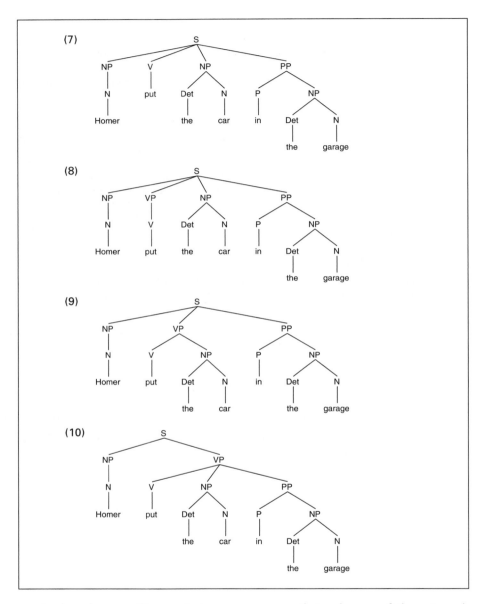

Again using constituency tests, we can argue that only one of these trees is correct, namely, (10).

 **EXERCISE**   Construct an argument for this conclusion parallel to the one given above with *chase*, but using ellipsis and dislocation instead of conjunction and proform replacement.

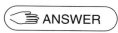 **? QUESTION**   Given that (10) is the correct tree, what do you observe about the relation between the verb *put* and its complement NP and PP? Where must the latter two phrases occur in relation to the verb that selects them?

In reflecting on the questions posed above, you have probably come to an answer something like this:

 **ANSWER**   The verb and its complements must occur together in their own constituent, VP.

For example, with *chase* we see that the verb and its complement form a constituent, [*chase Bart*], that excludes the subject NP. It's not enough that the object simply follow the verb; the two must be grouped together structurally. Likewise, with *put* we see that the verb, its object, and its location phrase must all form a single constituent that excludes the subject: [*put the car in the garage*]. It's not enough that NP and PP follow the verb (as in Trees (7) and (8)), nor is it enough for only one of the complements to be grouped with the verb (as in Tree (9)).

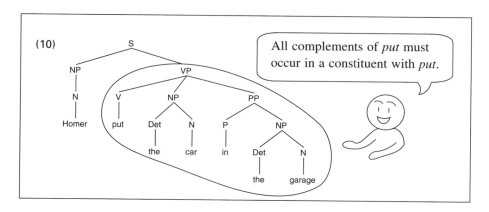

(10)

All complements of *put* must occur in a constituent with *put*.

Furthermore, notice that not only do the verb *put* and its complements form a constituent—they in fact form a constituent whose category is related to V. To see this point more clearly, let's consider a different class of examples—one not involving verbs.

Complements of P

Consider the two boldfaced items in (11):

> (11)   a.   Homer put the pork chop **in the refrigerator**.
>   b.   Homer put the pork chop **down**.

We have identified the first one as a PP. In fact, it is plausible to analyze both of these expressions as PPs, the former having the structure in (12), and the latter having the structure in (13).

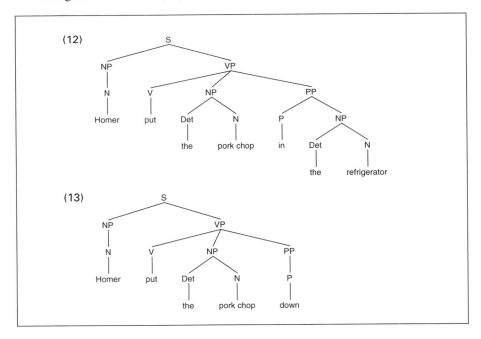

? QUESTION | What evidence is there that *down* is a P? Think of other examples in which *down* occurs.

Notice that under this analysis, *in* and *down* are similar to the verbs *chase* and *crawl*, respectively, introduced in Unit 15:

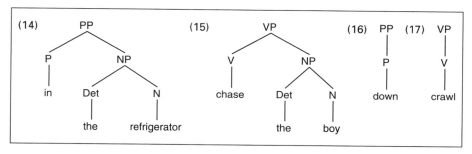

Chase is a verb that selects a complement, and *crawl* is a verb that selects no complements. In the same way, we can analyze *in* as a preposition that selects a complement, and *down* as a preposition that selects no complements. *In* (like *chase*) seems to need an additional phrase to complete its meaning; it makes little sense to speak of something as being "in."[1] By contrast, *down* (like *crawl*) seems to be able to stand on its own. This contrast is brought out by the following dialogue, spoken by two people standing in a stairwell beside a door:

Down seems to answer the question all by itself, but to the extent that *in* is acceptable in this context, we seem to have to understand it as elliptical for something like *in the door.*

---

1. Notice that even when we say things like *Overalls are not in this fall*, *in* is short for *in style*, a different use of *in*, but one that still requires an object.

Now notice that the same pattern of constituency seen with verbs and their complements holds with prepositions and their complements. That is, we can show by constituency tests that the structure of *Homer put the car in the garage* is as in (18), where P and its complement form a constituent:

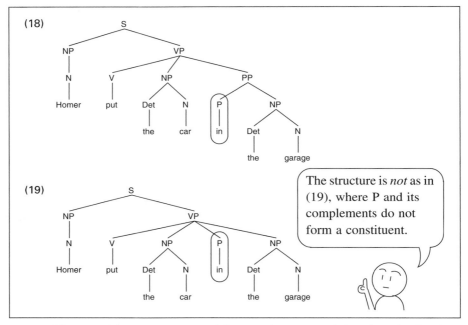

(18)

(19)

The structure is *not* as in (19), where P and its complements do not form a constituent.

Now consider the category of the constituent containing the selecting item and its complements. What is the category of the constituent that contains a verb and its complements? What is the category of the constituent that contains a preposition and its complements? The generalization or principle involved is clearly this:

Principle
An item X and its complements must occur together in a phrase headed by X.

A Locality Constraint

The principle that we have discovered is what is called a **locality constraint**: one that limits some phenomenon to hold within a certain local domain. Our results show that the selection of complements must occur within a minimal domain determined by the selecting element. Specifically, complements of an element X must occur within the phrase projected by X.

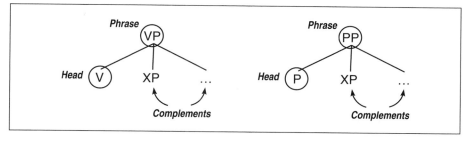

There are a number of ways of capturing this constraint.

Constraining Lexical Insertion

One way is by refining how subcategory features are understood relative to lexical insertion. Recall from Unit 13 that subcategory features constrain where we are allowed to place a word in a tree. Originally we put things very generally, interpreting features in this way:

Feature	Interpretation
[+ __]	"Insert me into a frame where nothing follows."
[+ __ NP]	"Insert me into a frame where a single NP follows."
[+ __ NP NP]	"Insert me into a frame where two NPs follow."
[+ __ NP PP]	"Insert me into a frame where an NP and a PP follow."

Suppose, however, that we interpret subcategory features more restrictively. We've seen that for a V, we want [+ __ NP] to mean "Insert me into a *VP* where a single NP follows." For a P, we want [+ __ NP] to mean "Insert me into a *PP* where a single NP follows." In short, we want the subcategory feature to be satisfied within a phrase that is projected by the feature-bearing item.

The following revised view of subcategory features and their interpretation takes account of these points:

Feature	Interpretation
[+ __]	"Insert me into a phrase that I head where nothing follows."
[+ __ NP]	"Insert me into a phrase that I head where one NP follows."
[+ __ NP NP]	"Insert me into a phrase that I head where two NPs follow."
[+ __ NP PP]	"Insert me into a phrase that I head where an NP and a PP follow."

Thus, if the lexical item to be inserted is a V, then the relevant frame for insertion is VP; if the item is a P, then the relevant frame is PP; and so on. This understanding of subcategory features will correctly prevent insertion of *chase* into a structure where it is followed by an NP that lies outside the VP headed by *chase*. Likewise, it prevents insertion of *in* into a structure where it is followed by an NP, but where P and NP don't form a PP:

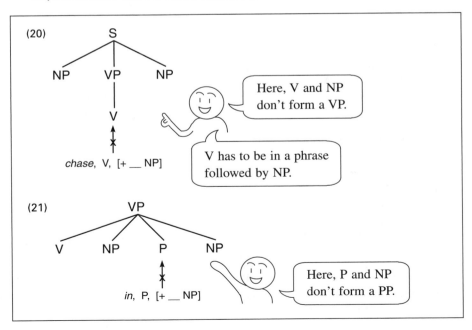

The only "frames" that count as legitimate for insertion are phrases that are headed by the selecting element and that contain the complement categories.

Subcategorization Frames as Features

An alternative way of capturing locality is to make use of the connection between heads and feature passing discussed in Unit 14, and to treat subcategorization frames as "shape features" of a special kind. To see how this works, consider the verb *put* and its lexical entry:

> (22) *put*, V, <agent, theme, location>, [+ __ NP PP]
> [+loc]

If [+ __ NP PP] is treated as a feature, then when *put* is inserted into a VP, this
[+loc]
feature will be inherited by VP according to Principle F from Unit 14 (see (23a)):

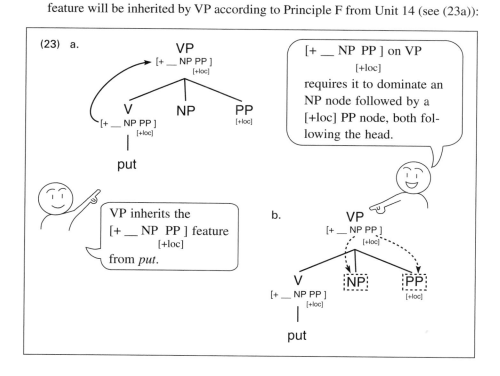

Suppose now that if a phrasal node bears the feature [+ __ NP PP], it is required
                                                          [+loc]
to dominate an NP node followed by a [+loc] PP node, both following the head
(23b). If the node bearing the subcategory feature fails to dominate the required
nodes, with their associated features, the tree is ill-formed. [+ __ NP PP] would,
                                                                     [+loc]
as it were, be a feature determining the shape of the phrasal node that bears it.
Since feature passing is local, from head to phrase, the proposed requirement
ensures the locality of selection within the phrase.

Notice that on this view, the verb *put* can be inserted into a tree that doesn't
meet its selection requirements. However, such a tree (and its associated sentence)
will end up being ungrammatical since VP will not have the right shape demanded
by its features.

Again, we will not try to choose between these two analyses of selection
locality, but simply consider them as potential ways of capturing the basic constraint.

Attaching Adjuncts

Review

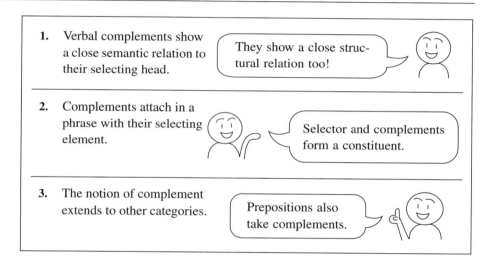

1. Verbal complements show a close semantic relation to their selecting head.

    They show a close structural relation too!

2. Complements attach in a phrase with their selecting element.

    Selector and complements form a constituent.

3. The notion of complement extends to other categories.

    Prepositions also take complements.

An Apparent Contradiction

Our results show that the close semantic relation between a head and its complements is matched by a close structural relation in the tree. What about the relation between a head and its associated modifiers? We might expect it to be much "looser." Is it?

Verbal Adjuncts as *Inside* VP

Consider the pair of sentences (1a) and (1b), which differ only in the choice of verb, *put* versus *polish*:[1]

(1) a. Homer put the car in the garage.

    b. Homer polished the car in the garage.

We have analyzed *put* as a verb selecting two complements: an NP and a locational PP. In contrast, *polish* would seem to select just one complement, as suggested by the fact that the PP can be deleted with *polish*, but not with *put*:

(2) a. *Homer put the car.

    b. Homer polished the car.

Given this difference in selection, let us ask, Where is the PP attached in (1b)? One possibility is that it is attached in the same place as with *put*: namely, under the VP with the object. And in fact there is evidence that seems to support this conclusion. Consider the facts in (3):

(3) a. Homer polished the car in the garage and oiled the lawn mower.

    b. Homer polished the car in the garage and Bart did so too.

    c. Homer polished the car in the garage and Bart did Ø too.

    d. (Homer said he would polish the car in the garage and)
       Polish the car in the garage, Homer did!

In (3a), *polished the car in the garage* has been conjoined with a phrase whose category is clearly VP (*oiled the lawn mower*). Using the conjunction principle from Unit 9, we thus have evidence that *polished the car in the garage* is also of category VP:

---

1. For present purposes, think of (1b) on the reading where *in the garage* tells where the polishing took place. There is a subtly different reading where *in the garage* modifies *the car* rather than *polish*. On this second reading, it was the car-in-the-garage that got polished by Homer, and the polishing could have taken place somewhere other than in the garage. This second reading is one in which the PP modifies the object NP (*the car*). We will return to modifiers of NP in Unit 22.

> **Conjunction test**
> If a phrase whose category we are unsure about (X) can be conjoined with another phrase (Y) whose category we know, then we can generally conclude that X belongs to the same category as Y.

In (3b), *polished the car in the garage* has been replaced by *do so*, which we earlier identified as a proform of category VP (a VP proform). Using the substitution principle from Unit 9, we get further evidence that *polished the car in the garage* is a VP:

> **Substitution test**
> If a phrase whose category we are unsure about (X) can, without change of function, replace another phrase (Y) whose category we know, then we can conclude that X belongs to the same category as Y.

(3c) shows what looks very much like VP-ellipsis; and (3d) shows what looks very much like VP-fronting, with *polished the car in the garage* moved together as a single constituent phrase. Once again, we can conclude that *polished the car in the garage* is a single phrase of category VP.

Verbal Adjuncts as *Outside* VP

Keeping these results in mind, consider next the data in (4):

> (4) a. Homer polished the car and oiled the lawn mower in the garage.
> b. Homer polished the car in the garage and Bart did so in the driveway.
> c. Homer polished the car in the garage and Bart did Ø in the driveway.
> d. (Homer said he would polish the car in the garage and) Polish the car, Homer did, in the garage!

In (4a), *polished the car* is conjoined with the VP *oiled the lawn mower* and *in the garage* modifies both *polished the car* and *oiled the lawn mower* (that is, it says where both took place). Again using our conjunction principle, we find evidence here that *polished the car* is itself a VP and hence that *in the garage* lies outside VP.

In (4b), *polished the car* has been replaced by *did so*, a VP proform, and the counterpart of *in the garage* (that is, *in the driveway*) has been left stranded. Using our substitution principle, we find more evidence here that *polished the car* is a VP and that *in the garage* and *in the driveway* lie outside VP.

In (4c), VP-ellipsis has deleted *polished the car* and stranded *in the garage*. (4d) shows the same thing with VP-fronting: *polished the car* has moved as a single constituent phrase and *in the garage* has been left in place. Once again we can conclude that *polished the car* is a single phrase of category VP and hence that *in the garage* lies outside it.

Verbal Adjuncts as Inside *and* Outside VP

These results appear contradictory. Verbal adjuncts behave as if they are inside VP, but they also behave as if they are outside VP! On further thought, however, the situation isn't really contradictory. Can you see a way of resolving the puzzle? More exactly, can you see a way of drawing a tree diagram for *Homer polished the car in the garage* that (1) positions *in the garage* inside a VP that contains *polished the car* and (2) positions it outside a VP that contains *polished the car*?

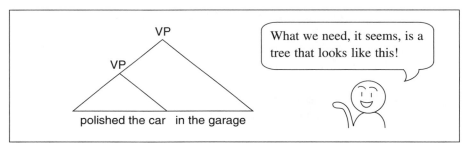

In this structure, there is a VP that contains the smaller string *polished the car*, but doesn't contain *in the garage*. *And* there is a VP that contains the smaller VP together with the modifier *in the garage*. With this picture, we can view the results in (3) as conjoining, replacing, deleting, and dislocating the larger VP:

(5) a. Homer [_{VP} polished the car in the garage] and [_{VP} oiled the lawn mower].

b. Homer [_{VP} polished the car in the garage] and Bart [_{VP} did so] too.

c. Homer [_{VP} polished the car in the garage] and Bart did [_{VP} Ø] too.

d. (Homer said he would [_{VP} polish the car in the garage] and) [_{VP} Polish the car in the garage], Homer did!

By contrast, we can view the results in (4) as conjoining, replacing, deleting, and dislocating the smaller, inner VP:

(6) a. Homer [_{VP} [_{VP} polished the car] and
       [_{VP} oiled the lawn mower] in the garage].

b. Homer [_{VP} [_{VP} polished the car] in the garage] and
   Bart [_{VP} [_{VP} did so] in the driveway].

c. Homer [_{VP} [_{VP} polished the car] in the garage] and
   Bart did [_{VP} [_{VP} Ø] in the driveway].

d. (Homer said he would [_{VP} [_{VP} polish the car] in the garage] and)
   [_{VP} Polish the car], Homer did [_{VP} ____ in the garage]!

Thus, the apparent contradiction is resolved.

Adjunction of Modifiers

Given our results, how exactly should the internal structure of the big VP containing a modifier look? What's inside the larger triangle? A simple proposal is this:

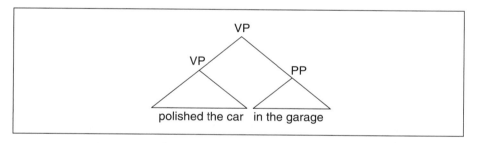

The idea is that modifying PPs are attached by a rule that expands VP, reintroducing another VP node underneath. More generally, we might add rules of this kind for all the types of modifiers mentioned in Unit 17:

VP → VP PP   (e.g., *polished the car **in the garage***)
VP → VP AdvP   (e.g., *polished the car **carefully***)
VP → VP NP   (e.g., *polished the car **that way***)

All of these rules have the same fundamental character: they expand VP as a VP plus a modifier (VP → VP Mod).

Recursion of Modifiers

The rules for attaching modifiers have an important property that we encountered earlier with conjunctions: they are *recursive*. The modifier rules introduce the same category on the right-hand side of the arrow that appears on the left-hand side of the arrow. This allows the rule to reapply to its own output, ad infinitum.

This outcome accommodates an important fact about modifiers that we noted earlier: they are *iterable*. In principle, a VP can have an unbounded number of modifiers attached to it:

(7) a.   Homer buttered the toast.
   b.   Homer buttered the toast carefully.
   c.   Homer buttered the toast carefully with a knife.
   d.   Homer buttered the toast carefully with a knife in the kitchen.
   e.   Homer buttered the toast carefully with a knife in the kitchen at midnight.
   f.   Homer buttered the toast carefully with a knife in the kitchen at midnight without waking Marge.
   g.   Homer buttered the toast carefully with a knife in the kitchen at midnight without waking Marge in order to satisfy a craving.
   h.   Homer buttered the toast carefully with a knife in the kitchen at midnight without waking Marge in order to satisfy a craving although he knew he shouldn't be eating.

The limitation on how many modifiers can follow the verb seems to be a matter of how many consistent, informative things we can find to say about Homer's toast buttering, and not a matter of grammar only allowing us a fixed number. For example, we couldn't attach both *at midnight* and *shortly after dawn* since these are inconsistent. Likewise, we couldn't attach a directional adjunct like *into the house* since buttering doesn't seem to involve motion toward a spatial goal of this kind.

With recursive rules, we can assign (7b–d), for example, the structures shown in (8a–c):

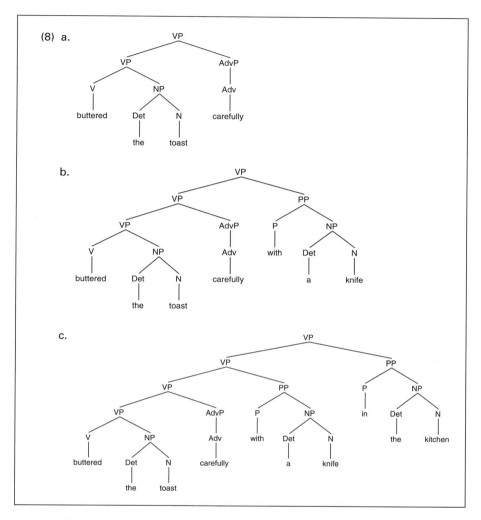

Clearly we could go on like this, stacking up more and more modifiers recursively onto the top VP node.

Complements: Sister of V – Modifiers: Sister of VP

These results give us a tidy way of distinguishing complements and modifiers, one that tracks our notion that the former are more closely related to the verb than the latter. Notice that while verbal complements and modifiers both occur within VP, the former always occur within the *smallest* VP, where they are *sisters to the verb*. On the other hand, the latter always occur within a *larger* VP, where they are *sisters to a VP*. Thus, in (8a–c), [_{NP} *the toast*] is a complement of the transitive verb *butter*, and it occurs within the smallest VP, where it is sister to [_V *buttered*]. By contrast, [_{AdvP} *carefully*] is an adjunct modifier of the verb, and not a complement. Correspondingly, it occurs higher up, attached as sister to a VP, not as sister to the V.

This result has the consequence that similar-looking strings may have very different structures. We saw in Unit 17 that *behave* selects a manner adverbial complement, whereas *write* does not. It follows that (9a,b) should receive different structures, despite their very similar appearance:

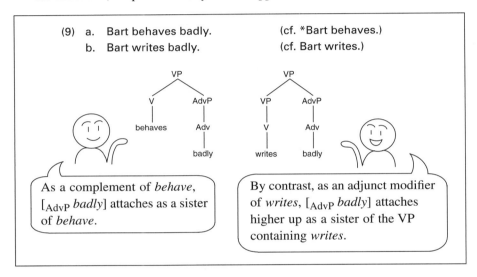

(9) a.   Bart behaves badly.   (cf. *Bart behaves.)
     b.   Bart writes badly.   (cf. Bart writes.)

As a complement of *behave*, [_{AdvP} *badly*] attaches as a sister of *behave*.

By contrast, as an adjunct modifier of *writes*, [_{AdvP} *badly*] attaches higher up as a sister of the VP containing *writes*.

Order of Verbal Complements and Adjuncts

Our account of verbal complements and adjuncts makes some simple predictions about the ordering of phrases. Consider the pairs in (10) and (11):

(10) a.   Homer buttered [the toast] [carefully].
      b.   ?*Homer buttered [carefully] [the toast].
(11) a.   Homer and Marge mentioned [their vacation] [on Thursday].
      b.   ?*Homer and Marge mentioned [on Thursday] [their vacation].

In each case, the (a) member of the pair is more natural than the (b) member; to make the latter acceptable, we seem to need a special intonation where the final

NP gets heavy stress. The generalization we arrive at is apparently this: complement NPs occur to the left of adjunct AdvPs or PPs.

Our tree structures for VP predict this result. Complements occur within the smallest VP as sisters of V, whereas adjuncts occur farther out, as sisters of VP. This means that when both occur to the right of V, the complement will need to occur closer to V than the adjunct. In turn, this means that the complement will occur before (to the left of) the adjunct:

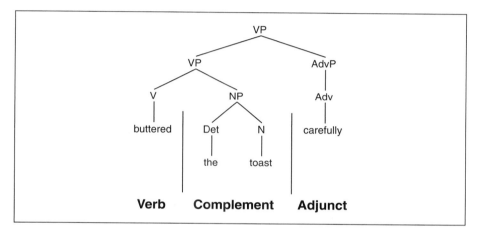

EXERCISES

1. For each of the words in (1)–(8), give lexical entries and example sentences. Be as complete as you can, but be mindful of understood material.

   Example

   bake, V, [+ __ NP]   Homer baked a cake.
          [+ __ NP PP]   Homer baked a cake for Marge.

   (1) *give*, V,

   (2) *send*, V,

   (3) *donate*, V,

   (4) *break*, V,

   (5) *live*, V,

   (6) *walk*, V,

   (7) *promise*, V,

   (8) *read*, V,

2. Look at the example sentences in (1)–(6) and decide what the lexical entry for each corresponding italicized word should be. (Briefly explain your answer.)

   Example

   tell, V

                      Homer told the story.
   [+ __ NP PP]   Homer told the story to Bart.

   Explanation: In *Homer told the story*, there is an understood hearer (*Homer told the story **to someone***); so the first seems to be an elliptical version of the second.

   (1) *talk*, V

                Marge talked.
                Marge talked to Bart.

   (2) *sneeze*, V

                Marge sneezed.
                Marge sneezed a (little) sneeze.

(3) *behave*, V

> Bart behaved poorly.
> Bart behaved.

(4) *leave*, V

> Homer left.
> Homer left the house.
> Homer left the house dirty.

(5) ~~sad~~ happy, A

> Homer is happy.
> Homer is happy about his promotion.
> Homer is happy that he was promoted.

(6) *since*, P

> (Bart hasn't been there) since that day.
> (Bart hasn't been there) since.
> (Bart hasn't been there) since Homer left.
> (Bart hasn't been there) since before Homer left.

3. Below is set of phrase structure rules allowing for a broad range of complement and adjunct patterns in the verb phrase:

S → NP VP	VP → V
NP → Det N	VP → V NP
NP → N	VP → V PP
Det → NP Poss	VP → V S
AdvP → Adv	VP → V AdvP
AP → A	VP → V NP NP
PP → P NP	VP → V NP PP
	VP → V NP AdvP
	VP → V NP AP
	VP → V NP S
	VP → V PP PP
	VP → VP PP
	VP → VP AdvP
	VP → VP AP

Here is a set of sentences:

(1) Homer jumped.

(2) Homer jumped the fence.

(3) Homer jumped over the fence.

(4)   Lisa spoke.

(5)   Lisa spoke those words.

(6)   Lisa spoke those words carefully.

(7)   Lisa spoke to Homer.

(8)   Lisa spoke about Bart.

(9)   Lisa spoke to Homer about Bart.

(10)   Bart's teacher told a story to Bart.

(11)   Bart's teacher told Bart a story.

(12)   Bart's teacher told Bart he passed.

(13)   Bart said those words.

(14)   Bart said those words to Homer.

(15)   Bart said he passed.

(16)   Lisa showed the picture to Maggie.

(17)   Lisa showed Maggie the picture.

(18)   Marge awarded the prize to Bart.

(19)   Marge awarded Bart with the prize.

(20)   Marge awarded Bart the prize.

(21)   Marge phrased her answer carefully.

(22)   Homer's job pays well.

(23)   Marge drinks her coffee black.

(24)   Homer arrived tired.

A.   Create a lexicon that will interact with the rules given above to do the following:

- Generate trees for all of the sentences given, and
- Correctly analyze the sentences in terms of complements and adjuncts.

B.   Check to see that your lexicon doesn't allow ungrammatical outputs like these:

(25)   a.   *Lisa spoke he passed.

       b.   *Bart's teacher told he passed.

       c.   *Bart's teacher said Bart he passed.

       d.   *Bart's teacher told to Bart.

    e.   *Bart's teacher said to Bart.

    f.   *Lisa showed Maggie with the picture.

(To be thorough, you should check your grammar against additional ungrammatical sentences of your own.)

4. Here is a set of structural rules for noun phrases:

NP → N

NP → Det N

    Here are a set of well-formed NPs (1) and a set of ill-formed NPs (2):

(1)   [NP the man]   [NP one boy]   [NP some girls]
       [NP Bart]   [NP some girl]   [NP both girls]
       [NP each baby]   [NP no baby]   [NP the girls]
       [NP a boy]   [NP two boys]

(2)   *[NP **the Maggie**]   *[NP **each babies**]
      *[NP some Marge]   *[NP a boys]
      *[NP every Homer]   *[NP **both boy**]
      *[NP no Lisa]   *[NP one girls]

    Now do the following:

A.   Create a lexicon to go with the structural rules that will allow all of the examples in (1) to be generated, but none of the examples in (2). (Hint: You will need to use features on the complements to do this.)

B.   For each of the the boldfaced NPs in (2), explain how your lexicon blocks it from being generated.

    Here are some additional facts:

(3)   *[NP boy]   (ran)   [NP boys]   (ran)
      *[NP baby] (cried)   [NP babies] (cried)

    Now do the following:

C.   Discuss whether the grammar you created in Question A will produce all these NPs.

D.   State how you might change your lexicon so that the ill-formed NPs in (3) are not generated. Can you prevent the NPs in (3) by specifying complements in some way?

E.   Suppose all NPs are really of the form [NP Det N] (so that the rule NP → N is discarded). Suppose further that the NPs in (3) actually contain an unpronounced determiner SOME. Does this help with the job of ruling out the ill-formed NPs in (3)? (Hereafter *N* will be used for all nouns, both common and proper.)

5. For each of the sentences in (1)–(6), state whether the boldfaced word or phrase is an adjunct or complement of the verb, and briefly give the reason for your choice.

Example

Homer worded the message **carefully**.

 The adverb *carefully* is a complement of the verb *worded*. This is shown by the fact that it cannot be deleted without causing incompleteness: **Homer worded the message*.

 (1) Marge signaled **to Bart**.

 (2) Lisa slept **two days** in the hospital.

 (3) Homer's job pays **well**.

 (4) It bothers Homer **when he has no beer**.

 (5) Homer stood the ladder **in the corner**.

 (6) Lisa persuaded Homer **that he should give up beer**.

6. Consider the APs in (1):

 (1) a. Marge is [$_{AP}$ fond [$_{PP}$ of Homer]].

   b. Marge is [$_{AP}$ fond [$_{PP}$ of Homer] [$_{PP}$ in many ways]].

   c. Marge is [$_{AP}$ terribly fond [$_{PP}$ of Homer] [$_{PP}$ in many ways]].

   d. Marge is [$_{AP}$ so terribly fond [$_{PP}$ of Homer] [$_{PP}$ in many ways]].

 Further, consider these facts:

 (2) a. **Fond of Homer** though Marge is, she won't buy him a motorcycle.

   b. **Fond of Homer in many ways** though Marge is, she won't buy him a motorcycle.

   c. **Fond of Homer** though Marge is *in many ways*, she won't buy him a motorcycle.

 (3) a. Marge is fond of Homer in some ways, but less **so** than Bart.

   b. Marge is fond of Homer in some ways, but less **so** in other ways than Bart.

 On the basis of these facts (and any others that you might suggest yourself), do the following:

A. Propose structures for (1a–d).

B. Argue that your structures are correct.

7. Adjectival modifiers in NP seem to prefer certain orderings. Consider the facts in (1)–(4):

   (1)   a.   a big gray brick house

         b.   *a brick gray big house

         c.   *a brick big gray house

   (2)   a.   a beautiful blue South African diamond

         b.   ??a blue beautiful South African diamond

         c.   *a South African blue beautiful diamond

   (3)   those large new red English wooden chairs

   (4)   those aforementioned marvelous beautiful red wooden chairs

         Do the following:

   A.   Classify the various adjectives into different categories.

   B.   Construct phrase structure rules that generate adjectives in the right order using your adjectival categories.

8. Consider the PP in (1) and suppose that it is a modifier of A:

   (1)   Marge is [_AP smarter [_PP than Homer]].

         What difficulties are raised by the data in (2)?

   (2)   a.   Burns is a smart man.

         b.   Burns is a man smarter than Homer.

         c.   Burns is a smarter man than Homer.

         d.   *Burns is a smarter than Homer man.

9. Consider the phrase markers (trees) in (1) and (2):

   A.   Complete the phrase markers by inserting appropriate terminal elements (words!). Note carefully the differences between the two structures.

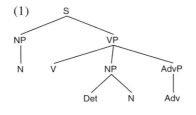

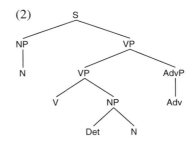

B.   Complete the following statements:

In Tree (1), AdvP is a(n) _____ . (complement, adjunct)

In Tree (2), AdvP is a(n) _____ . (complement, adjunct)

10. Here are two examples:

(1)   Lisa received a letter from Milhouse through the mail during last week.

(2)   Bart twice behaved rudely deliberately.

Give phrase markers (trees) for the sentences in (1) and (2). For (2), assume that *rudely* and *deliberately* are adverbs (Advs) introduced by this rule:

(3)   AdvP → Adv

Assume also the following rules introducing adjunct PPs and AdvPs:

(4)   a.   VP → VP PP

      b.   VP → VP AdvP

      c.   VP → AdvP VP

11. Consider the pair of examples in (1). Suppose both are spoken "out of context" (i.e., without significant previous discussion).

(1)   a.   Lisa played the saxophone in the street.

      b.   Lisa played in the street.

A.   Is it correct to analyze (1b) as an elliptical version of (1a)? Why or why not?

B.   On the basis of your decision above, what is/are the lexical entry/entries for *play*?

12. We have proposed the following principle relating complement/adjunct status to tree structure:

Principle

Verbal complements attach as sisters to V, whereas verbal adjuncts attach as sisters to VP.

A.   Now consider the following examples involving the adverb *surreptitiously*:

(1)   a.   **Surreptitiously** Smithers put the package in the car.

      b.   Smithers **surreptitiously** put the package in the car.

      c.   Smithers put the package **surreptitiously** in the car.

      d.   Smithers put the package in the car **surreptitiously**.

Offer a tree diagram for each sentence. Do any of the examples raise a problem for the proposed principle? Explain the problem(s) clearly and suggest a solution if you can.

B.   Assume the following judgment:

(2)   *Homer went to the ball game and Smithers **did so** to the power plant. (Meaning: 'Homer went to the ball game and Smithers went to the power plant.')

Now answer the following questions:

    a.   What string of words does *did so* (attempt to) replace in (2)?

    b.   What does the ungrammaticality of (2) suggest about the category of the string *did so* replaces?

    c.   On the basis of your answers, can you decide whether *to the ball game* in (2) is an adjunct or a complement?

C.   Look at the following conversations:

(3)   A: Where's Marge?

      B: She went.

(4)   A: Huge party, wasn't it?

      B: Yes, even Marge went.

How should we handle the subcategory features of *go* in these cases?

13. Examples (1a) and (1b) are nearly identical in surface form:

(1)   a.   Burns considered Smithers carefully.

    b.   Burns considered Smithers careful.

Suggest tree structures for the two examples. Carefully discuss your reasoning for the structures you assign.

14. For each of the phrases in (1)–(5), draw the appropriate tree diagram, assuming the lexical entries given.

Example

    a.   Phrase: chase the boy

    b.   Lexical entry: *chase*, V, [+ __ NP]

c.   Tree diagram:

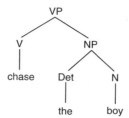

(1)   a.   Phrase: believe he is guilty

      b.   Lexical entry: *believe*, V, [+ __ S]

                    is, V, [+ __ AP]

                    guilty, A, [+ __]

      c.   Tree diagram:

(2)   a.   Phrase: persuade Homer he is guilty

      b.   Lexical entry: *persuade*, V, [+ __ NP S]

      c.   Tree diagram:

(3)   a.   Phrase: tell Homer the job pays well

      b.   Lexical entry: *tell*, V, [+ __ NP S]

                    pays, V, [+ __ AdvP]

      c.   Tree diagram:

(4)   a.   Phrase: glad Bart bet Lisa he would win

      b.   Lexical entry: *glad*, A, [+ __ S]

                    bet, V, [+ __ NP S]

                    will/would, V, [+ __ VP]

                    win, V, [+ __]

      c.   Tree diagram:

(5)   a.   Phrase: because of the fact Homer asked Lisa about Marge

      b.   Lexical entry: *because-of*, P, [+ __ NP]

                    fact, N, [+ __ S]

                    ask, V, [+ __ NP PP]

      c.   Tree diagram:

PART VI Following the Consequences

Scientific theories generate questions, and a good one will generate many interesting questions. Some arise when we bump up against new data and wonder, What can our theory say about this? In other cases, our theory makes specific predictions that need to be checked against the facts. In the event of conflict, we must be prepared to make changes. In still other cases, our theory may have broad conceptual implications that push us in certain directions.

With any science, most day-to-day work lies in pursuing consequences of this kind. In fact, the philosopher of science Thomas Kuhn referred to this simply as "normal science." Scientists are trained and work within what Kuhn called a **paradigm**, a mode of scientific practice involving theory, data, apparatus, and technique, and most of their work consists in fleshing out this paradigm:

The success of a paradigm ... is at the start largely a *promise* of success discoverable in selected and still incomplete examples. Normal science consists in the actualization of that promise ... achieved by extending the knowledge of those facts ... , by increasing the extent of the match between those facts and the paradigm's predictions, and by further articulation of the paradigm itself.
—*The Structure of Scientific Revolutions*, pp. 23–24

Thomas Kuhn
1922–1996
Photo courtesy MIT Museum.

So far, we have developed a number of analytical ideas and techniques for approaching human language, as well as a selected range of examples to which we have applied them. But at this point our domain of inquiry constitutes only a small fraction of linguistic data. A great deal of work therefore lies ahead in seeing whether our ideas can be applied to a wider domain, what challenges arise when we do, and where those challenges will lead us.

In Units 19–23, we will follow the consequences of some of our ideas by looking at the domain of sentential complements, and some surprising and far-reaching connections that our investigation brings to light.

Complement Sentences I

Review

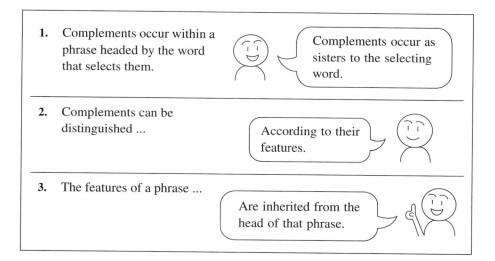

1. Complements occur within a phrase headed by the word that selects them.

   Complements occur as sisters to the selecting word.

2. Complements can be distinguished ...

   According to their features.

3. The features of a phrase ...

   Are inherited from the head of that phrase.

Sentence Forms

Sentences come in different forms, corresponding roughly to the ways they are used. For instance, the **declarative form** is typically used in making statements. Sentences in this form are called **declaratives**:

(1) a. Marge is a genius.
     b. Lisa has been very thoughtful.

The **interrogative form** is typically used to ask questions. Sentences in this form are called **interrogatives**:

> (2) a. Is Marge a genius?
>   b. How thoughtful has Lisa been?

The **exclamative form** is used to express surprise or astonishment. Sentences in this form are called **exclamatives**:

> (3) a. What a genius Marge is!
>   b. How thoughtful Lisa has been!

In spoken English, we distinguish these forms by word order and by the presence of items like *what* and *how*. Other languages use different means.

The form of a sentence is not always a sure indicator of how it is or can be used. For example, if we utter (1a) or (1b) with a **rising intonation**, then these sentences can have the force of questions, even though they are in the declarative form. Any declarative can be turned into a question this way.

> (4) Marge is a genius

Nonetheless, the matchup between form and use is generally a strong one. We would not use the sentences in (2) or (3) to express statements, for example. Nor would we use the sentences in (3) to ask a question.

A Further Distinction in Interrogatives

Within the general set of interrogative sentences, it's useful to recognize two kinds, distinguished by the types of answers they receive. Consider the questions in (5) versus the questions in (6). The questions in (5) can be answered with a simple *yes* or *no*. By contrast, a proper answer to the questions in (6) requires some sort of contentful word or phrase; a simple *yes* or *no* is not enough.

> (5) a. Did Marge eat those pizza slices?
>   (potential answer: *yes* or *no*)
>   b. Will Lisa go to her lab today?
>   (potential answer: *yes* or *no*)
> (6) a. Which pizza slices did Marge eat?
>   (potential answer: *Those slices on the table*)
>   b. Who will go to her lab today?
>   (potential answer: *Lisa*)
>   c. Where will Lisa go today?
>   (potential answer: *Her lab*)
>   d. When will Lisa go to her lab?
>   (potential answer: *Today*)
>   e. Why will Lisa go to her lab today?
>   (potential answer: *To run an experiment*)

Questions that can be answered with a *yes* or a *no*, like (5a,b), are called **polarity questions** or **yes-no questions**. Questions that must be answered with a contentful word or constituent are called **constituent questions**, or sometimes ***wh-questions***, because they typically involve a word like *who*, *what*, *where*, *when*, *why*, or *which*, which begin with *wh-*. (*How* also counts as one of these words.)

In this unit, we will mainly concentrate on declaratives and interrogatives (polarity and constituent), putting exclamatives aside.

Sentences inside Sentences

We've seen in earlier units that sentences can contain a variety of phrases, including noun phrases, verb phrases, prepositional phrases, and adverbial phrases:

> (7) a. **The woman** told her story to the child more quickly than Homer.
>   (NP)
>   b. The woman **told her story to the child** more quickly than Homer.
>   (VP)
>   c. The woman told her story **to the child** more quickly than Homer.
>   (PP)
>   d. The woman told her story to the child **more quickly than Homer**.
>   (AdvP)

In addition, sentences can contain other sentences. Consider the pairs in (8)–(10), for instance. The first member of each pair is an independent sentence, which occurs inside the second member of the pair:

(8)   a.   Marge left.
      b.   Bart said **Marge left**.
(9)   a.   Marge could climb the mountain.
      b.   Bart persuaded Lisa that **Marge could climb the mountain**.
(10) a.   Bart likes peanuts.
      b.   That **Bart likes peanuts** is obvious.

The embedding of one sentence inside another can be compounded. (11a) is a sentence containing a sentence (11b), containing yet another sentence (11c):

(11) a.   Moe persuaded Lisa that **Bart believed Marge left**.
      b.   Bart believed **Marge left**.
      c.   Marge left.

It's easy to see that we could take things even further, putting (11a) inside another sentence, putting the result inside yet another sentence, and so on.

Constituency

Arguments of a familiar kind can be used to show that the boldfaced strings in (8b), (9b), and (10b) are constituents within the larger sentences. Consider the evidence from conjunction, proform replacement, and ellipsis shown in (12):

(12) a.   Bart said [**Marge left**] and [**Homer stayed**].
      b.   Bart said **Marge left**. Lisa already knew **that**.
      c.   Bart said **Marge left**. Lisa already knew Ø.

On the basis of these data, we can construct an argument that the structure of *Bart said Marge left* should be as in (13a), where *Marge left* forms a constituent S, and not as in (13b), where *Marge left* is not a constituent.

(13) a.
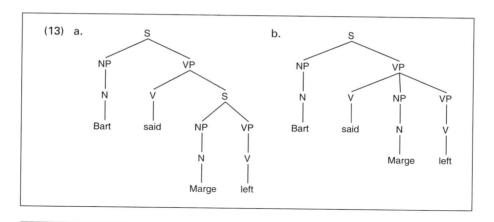

😊 EXERCISE | Using the data in (12), construct the argument for (13a) versus (13b).

Embedded Sentences of Different Types

The sentences occurring within other sentences include all of the types that we surveyed above. For example, (14a) contains an embedded declarative; (14b) contains an embedded polarity interrogative; (14c) contains an embedded constituent question; and (14d) contains an embedded exclamative:

(14) a. Bart believes that **Marge is a genius**.
(embedded declarative)

b. Bart asked **whether Marge was a genius**.
(embedded polarity interrogative)

c. Bart wondered **how thoughtful Lisa had been**.
(embedded constituent interrogative)

d. Bart couldn't believe **how thoughtful Lisa had been**.
(embedded exclamative)

Notice that *containing* a sentence of a certain kind is different from *being* a sentence of that kind. (14b) and (14c) contain interrogatives, but they are not interrogatives themselves; rather, they are declaratives. Neither (14b) nor (14c) asks a question; rather, they make statements that involve someone asking a question or wondering about its answer. More precisely, (14b) is a declarative containing an embedded polarity interrogative. And (14c) is a declarative containing an embedded constituent interrogative.

In general, the type of the containing or **matrix** sentence is independent of the type of the contained or **embedded** sentence. In addition to the possibilities in (14), we also find matrix interrogatives containing embedded declaratives (15a); matrix interrogatives containing embedded interrogatives (15b,c); and so on:

(15) a. Does Bart believe that **Marge is a genius**?
      b. Which persons wondered **how thoughtful Lisa had been**?
      c. Who couldn't believe **how thoughtful Lisa had been**?

 EXERCISE

As a test of your understanding, give sentences illustrating all of the following combinations of matrix and embedded sentence-types:

- Matrix declarative containing embedded declarative.
- Matrix declarative containing embedded polarity interrogative.
- Matrix declarative containing embedded constituent interrogative.
- Matrix polarity interrogative containing embedded declarative.
- Matrix constituent interrogative containing embedded declarative.
- Matrix polarity interrogative containing embedded constituent interrogative.
- Matrix constituent interrogative containing embedded polarity interrogative.
- Matrix polarity interrogative containing embedded polarity interrogative.
- Matrix declarative containing embedded polarity interrogative containing embedded declarative.

Selection for Sentence Type

In completing the exercise above, you will have noticed that the type of the embedded sentence depends strongly on the choice of the matrix verb.

(16) a.   Marge believed / expected that Bart stole the pizza.
      b.   *Marge believed / expected whether Bart stole the pizza.

Verbs like *believe* and *expect* always take an embedded declarative, and never take an interrogative.

(17) a.   *Marge wondered / inquired that Bart stole the pizza.
      b.   Marge wondered / inquired whether Bart stole the pizza.

Verbs like *wonder* and *inquire* always take an embedded interrogative, and never a declarative.

(18) a.   Marge knew / guessed that Bart stole the pizza.
      b.   Marge knew / guessed whether Bart stole the pizza.

Verbs like *know* and *guess* seem to take both.

The matchup that we see between specific verbs and complement types makes a good deal of intuitive sense. Consider *believe* and *expect*, for instance. Presumably one believes or expects *that various things will be true*. That-something-is-true is the kind of thing expressed by a declarative. Hence, it is natural for *believe* and *expect* to take declaratives. Likewise, consider *wonder* and *inquire*. One wonders and inquires about *the answers to questions*. Questions are what is expressed by an interrogative. Hence, it is natural for *wonder* and *inquire* to take interrogatives. Finally, consider *know* and *guess*. Intuitively, one can know or guess *that something is true*, or know or guess *the answer to a question*. Correlatively, *know* and *guess* take both declaratives and interrogatives.

Recalling structure (13a), a simple approach to these facts is to think of the type of a complement sentence as a feature that can be selected by the higher, sentence-taking verb. Concretely, suppose that declarative sentences bear the feature [+D] and that interrogative sentences bear the feature [+Q]. Then we can classify our verbs as follows:

> (19) a. *believe*, V, [+ __ S] (similarly for *expect*)
>   [+D]
>
>   b. *wonder*, V, [+ __ S] (similarly for *inquire*)
>   [+Q]
>
>   c. *know*, V, [+ __ S], [+ __ S] (similarly for *guess*)
>   [+D]   [+Q]

Complementizers

Our picture of complement-type selection can be refined in an interesting way by considering the embedded sentences in (16)–(18) more closely. Notice that in all of these examples, the type of the complement sentence is marked or determined by a special word or phrase that precedes it. For instance, the interrogative status of the complement in (18b) is marked by the presence of the word *whether*, which precedes the clause. An interrogative complement requires a word like *whether*, *when*, *where*, or *why* to "introduce" it.

> (20) **Interrogative introducers**: *whether / if / when / where / why / who / what*
>   a. Bart wonders whether / if / when / where / why Marge left.
>   b. Bart wonders who / what left.

By contrast, the declarative status of the complement in (18a) is marked by the presence of the word *that*. A (tensed) declarative complement requires *that* to be present, or else no complement-introducing word at all (Ø):

> (21) **Declarative introducers**: *that / Ø*
>   a. Bart thinks that Marge left.
>   b. Bart thinks Marge left.

Words like *whether* and *that*, which serve to introduce complement sentences, and which mark their type, are called **complementizers**. We will assign complementizers to the category C.

Constituency

How do complementizers fit into the sentence? What are their constituency relations with other elements?

When we look at a simple example like (22), at least three possibilities suggest themselves. First, the complementizer might be a daughter of the upper VP. This situation is pictured in (23a). Second, C might be a daughter of the embedded S. This situation is pictured in (23b). Finally, C might be a daughter of a separate constituent, one identical to neither VP nor S. This last would represent a kind of intermediate possibility, as shown in (23c):

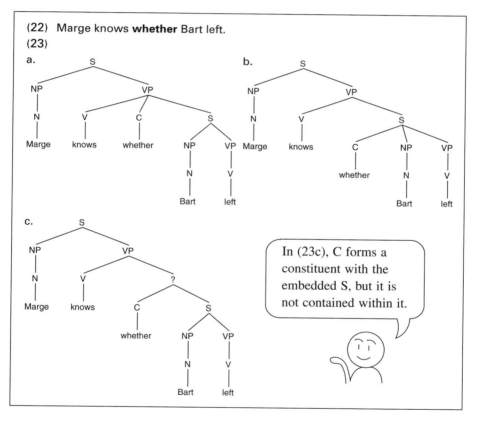

(22) Marge knows **whether** Bart left.

(23)

In (23c), C forms a constituent with the embedded S, but it is not contained within it.

Familiar kinds of data clearly indicate that structure (23c) is the correct one. Consider (24a–e):

> (24) a. Marge knows whether Bart left and whether Homer arrived.
>   b. Marge asked whether Bart left, but Homer didn't ask this.
>   c. Marge asked whether Bart left. Homer didn't know.
>   d. Whether Bart left, Marge didn't know.
>   e. Marge knows whether Bart left and Homer arrived.

 **EXERCISE**   On the basis of these data and the principles that you know for testing constituency, argue that structure (23c) is correct. Use all of the data in arguing for your conclusion. Give phrase markers wherever relevant to illustrate your points.

The Category CP

Accepting the structure in (23c), what is the identity of the category marked "?" in that tree? To get some insight into the answer, reflect on the following points:

> • Verbs may select for complement type (as seen in (16)–(18)).
>
> • Complement type is featural information (as shown in (19)).
>
> • Complement type is marked/determined by the complementizer (as noted in (20)–(21)).
>
> • Features of a phrase are inherited from the head of the phrase.

A verb selects featural information in its complements. And from Unit 15, we know that complements of a verb occur as sisters to it. This entails that when a verb selects for complement type, it must be selecting for featural information in its sister category ?. Thus, a verb like *wonder* selects for a [+Q] feature on ?, and a verb like *think* selects for a [+D] feature on ?:

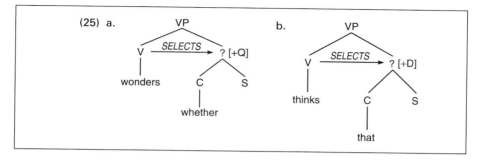

The notion that a complementizer determines complement type is naturally interpreted as meaning that the complement inherits its complement-type feature from C. Thus, a sentential complement containing *whether* inherits its [+Q] from *whether*. And a sentential complement containing *that* inherits its [+D] from *that*:

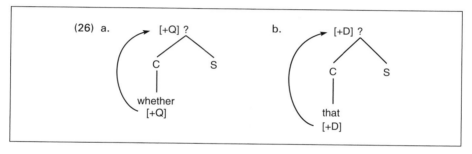

Finally, the principle that a phrase inherits featural information from its head suggests that C is in fact the head of the phrase labeled "?". Or, to put things differently, what these points suggest is that ? is in fact a projection of the complementizer, which we may therefore label "CP."

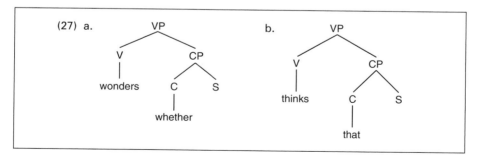

From now on, we will refer to expressions of category S as **sentences**, and we will refer to expressions of category CP as **clauses**, understanding that every clause contains a sentence.

Selection of CP

The picture of clausal complements and complement selection that emerges from these observations is ultimately a simple one. We have seen that VPs can consist of a verb followed by a clause (CP) and that clauses in turn consist of a complementizer (or "clause introducer") followed by a sentence:

> (28)   a.   VP → V CP
>   b.   CP → C S

A complementizer determines the type of its clause, where clause types include declarative (designated by the feature [+D]) and interrogative (designated by the feature [+Q]). *That* heads a [+D] clause, and *whether* heads a [+Q] clause:

> (29)   a.   *whether*, C, [+Q]
>   b.   *that*, C, [+D]

Specific verbs select for specific complement types. Thus, some verbs (like *think*) select for [+D] CP complements, other verbs (like *wonder*) select for [+Q] CP complements, and still other verbs (like *know*) select for both:

> (30)   a.   *think*, V, [+ __ CP] (similarly for *believe, expect*)
>   [+D]
>   b.   *wonder*, V, [+ __ CP] (similarly for *inquire*)
>   [+Q]
>   c.   *know*, V, [+ __ CP], [+ __ CP] (similarly for *guess*)
>   [+D]   [+Q]

The usual inheritance of features between heads and phrases brings the information together. V selects for complement type in its sister CP; those features are inherited by CP from its C head:

(31) a.

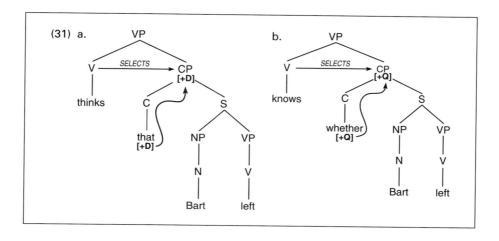

Complement Sentences II

Review

1. VPs can consist of a verb
    followed by a clause.

    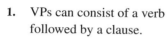

    Clauses consist of a comple-
    mentizer followed by a
    sentence.

2. The complementizer *that*
    heads a declarative clause.

    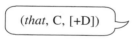

    Whether heads an
    interrogative clause.

3. Specific verbs select for spe-
    cific clausal complement
    types.

    Some verbs (like *think*) select a
    CP that is [+D]; others (like
    wonder) select a CP that is [+Q];
    still others (like *know*) select
    either!

Finite versus Nonfinite Clauses

Differences between embedded clauses go beyond differences in clause type (declarative, interrogative, emphatic, etc.). The boldfaced pairs in (1)-(3) are all declarative clause complements. But they differ in an important way.

---

(1) a. Marge believes that **Bart skates well**.
    b. Marge believes **Bart to skate well**.
(2) a. Marge hopes that **Bart will win the race**.
    b. Marge hopes for **Bart to win the race**.
(3) a. Marge judged that **Bart had stolen the pizza**.
    b. Marge judged **Bart to have stolen the pizza**.

How are they different?

The first member of each pair is what is called a **finite clause**. A finite clause contains a tensed main verb (*skates*), a modal (*will*), or a tensed auxiliary verb (*had*). By contrast, the second member of each pair is what is called a **nonfinite** or **infinitival clause**. A nonfinite clause lacks a tensed verb or modal. Instead the particle *to* occurs, and the verb appears in its untensed form (*skate, win, have*).

Similarities between Finite and Nonfinite Complements

Finite and nonfinite complements share many attributes. The pairs in (1)–(3) are clearly similar in form: both contain a subject (*Bart*) and a parallel verb phrase (*skates well/to skate well, will win the race/to win the race*, etc.). Furthermore, the position occupied by the tensed verb or modal in the finite clause is matched by that of *to* in the nonfinite clause.

The nonfinite forms also seem to involve their own complementizer element. The item *for* that appears in (2b) seems to occupy a position parallel to *that* in (2a). And in certain cases, *for* seems to be deletable, just like *that*:

---

(2) a. Marge hopes **that** Bart will win the race.
    b. Marge hopes **for** Bart to win the race.
(4) a. Marge expects **that** / **Ø** Bart will win the race.
    b. Marge expects **for** / **Ø** Bart to win the race.

Finally, the finite-nonfinite pairs in (1)–(4) also seem to carry approximately the same meaning. Thus, *Bart to skate well* appears to contribute nearly the same meaning to (1b) that *Bart skates well* contributes to (1a). The same is true with (2a,b), (3a,b), and (4a,b).

Constituency

It is possible to make constituency arguments for the nonfinite complement clauses parallel to those given earlier for the finite cases. On the basis of conjunction and proform replacement facts like (5a–c), for example, we can argue for the structure in (6) over alternatives:

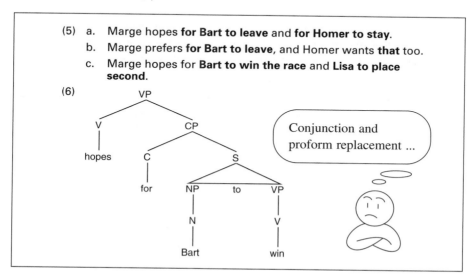

(5) a. Marge hopes **for Bart to leave** and **for Homer to stay**.
     b. Marge prefers **for Bart to leave**, and Homer wants **that** too.
     c. Marge hopes for **Bart to win the race** and **Lisa to place second**.

(6)

 **EXERCISE** On the basis of principles you know for testing constituency, argue that the structure in (6) correctly explains the data in (5). Use all of the data in arguing for your conclusion. As a test of your understanding, suggest alternative phrase markers that would *not* make the same predictions as (6) or explain the data correctly.

Differences between Finite and Nonfinite Complements

Although similar in many ways, finite and nonfinite clauses also show important differences. First, whereas finite clauses can occur as freestanding sentences, nonfinite clauses cannot. Thus, the finite clause complement *Marge left* can occur embedded, as in (7a), or it can stand on its own as an independent sentence, as in (7b). In contrast, the nonfinite clause *Marge to leave* embedded in (8a) cannot occur as an independent sentence (8b). Independent sentences typically require a tensed verb or modal, and nonfinite clauses simply lack this:

(7) a. Homer said **Marge left**.
     b. Marge left.
(8) a. Homer wanted **Marge to leave**.
     b. *Marge to leave.

A second important difference between finite and nonfinite clauses is illustrated in (9a,b) versus (10a,b). Notice that whereas a finite complement clause must always contain a subject, on pain of ill-formedness, infinitival complements may occur without one (10b):

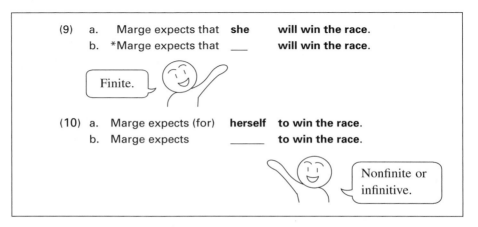

(9)   a. Marge expects that   **she**   **will win the race**.
      b. *Marge expects that ___   **will win the race**.

Finite.

(10) a. Marge expects (for) **herself** **to win the race**.
      b. Marge expects   _____   **to win the race**.

Nonfinite or infinitive.

Examples like (10b) might be called **subjectless infinitives**. However, we will see reasons in Unit 21 for thinking that such complements contain subjects after all.

Selection for Finiteness

We saw above that choice among declarative complementizers depends on the finiteness or nonfiniteness of the embedded sentence. The declarative complementizer *that* always goes with finite complements (11a), whereas the declarative complementizer *for* always goes with nonfinite complements (11b):

(11) a. Marge expected that / *for Bart stole the pizza.
      b. Marge expected *that / for Bart to steal the pizza.

A similar correlation occurs with interrogative complementizers. *Whether* may occur with either finite or nonfinite complements (12); however, the synonymous form *if* only occurs with finite clauses (13):

---

(12) a.   Marge wondered whether she should steal the pizza.

        b.   Marge wondered whether to steal the pizza.

(13) a.   Marge wondered if she should steal the pizza.

        b.   *Marge wondered if to steal the pizza.

Thinking about the structure of CP, a simple approach to these facts is to think of the finiteness or nonfiniteness of a complement sentence as a feature that can be selected by the higher complementizer. Concretely, suppose that finite sentences—ones containing a tensed verb or a modal verb—bear the feature [+TNS]. And suppose that nonfinite sentences bear the feature [–TNS]. Then we can refine our lexical entries for the complementizers as follows:

---

(14) a. *that*, C, [+D], [+ __ S]
                     [+TNS]

       b. *for*, C, [+D], [+ __ S]
                   [–TNS]

       c. *if*, C, [+Q], [+ __ S]
                   [+TNS]

       d. *whether*, C, [+Q], [+ __ S], [+ __ S]
                        [+TNS]   [–TNS]

> *Whether* can take finite or nonfinite!

Let us look into selection for finiteness or nonfiniteness a bit further.

What Determines Finiteness?

We noted briefly above that the finiteness of a clause depends on the presence or absence of certain key items. Specifically, a clause is finite if it contains a tensed verb or a modal. A clause is nonfinite if it contains the particle *to*.

Tensed verbs include garden-variety **main verbs** like *goes*, *walks*, *eats*, *sleeps*, *went*, *walked*, *ate*, and *slept*. They also include tensed **auxiliary verbs** like so-called **perfective *have*** and **progressive *be***. Roughly speaking, perfective *have* is used to express that an action is completed. Progressive *be* is used to express that an action is in progress. Simple tensed main verbs are illustrated in (15), and tensed auxiliary verbs are illustrated in (16):

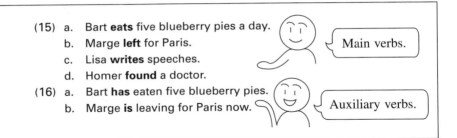

(15) a. Bart **eats** five blueberry pies a day.
      b. Marge **left** for Paris.
      c. Lisa **writes** speeches.
      d. Homer **found** a doctor.

(16) a. Bart **has** eaten five blueberry pies.
      b. Marge **is** leaving for Paris now.

Modals are verblike words that express possibility (*can*), necessity (*must*), permission (*may*), or obligation (*should*). Examples with modals are given in (18):

(17) **Modal verbs:** *can / could / may / might / must / shall / should / will / would / have-to / ought-to / need-to / used-to*

(18) a. Bart **can** eat five blueberry pies.
      b. Marge **may** be leaving for Paris.
      c. Lisa **should** write her speech.
      d. Homer **ought-to** have found a doctor.

The particle *to* occurs in a nonfinite clause between the subject and the predicate. *To* cannot cooccur with a modal (19a). However, it can occur with an untensed main verb (19b,c) or an untensed auxiliary verb (19d,e):

(19) a. *Marge expects Bart **to can** / **could** / **may** / **might** / **must** eat five blueberry pies.
      b. Marge expects Bart **to go** / **walk** / **eat** / **sleep**.
      c. Homer believes Marge **to like pizza** / **to write novels**.
      d. Marge expects Bart **to have** left.
      e. Marge expects Bart **to be** leaving.

Notice in the above examples that modals and *to* pattern similarly. The two seem to occur in the same position in the sentence between the subject and the verb phrase. Indeed, the two seem to compete for the very same slot since they do not *co*occur. Furthermore, when either a modal or *to* appears, the accompanying main verb of the sentence occurs in untensed form. Given their similarities, let us provisionally assign modals and *to* to the same category T (for "Tense") and assume that T is introduced directly under S by this rule:

(20) S → NP T VP

We'll return to the issue of T in a sentence with a normal tensed verb in a moment.

S Is TP!

To say that tensed verbs, modals, and *to* determine the finiteness of a sentence has very interesting consequences for our analysis of the category of sentences. Up to this point, we've given sentences their own special category: S. We have taken S to be an exocentric category—one lacking a head. But our reflections on finiteness indicate something surprisingly different.

We observed above that complementizers select for finiteness or nonfiniteness in the sentences that follow them. *That* selects a tensed sentence, *for* selects an infinitival sentence, and so on. In response, we suggested that finiteness be analyzed as a feature [±TNS] and that this feature occurs on sentences, where it can be "seen" and selected by higher complementizers like *that* and *for*.

Notice that if this is true, then since modals and *to* determine finiteness, it's natural to see a sentence as inheriting its [±TNS] status from the T element that it contains. Thus, if a sentence contains a modal, then it inherits the feature [+TNS]; and if it contains *to*, then it inherits the feature [–TNS]:

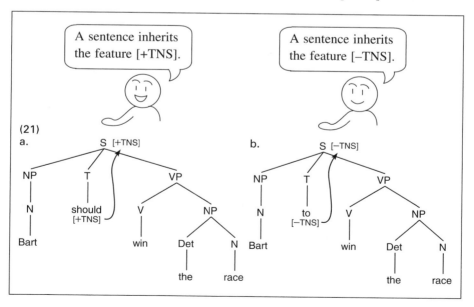

Now, our principle has been that *the features of a category are inherited from its head*. But then if the sentence category inherits its key features from T, it follows that *T must be the head of the sentence*. Or, to put it differently: the category of sentences must actually be TP.

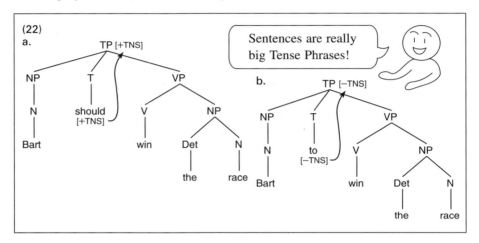

(22)

"Abstract" Tense

The conclusion that sentences are TPs may look doubtful at first. After all, what about the case where the sentence contains a tensed verb?

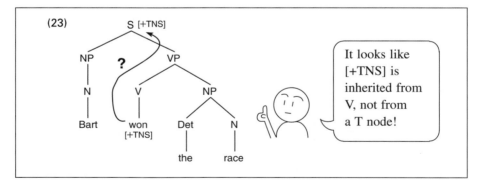

(23)

But there is a way of assimilating the analysis of tensed verbs to that of modals and *to*, while retaining the idea that T is the head of the sentence and that sentences are TPs. In his famous book *Syntactic Structures*, Chomsky (1957) makes the ingenious (and quite reasonable) proposal that tensed verbs should be divided into an untensed verb stem and a separate, "abstract" tense part. There are two such tenses in English: present tense, *PRES*, and past tense, *PAST*.

On this idea, the present tense verb *walks,* for example, consists of the stem *walk* plus the present tense morpheme *PRES* (where *morpheme* refers to a minimal unit of word form having independent meaning). Likewise, the past tense *walked* consists of *walk* plus the past tense morpheme *PAST.* In the case of regular verbs, such as *walk, PRES* is "spelled out" as the ending *-s* with third person singular subjects, and *PAST* is spelled out as the ending *-ed* (24a). In the case of irregular verbs, such as *win* and *be,* the spelling out of the tense elements is more idiosyncratic (24b,c):

(24) a. walks   = walk + PRES = walk + -s
          walked = walk + PAST = walk + -ed
      b. wins   = win + PRES = win + -s
          won   = win + PAST
      c. is   = be   + PRES
          was   = be   + PAST

When verbs and tenses are separated in this way, sentences with tensed verbs can be given the same general structure as sentences with modals and *to.* Thus, *Bart won the race* is assigned, not the structure in (23), but the one in (25), where *PAST* occupies the same position under T that modals and *to* occupy. The verb *win* and the tense *PAST* join up at some point to create *win+PAST,* which is ultimately spelled out as the form *won.* Assuming that *PRES* and *PAST* both carry the feature [+TNS], these elements will determine that a sentence with a tensed verb is [+TNS], in much the same way as what happens with modals:

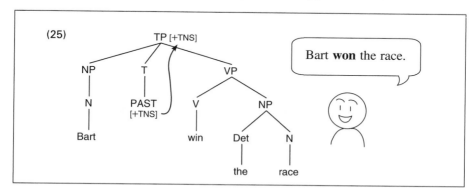

On this analysis, a sentence always involves a T element together with an untensed verb. T may be an actual word, like a modal or *to,* as in (22); or it may be an abstract tense element like *PRES* or *PAST,* as in (25). In all cases, however,

T counts as the head of the sentence since it is T that determines whether the sentence is [+TNS] or [–TNS].

Selection of TP by C

As in the case of clausal complements and complement selection, the picture that emerges from these observations is ultimately a simple one. We've seen that CPs consist of a complementizer followed by a sentence, which we now analyze as TP. TP in turn consists of a subject, followed by T, followed by the VP:

> (26) a.   CP → C TP
>   b.   TP → NP T VP

The element occurring in T determines whether the clause is finite ([+TNS]) or nonfinite ([–TNS]). In particular, modals like *can*, *could*, *may*, *might*, *must*, *shall*, and *should* are [+TNS], and so are the abstract tense elements *PRES* and *PAST*. The particle *to* is [–TNS]:

> (27) a.   *can,*   T, [+TNS]
>   b.   *could,* T, [+TNS]
>   c.   *may,*   T, [+TNS]
>   d.   *might,* T, [+TNS]
>
>   ...
>
> (28) a.   *PRES,* T, [+TNS]
>   b.   *PAST,* T, [+TNS]
> (29)   *to,*   T, [–TNS]

Specific complementizers select for finiteness. Thus, some complementizers (like *that* and *if*) select for [+TNS] TP complements, other complementizers (like *for*) select for [–TNS] TP complements, and still other complementizers (like *whether*) select for both:

(30) a. *that*, C, [+ __ TP]
          [+TNS]

      b. *for*, C, [+ __ TP]
          [−TNS]

      c. *whether*, C, [+ __ TP], [+ __ TP]
          [+TNS]   [−TNS]

> Finiteness depends on the complementizer.

Inheritance of features between heads and phrases brings the information together. C selects for finiteness features in its sister TP; those features are inherited by TP from its T head:

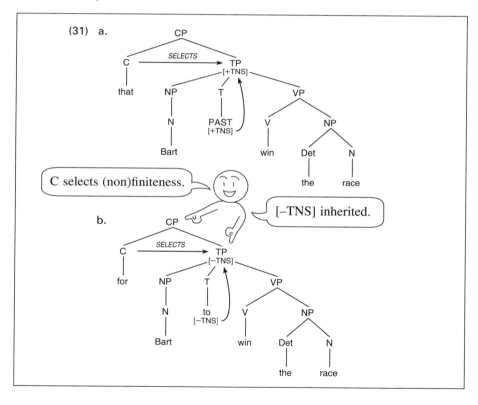

(31) a.

> C selects (non)finiteness.

> [−TNS] inherited.

b.

EXERCISE   Above we gave a structure like (i) for the constituency of T in a sentence.

(i)

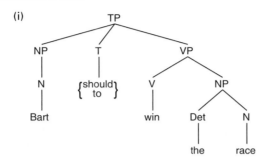

Consider the facts in (ii) and (iii), however.

(ii)   a.   Marge knows that Bart **should leave** and **could travel to Paris**.

     b.   Marge knows that Bart **should leave** and **travel to Paris**.

     c.   Bart **will travel to Paris**, and Homer Ø too.

(iii)   a.   Marge wants Bart **to leave** and **to travel to Paris**.

     b.   Marge wants Bart **to leave** and **travel to Paris**.

     c.   Marge wants Bart **to travel to Paris**, and Homer Ø too.

These data, and the principles that you know for testing constituency, argue for a somewhat more articulated structure than (i). Give the structure, and argue for its correctness using the data in (ii) and (iii).

Invisible Lexical Items

Review

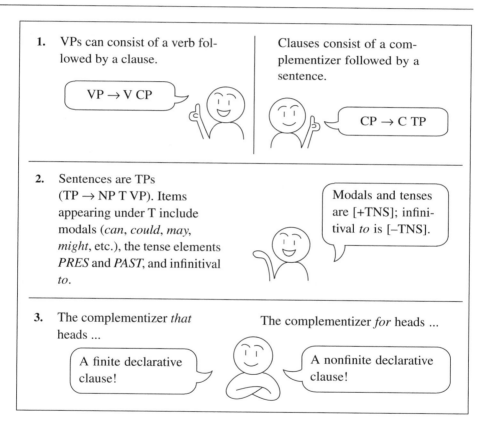

1. VPs can consist of a verb followed by a clause.

   VP → V CP

   Clauses consist of a complementizer followed by a sentence.

   CP → C TP

2. Sentences are TPs (TP → NP T VP). Items appearing under T include modals (*can*, *could*, *may*, *might*, etc.), the tense elements *PRES* and *PAST*, and infinitival *to*.

   Modals and tenses are [+TNS]; infinitival *to* is [–TNS].

3. The complementizer *that* heads ...

   A finite declarative clause!

   The complementizer *for* heads ...

   A nonfinite declarative clause!

Subjectless Infinitives and *PRO*

In the last unit, we noted an important difference between finite and nonfinite clauses: whereas the former must always contain a subject (cf. (1a,b)), the latter may occur without one (cf. (2a,b)):

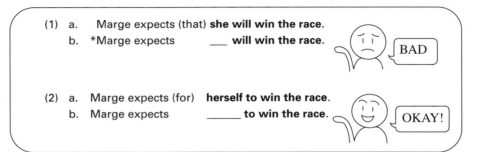

(1) a.   Marge expects (that) **she will win the race.**
     b.   *Marge expects   ___ **will win the race.**   BAD

(2) a.   Marge expects (for) **herself to win the race.**
     b.   Marge expects   _____ **to win the race.**   OKAY!

There are two possible analyses of the situation in (2b). The first is what we might call the **no-subject analysis**. On this view, (2b) contains exactly what it appears to contain, nothing more and nothing less:

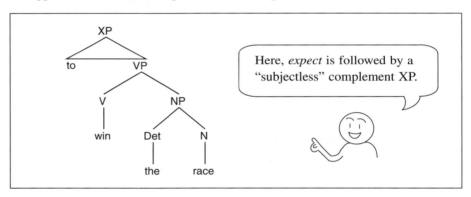

Here, *expect* is followed by a "subjectless" complement XP.

The second is what we might call the **hidden-subject analysis**. On this view, the structure of (2b) is more directly parallel to that of (2a), except that it contains a subject that is inaudible or "unpronounced." We will label the hidden subject in (2b) ***PRO***:

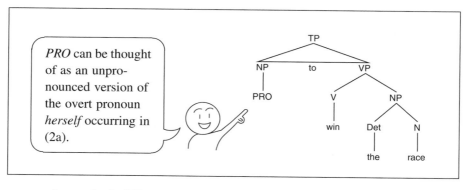

It may look difficult at first to choose between the two accounts. However, there are advantages to the second approach, which assumes *PRO*.

PRO Simplifies Our Account of Selection

The hidden-subject analysis appears to simplify our account of the selectional properties of the higher Vs. If we say that what follows *expect* in (2b) is a clause (see (3a)), then a single subcategorization frame will account for all of our examples. But if we say that what follows *expect* in (2b) is some other category XP, then we will need at least two different frames, (3a) *and* (3b):

(3) a.   *expect,* V, [+ __ CP]
                    [+D]
    b.   *expect,* V, [+ __ XP]
                    [+D]

A similar point arises in relation to (4) and (5).

(4) a.   Marge wondered / inquired **whether   she   should leave.**
    b.   Marge wondered / inquired **whether   ___   to leave.**
(5) a.   Marge knew / guessed **who   she   should visit.**
    b.   Marge knew / guessed **who   ___   to visit.**

We saw earlier that *wonder* and *inquire* always select an interrogative complement and that *know* and *guess* may do so. Under the no-subject analysis, the (b) examples cannot be assimilated straightforwardly to the (a) examples. Instead, we would seem to have to speak about "interrogative XPs" and to allow *wonder, inquire, know,* and *guess* to select for "interrogative XPs."

By contrast, under the hidden-subject analysis, the (b) examples become clausal, and directly analogous to the (a) examples:

(4b) Marge wondered / inquired **whether PRO to leave**.

(5b) Marge knew / guessed **who PRO to visit**.

> If we assume *PRO*, we can stick with simple clausal selection frames for all of these verbs.

PRO Simplifies Our Semantics

The hidden-subject analysis also gives a direct explanation for why (2a) and (2b) appear to mean the same thing. Under this analysis, essentially the same elements are present in both sentences in the same positions. It's simply that the latter contains an invisible form of the pronoun.

By contrast, the no-subject analysis must provide some independent explanation for why (2a) and (2b) mean the same thing, despite having different structures.

Conjunction Facts

Some simple conjunction facts also appear to favor the hidden-subject analysis. Recall our principle that conjunctions join expressions of like category. Consider (6a–c) in this light:

---

(6) a. Marge expects [**herself to win the race**] and [**Bart to place second**].

  b. Marge expects [**to win the race**] and [**to take home the trophy**].

  c. Marge expects [**to win the race**] and [**Bart to place second**].

(6a) shows that it is possible to conjoin two infinitives with overt subjects. Likewise, (6b) shows that it is possible to conjoin two infinitives that lack an overt subject. Interestingly, (6c) shows that it also seems possible to conjoin an infinitive *without* a subject and an infinitive *with* a subject.

This last possibility is unexpected if *to win the race* is an XP and *Bart to place second* is a sentence. If that were so, the two conjuncts would be of different categories. However, if the first conjunct in (6c) contains a *PRO* subject, then the example just represents a conjunction of sentences, parallel to (6a):

(6c)   Marge expects [~TP~ **PRO to win the race**] and [~TP~ **Bart to place second**].

The possibility of conjunctions like this favors *PRO*.

Other Cases of Inaudible Subjects

There seem to be other cases as well, in English and in other languages, where we want to talk about inaudible subjects.

Consider English imperative sentences like (7a–c):

(7)   a.   Eat your brussels sprouts!
            (cf. You eat your brussels sprouts!)
      b.   Come back with my brisket!
            (cf. You come back with my brisket!)
      c.   Express yourself!
            (cf. You express yourself!)

None of these examples contain an overt, "audible" subject; nonetheless, a subject is plainly understood. In each case, we understand the subject to be equivalent to the second person pronoun *you*. This idea is supported by the appearance of *yourself* in (7c). The reflexive pronoun *yourself* typically requires an occurrence of the pronoun *you* to refer back to. A natural idea, then, is that English imperatives contain a subject, despite surface appearances. This subject is just an unpronounced version of the pronoun *you*: *YOU*. Inaudible subjects also appear to occur in other languages. For example, consider the question-and-answer exchange in (8), from Japanese. (8a) asks whether the individual Taroo went. The usual reply in Japanese involves repeating just the verb, although the answer is understood as if it contained an unpronounced subject pronoun, equivalent to English *he*.

(8)   a.   Taroo-wa ikimashita ka.
            Taroo   went   Q
            'Did Taroo go?'
      b.   Hai, ikimashita.
            yes went
            'Yes, he went.'

These kinds of facts are readily duplicated in many other languages. Thus, the appeal to unpronounced subjects, like *PRO*, is not unprecedented.

We see then that "subjectless infinitives" is not a good term for examples like *Marge expects to win the race*. We needn't regard such examples as subject-less, except in a superficial sense. And indeed there appear to be good reasons for assuming they do in fact contain a subject after all, even if an inaudible one.

"Invisible Elements": *Expect* versus *Persuade*

Assuming an inaudible *PRO* simplifies the analysis of clausal complements, as we've seen. But it complicates matters in another sense. To see why, consider an analogy from fiction. In *The Invisible Man* by H. G. Wells, a scientist invents a chemical potion that renders him invisible. The invisible scientist commits crimes and is pursued by the police. But the police face a very difficult task in tracking him down. In their search, they often enter rooms where no one can be seen. But are things as they seem, with no one really present? Or is the scientist hiding in the room in invisible form? How can they tell?

The Need for Logical Detective Work

Introducing invisible elements like *PRO* into our grammar raises a problem similar to that facing the police in the novel. Suppose that in investigating some area of grammar we encounter a given sentence. Are things as they seem, with nothing present beyond what we actually hear? Or are elements lurking in the sentence in inaudible form? And how do we tell?

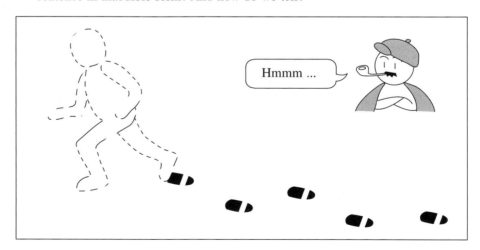

In *The Invisible Man*, the police use logic to detect their unseen foe. Even though an invisible man cannot be observed directly, his presence can be deduced from indirect evidence. A man, though invisible, still has weight and mass, so his presence can be detected in the footprints he leaves on a carpet or in the snow. And even when a man is invisible, he must breathe; thus, his presence could in principle be inferred from the consumption of oxygen in a room, or from the faint (but still detectable) air currents created by his breathing. So even when a thing can't be observed directly, there may still be many ways of inferring its presence. In general, the presence of an object can be inferred from its effects on things around it, whether it can be seen or not.

Presumably, in dealing with invisible grammatical elements, we must proceed like the police in the novel: not being able to hear *PRO*, we must attempt to infer its presence by looking carefully for its effects on its surroundings. To see concretely how this might go, we will consider a specific example in detail. We will compare the following two sentences, which appear quite similar at first:

			V	NP	to	VP
(9)	a.	Homer	**expected**	**Marge**	**to**	**win the race.**
	b.	Homer	**persuaded**	**Marge**	**to**	**win the race.**

On the surface, (9a,b) seem to involve the same sequence of categories: V NP *to* VP. A natural assumption is that the two sentences have the same structure and will behave the same way. As we will see, however, sentences with *expect* and *persuade* pattern quite differently, despite surface similarities. And these differences point to the presence of an "invisible" constituent that is lurking in one but not the other.

Subject Pleonastics

In addition to normal **referring pronouns**, English grammar includes what are sometimes called **dummy subject pronouns**, or **pleonastic pronouns**.

(10) a. **It** certainly is a tall building.
          It's a blimp, not a balloon!
      b. **What** certainly is a tall building?
          What is a blimp, not a balloon?

(11) a. **It** is a hot day.
          It is a long way to Tokyo.
          It seems that Marge likes anchovies.
      b. *__What__ is a hot day?
          *__What__ is a long way to Tokyo?

> Compare the instances of *it* in (10a) and (11a). They *look* similar, but we feel a clear difference.

The pronouns in (10a) would normally be used to refer to objects in the speaker's environment, perhaps accompanied by a pointing gesture to indicate the object in question. Because they are used to refer to something, it makes sense for someone to ask *what* thing is being referred to—for example, using questions like those in (10b), where *it* is replaced by the corresponding question word *what*. By contrast, the pronouns in (11a) are not understood as referring to anything and would not be accompanied by a pointing gesture. You can't say the first sentence in (11a), for instance, pointing to something that's a hot day. Correlatively, it is senseless to ask what *what* refers to in questions like those in (11b). The *it*-pronouns in (11a) are not referring pronouns that designate something; they are empty or pleonastic pronouns.

A similar (but somewhat subtler) contrast holds between the instances of *there* in (12) and (13):

(12) a. **There** is the place I was talking about.
          There would be a good place to land.
      b. **Where** is the place you were talking about?
          Where would be a good place to land?

(13) a. **There** is a fly in my soup.
          There is a pizza on the veranda.
      b. ??**Where** is a fly in my soup?
          ??**Where** is a pizza on the veranda?
      c. A fly is in my soup.
          A pizza is on the veranda.

The sentences in (12a) contain the **locative proform** *there*, which is normally used to refer to a spatial location, and which can also be accompanied by a pointing gesture to indicate the intended place. Because *there* is being used to refer to a location in (12a), it makes sense to ask *which location* using questions like those in (12b), which contain the question word *where*. The instances of *there* in (13a) are different, however, at least when pronounced with their normal unstressed intonation. In these cases, *there* is not being used to refer to a place. Notice that the examples in (13a) could not normally be used to answer the questions in (13b). The question *Where is a fly in my soup?* can't be answered with *There is a fly in my soup*, spoken in its usual way without heavy stress on *there*. The *there* occurring in (13a) is not locative *there*; rather, it is **pleonastic *there***.

Pleonastic Pronouns as a Test for Subjecthood

There are many interesting facts about the distribution of pleonastic pronouns, but for our purposes the crucial property of pleonastic *it* and *there* is that they seem to be *confined to subject position*. Whenever the word *it* occurs in nonsubject position, it must be understood as **referential *it***, and not as **pleonastic *it***. Likewise, whenever the word *there* occurs in nonsubject position, it must be understood as **referential *there***, not as **pleonastic *there***. To convince yourself of this, consider (14a,b):

> (14) a. Homer bought **it**.   (cf. What did Homer buy?)
>   b. Homer lives **there**. (cf. Where does Homer live?)

The *it* in object position in (14a) must be understood as picking out some object. Accordingly, if we hear (14a), it is always legitimate to ask *which thing* the speaker is referring to. Likewise, the *there* in postverbal position in (14b) must be understood as picking out some specific place; thus, it always makes sense to ask *which place* the speaker is referring to. In view of this behavior, pleonastic pronouns can be used as a test for subjecthood. If *it* or *there* occurs in a given position and can be understood as a pleonastic in that position, then the latter must be a subject position.

> **Principle**
> Pleonastic pronouns occur only in subject position.

With these points in mind, consider the pairs in (15) and (16), containing *it* and *there* following *expect* and *persuade* (recall that "#" indicates anomaly):

---

(15) a. Homer expected   **it** to be a hot day.

                     it to be a long way to Tokyo.

                     it to seem that Marge likes anchovies.

      b. Homer expected   **there** to be a fly in my soup.

                     there to be a pizza on the veranda.

(16) a. #Homer persuaded   **it** to be a hot day.

                     it to be a long way to Tokyo.

                     it to seem that Marge likes anchovies.

      b. *Homer persuaded   **there** to be a fly in my soup.

                     there to be a pizza on the veranda.

The infinitives in (15) are fully well-formed. Furthermore, the instances of *it* and *there* that appear can have the same pleonastic interpretation that they show in (11a) and (13a). The situation in (16) is quite different, however. The sentences in (16a) seem to require us to understand *it* as a referring form. When most people hear *Homer persuaded it to be a hot day*, their immediate reaction is to ask, *Homer persuaded WHAT to be a hot day?*, showing that they are forced to understand *it* as referential. The sentences in (16b) are even worse and don't seem to be interpretable at all.

So although *expect* and *persuade* look similar in their surface syntax, their behavior with respect to pleonastic pronouns is quite different. *Expect* can be followed by a pleonastic pronoun, but *persuade* cannot. Given our principle above, this suggests that the NP trailing *expect* in its infinitive pattern is a *subject*, and so can be a pleonastic pronoun. And it suggests that the NP trailing *persuade* in its NP-*to*-VP pattern is *not a subject*, and so cannot be a pleonastic:

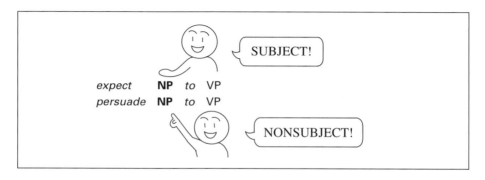

Sentence Idioms with *Expect* and *Persuade*

We are all familiar with the phenomenon of phrases whose meaning cannot be determined from their parts without special explanation. Slang is the commonest example. Consider the slang phrase *toss my/his/her/their cookies*. This expression is not literally about throwing cookies through the air. Rather, the whole expression is equivalent in meaning to the simple verb *vomit*. The meaning of the expression *toss my/his/her/their cookies* cannot be predicted from the meanings of the separate items *toss*, *my/his/her/their*, *cookies* and their mode of combination. Instead, the whole expression must be learned separately, as a single "chunk," so to speak. Expressions like these, whose meaning cannot be predicted from the meanings of their parts and their mode of combination, are called **idioms** or **idiomatic phrases**.

There are many kinds of idioms in English, including phrases like those in (17), and even whole sentences. (18a–d) are examples of **sentence idioms** and their approximate glosses:

(17)	a.	toss one's cookies	'vomit'
	b.	go to the dogs	'decline in quality'
	c.	put X through the wringer	'cause great trouble for X'
	d.	throw X to the wolves	'sacrifice X'
(18)	a.	The chickens have come home to roost.	'The effects of someone's actions have come back to him or her.'
	b.	The cat is out of the bag.	'Secrets have been revealed.'
	c.	The fur flew.	'There was a big fight.'
	d.	The shit hit the fan.	'There was trouble.'

Idioms as a Test for Constituency

A reasonable idea about sentence idioms, and about idioms in general, is that they are represented structurally as constituents. In other words, their semantic status in being *understood* as "chunks" is matched by a structural status in being *represented* as chunks. Under this view, an idiomatic understanding of the words *going to the dogs* in a sentence like (19a) must correspond to a tree structure in which that string of words forms a constituent—for example, (19b):

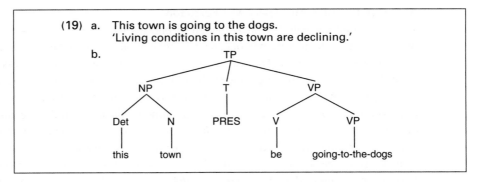

(19) a.   This town is going to the dogs.
          'Living conditions in this town are declining.'

     b.

Assuming this idea is correct, it can thus be used as a test for constituency. To state it in the form of a principle:

Principle
If a string of words XYZ is understood as an idiom in sentence S, then XYZ form a constituent in S.

With these points in mind, consider the examples in (20) and (21), containing *expect* and *persuade* followed by strings that could potentially be understood as sentence idioms:

(20) a.   Homer expected   **the chickens to come home to roost.**
     b.   **the cat to get out of the bag.**
     c.   **the shit to hit the fan.**
(21) a.   Homer persuaded   **the chickens to come home to roost.**
     b.   **the cat to get out of the bag.**
     c.   **the shit to hit the fan.**

The boldfaced infinitives in (20) can have their **idiomatic interpretation**. Thus, (20b) can mean something like 'Homer expected secrets to have been revealed'. Likewise, (20c) can mean 'Homer expected there to be trouble'. And so on. The situation in (21) is quite different, however. The presence of *persuade* in (21) seems to force us to understand the boldfaced words literally. When we hear *Homer persuaded the chickens to come home to roost*, our only mental image is of Homer cajoling chickens, and similarly for (21b). (21c) requires us to summon up a bizarre picture of Homer talking to excrement. It is simply not possible to interpret the boldfaced elements following *persuade* as sentence idioms.

Again, despite similarities in their surface syntax, *expect* and *persuade* behave quite differently. An NP-*to*-VP sequence following *expect* can be understood as a sentence idiom, but the same sequence following *persuade* cannot. Given our principle above, what these facts suggest is that an NP-*to*-VP sequence following *expect* is a *constituent sentence*, and so can be understood as a sentence idiom. By contrast, these same facts suggest that the NP-*to*-VP sequence following *persuade* is *not a constituent sentence*, and so cannot be understood as a sentence idiom:

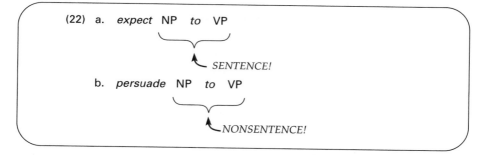

Finite Clause Complements

Finally, consider variants of (9a,b) (repeated below) that involve finite clause complements instead of infinitives:

(9)	a.	Homer expected	**Marge to win the race.**
	b.	Homer persuaded	**Marge to win the race.**
(23)	a.	Homer expected	**that Marge would win the race.**
	b.	Homer persuaded	**Marge that she should win the race.**

With *expect*, the infinitive *Marge to win the race* in (9a) surfaces as the finite CP complement *that Marge would win the race* in (23a). With *persuade*, however, something different happens. The sequence *Marge to leave* separates into *two* complements: an NP object *Marge*, followed by an independent CP *that she should win the race*. So even though *expect* and *persuade* look similar with infinitives, as soon as we switch to finite complements the similarity disappears. *Expect* takes one complement, but *persuade* takes two.

Putting It Together

What exactly is going on here? Clearly, *expect* and *persuade* diverge syntactically in a number of important ways. Do they have different structure? And if they do have different structure, then why do they show the same surface form with infinitives?

Why They Behave Differently: Thematic Structure

The key to the differences between *expect* and *persuade* lies in the facts of (23), which show that *expect* takes one complement, but *persuade* takes two. In Unit 15, we saw that the number of complements that a given verb takes depends on its **thematic structure**. The thematic structure of a verb is like a script, specifying how many participants the verb involves and what roles they play.

Intuitively, a situation or state of expectation seems to involve two things:

> - The experiencer of the state X: the "expecter," and
> - The theme of the state Y: the thing that is expected.
>
> $$\text{expect} (\ X \ , \ Y \ )$$
> *EXPERIENCER*⤴   ⤴ *THEME*

In the simple transitive example (24a), the experiencer/expecter is Homer, and the theme/expectee is Marge. In example (24b) with a finite clause complement, the experiencer is again Homer, but the theme is what is given by the clause *that Marge will leave*. The latter describes an event that Homer is expecting, or some proposition that he expects to be true.

> | | | **Experiencer** | | **Theme** |
> |------|----|-----------------|---------|----------------------|
> | (24) | a. | Homer | expects | Marge. |
> | | b. | Homer | expects | that Marge will leave. |

Now consider the thematic relations involved with *persuade*. They are very different from those of *expect*. Intuitively, an act of persuasion involves not two things, but *three*, and the roles are different:

> - The agent of the action X: the "persuader,"
> - The theme of the action Y: the individual that is persuaded, and
> - The goal of the action Z: what the theme is persuaded of.
>
> $$\text{persuade} (\ X \ , \ Y \ , \ Z \ )$$
> *AGENT*⤴ ⤴ *THEME* ⤴ *GOAL*

In the ditransitive example (25a), the agent is Homer and the theme is Marge; the goal of the action—what Homer is trying to persuade Marge of—is his honesty. In example (25b) with a finite clause complement, the agent is Homer, the theme is Marge, and the goal is what is given by the clause *that she should leave*—which describes an action that Homer has persuaded Marge to undertake, or some proposition that he persuaded her was true:

> **Agent** **Theme Goal**
>
> (25) a. Homer persuaded Marge of his honesty.
>
> b. Homer persuaded Marge that she should leave.

Now let's consider the infinitive cases. Given the pattern with *expect* above, the experiencer in (26) should be Homer, and *Marge to leave* should correspond to a *single* complement serving as theme. In other words, (26) should have the same structure as (24b), but with a nonfinite clause where the finite clause appears:

> **Experiencer** **Theme**
>
> (26) Homer   expects [Marge to leave].

The pattern with *persuade* requires something different, however. The agent in (27) should be Homer, but *Marge to leave* should correspond to two complements: one serving as theme, the other serving as goal. In other words, in order for it to fit the selectional requirements of *persuade*, we must see the string *Marge to leave* as factoring into two separate complements, equivalent to what we find in (25b):

> **Agent** **Theme Goal**
>
> (27) Homer persuaded Marge to leave.

This division may look odd at first since what follows *Marge* looks like a sentence fragment, *to leave*. But we can make things look more normal, and establish an exact correlation between the finite and nonfinite cases, if we reanalyze *to leave* as *PRO to leave* with an invisible subject. Then the analysis of *Homer persuaded Marge to leave* is not as in (27); rather, it is this:

> | | **Agent** | | **Theme** | **Goal** |
> | --- | --- | --- | --- | --- |
> | (28) | Homer | persuaded | Marge | PRO to leave. |

Now (28) is fully parallel to (25b); it contains an object (*Marge*) and a full clause (*PRO to leave*).

This account shows us why *expect* and *persuade* pattern so differently. The NP-*to*-VP sequence following *expect* forms a constituent sentence (29a), with NP as its subject. Since NP is a *subject*, it can be a pleonastic pronoun (29b). And since NP-*to*-VP is a *constituent sentence*, it can be understood as a sentence idiom (29c):

> (29) a.   Homer expected [Marge to win the race].
>   b.   Homer expected [**it** to be hot today].
>   c.   Homer expected [**the fur to fly**].

By contrast, the NP-*to*-VP sequence following *persuade* is really an NP object followed by a sentence with a hidden *PRO* subject (30a). Since NP itself is not a subject, it cannot be a pleonastic pronoun (30b). And since NP-*to*-VP does not form a constituent, it cannot be understood as a sentence idiom (30c):

> (30) a.   Homer persuaded [Marge] [PRO to win the race].
>   b.   *Homer persuaded [**it**] [PRO to be hot today].
>   c.   *Homer persuaded [**the fur**] [PRO **to fly**].

Why They Look the Same: PRO!

This analysis also explains why *expect* and *persuade* look alike, despite their very different syntax and thematic structure. The culprit that disguises their difference is *PRO*! Exactly because we can't hear *PRO*, we can't see that the overt NP after *persuade* is not the subject of the following infinitive. Rather, the subject is an invisible element that occurs in between NP and *to*-VP. It is the inaudibility of *PRO* that hides this crucial difference.

Summing Up

We see then that by assuming "invisible elements," we can simplify our overall theory—for example, by making the statement of selectional patterns more regular. But "invisibilia" complicate our life in another sense. Specifically, the presence of inaudible elements makes it much harder for us to know what we are actually hearing when we hear it. If there can be more to a sentence than what "meets the ear," then we must be constantly alert for the presence of such elements. We have seen that *PRO* can make its presence clearly felt, even though it is inaudible. The very different behaviors of *expect* and *persuade*, despite their surface similarities, lead us directly to the view that the latter can involve a silent subject.

NP Structure

Review

1. Clauses come in a variety of types (declarative, interrogative, exclamative, imperative).

   They may be either finite (tensed) or nonfinite (untensed).

2. Verbs may select for ...

   The type of their complement clauses (CPs).

3. Complementizers may select for ...

   The tensed or untensed status of their complement sentences.

4. Embedded nonfinite clauses may contain an "invisible" subject, *PRO*.

   This makes analysis both simpler and more complicated!

Sentencelike NPs

Up to this point, the English NPs we have considered have been either proper NPs like (1a) or determiner-noun combinations like (1b):[1]

> (1) a. [$_{NP}$ [$_N$ Bart]]
>   b. [$_{NP}$ [$_{Det}$ the] [$_N$ boy]]

Beyond these simple cases, however, there is a wide variety of other NP structures in English, including ones whose form closely resembles the clausal complement constructions we considered in the last units. Compare the triples in (2)–(4). The (a) examples contain clausal complements, showing a complementizer, a subject, and a tensed or nontensed verb:

> (2) a. Marge predicted [$_{CP}$ **that Bart would destroy the evidence**].
>   b. Marge predicted [$_{NP}$ **Bart's destroying (of) the evidence**].
>   c. Marge predicted [$_{NP}$ **Bart's destruction of the evidence**].
> (3) a. Lisa preferred [$_{CP}$ **for Bart to choose Milhouse**].
>   b. Lisa preferred [$_{NP}$ **Bart's choosing (of) Milhouse**].
>   c. Lisa preferred [$_{NP}$ **Bart's choice of Milhouse**].
> (4) a. Burns regretted [$_{CP}$ **that Homer lost the uranium**].
>   b. Burns regretted [$_{NP}$ **Homer's losing (of) the uranium**].
>   c. Burns regretted [$_{NP}$ **Homer's loss of the uranium**].

The (b) examples contain **gerundive nominals**, with a possessive NP that functions like a subject, and a noun that has been created from a verb by attaching the gerundive inflection *-ing*:[2]

---

1. Recall that in Unit 10, we assimilated possessive NPs like *his father* and *Homer's father* to the second case. We treated the first as containing a simple possessive determiner (*his*) and the second as containing a complex possessive determiner, formed from an NP (*Homer*) and a possessive element (*'s*):

> (i) a. [$_{NP}$ [$_{Det}$ his] [$_N$ son]]
>   b. [$_{NP}$ [$_{Det}$ [$_{NP}$ Homer] [$_{Poss}$'s]] [$_N$ son]]

2. The preposition *of* is typically optional after the gerund. If *of* does occur, we have a so-called **nominal gerund**; if *of* does not occur, we have a **verbal gerund**.

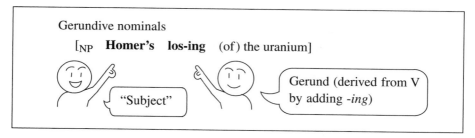

The (c) examples contain so-called **derived nominals**. Like gerunds, these include a subjectlike possessive NP, but here N shows a more indirect relation to V. Some derived nominals are created from the corresponding V by attaching an affix like *-tion* (*destroy~destruction, discuss~discussion, concede~concession, create~creation*) or *-ment* (*develop~development, discourage~discouragement, improve~improvement*). But with many derived nominals, the "shape relation" between the noun and the matching verb is not predictable (*choose~choice, lose~loss, give~gift, promise~promise*, etc.).

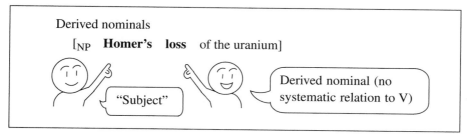

The obvious parallels between the clausal structures with verbs and the nominal structures with gerunds and derived nominals suggest that ideas we have developed for the former may apply to the latter as well. Let us look into this more closely, concentrating on derived nominals.

Complements of N

Consider the example pairs in (5)–(7). Notice that the relation between the verbs and the boldfaced elements in the (a) examples closely parallels the relation between the nouns and the boldfaced elements in the (b) examples:

(5) a. Homer [$_V$ discussed] **his options.** (It was revealing.)
    b. Homer's [$_N$ discussion] **of his options** (was revealing).
(6) a. Homer and Marge [$_V$ argued] **about their vacation.** (It was unpleasant.)
    b. Homer and Marge's [$_N$ argument] **about their vacation** (was unpleasant).
(7) a. Lisa [$_V$ claimed] **that she had been abducted by aliens.** (It worried us.)
    b. Lisa's [$_N$ claim] **that she had been abducted by aliens** (worried us).

Using the tests from Unit 16, we can see that *his options* should be analyzed as a complement of *discussed* in (5a). Discussing always involves discussing something, and *his options* specifies the thing discussed; it "completes" the meaning of V. Furthermore, the NP following *discuss* cannot be iterated. But if this reasoning is correct, then it seems we should also analyze *of his options* as a complement of *discussion* in (5b). Again, (*of*) *his options* specifies the thing discussed and so completes the meaning of *discussion*. And again, this *of*-PP cannot be iterated (**Homer's discussion of his options of his plans*). The same reasoning applies to (6) and (7).

 **EXERCISE**   Apply the same reasoning to (6b) and (7b) to show that they contain complements.

Attaching Noun Complements

Analyzing a phrase as a noun complement has important implications for structure. Recall this principle from Unit 17:

Principle
An item X and its complements must occur together in a phrase headed by X.

Now consider the following three potential structures for *Homer's discussion of his options* (5b), where *of his options* is a (PP) complement of *discussion*:

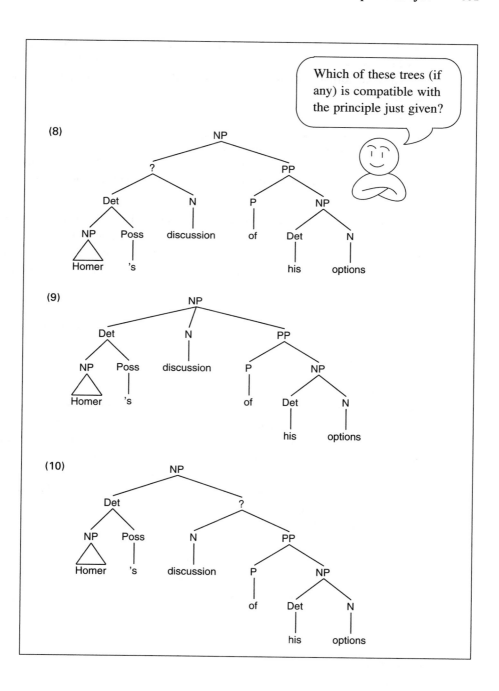

On reflection, only Trees (9) and (10) are compatible with the principle, because only there is [pp *of his options*] a sister to *discussion*, as required.

There are further data that can help us decide between (9) and (10). Examine the facts in (11a–c):

(11) a. Every **discussion of his options** and **examination of the consequences** (led to an impasse).
      b. This discussion of his options was more helpful than that **one**.
      c. This discussion of his options was more helpful than that **Ø**.

(11a) shows *discussion of his options* being conjoined with *examination of the consequences*. (11b) shows *discussion of his options* being replaced with the proform *one*. And (11c) shows *discussion of his options* being elided. By familiar principles, these results imply that *discussion of his options* must be a constituent. Only Tree (10) shows the correct constituency.

EXERCISE   Using the data in (11), construct a formal argument for Tree (10) versus Tree (9).

The Category N′

These results raise an immediate question about the nature of the constituent marked "**?**" in Tree (10). What category is this phrase? In discussing verbs, we said that a verb plus its complements create a VP—a projection of V. Applying the same reasoning here, it seems that a noun plus its complements should create a projection of N. So **?** should be some kind of nominal category.

Our first instinct might be to think that **?** in Tree (10) is just NP. But if *argument about their vacation* were an NP, we would expect it to occur where other NPs occur. (12) and (13) show this isn't always so.

(12) a.   They regretted [np that fight].
      b.   ??They regretted [? argument about their vacation].
(13) a.   [np Her statement] was silly.
      b.   *[? Claim that she was abducted by aliens] was silly.

Furthermore, if *argument about their vacation* and *discussion of his options* were NPs, we wouldn't expect them to be able to take determiners. But (14) and (15) show that they *do* take determiners:

(14) a. *They regretted [that [_{NP} that fight]].
b. They regretted that [? argument about their vacation].
(15) a. *The [_{NP} her statement] was silly.
b. The [? claim that she was abducted by aliens] was silly.

In general, strings like *argument about their vacation* and *discussion of his options* seem to behave as nounlike items that are "intermediate" in size between a simple lexical N and a full NP. Just to have a label, we will designate this intermediate kind of nominal as N′ (pronounced "N bar" or "N prime"), so that the completed tree for *Homer's discussion of his options* looks like this:

(16)

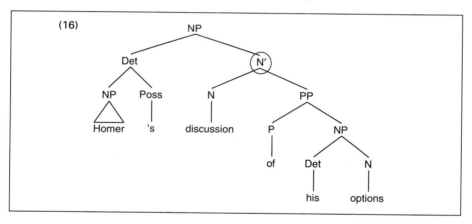

The new phrase structure rules needed to generate this structure are as follows:

(17) a. NP → Det N′
b. N′ → N PP

Notice that we still need to be able to generate simple NPs like *Bart* and *that boy*—we need to be able to handle the case where N has no complements at all. We could do this either by leaving things as they are, with rules that expand NP directly as N or Det N (18a,b). Alternatively, we could add a single rule allowing N′ to expand as N (18c):

(18)   a.   NP → Det N
       b.   NP → N
       c.   N′ → N

We will take the view here that extra structure isn't generated except when motivated by the presence of lexical items. If so, then [NP *Bart*], [NP *that discussion*], and [NP *that discussion of Bart*] have the structure shown in (19a–c):

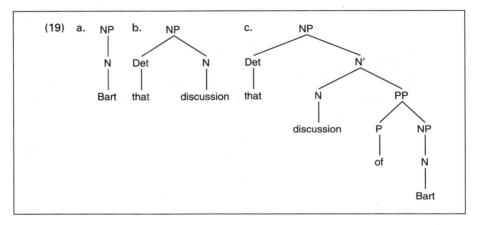

Differences between Noun and Verb Complements

In motivating the idea of noun complements, we looked at pairs like (5a,b), noting the similar relations that N and V bear to the boldfaced elements:

(5)   a.   Homer [V discussed] **his options**. (It was revealing.)
      b.   Homer's [N discussion] **of his options** (was revealing).

Along with the similarities, however, there are important differences. First, whereas verbs can take simple NP complements, as in (20a), derived nominals cannot (20b); instead, they require a PP:

(20)   a.   Homer [V discussed] his options. (It was revealing.)
       b.   *Homer's [N discussion] his options was revealing.

With V-N pairs in which the verb takes an NP object, the derived nominal usually takes a PP containing the preposition *of*.

A second difference is that whereas the NP complements of V are typically obligatory, the corresponding PP complements of N are not. A verb like *discuss* feels incomplete without a following NP (21a), but the noun *discussion* gives no such sense of incompleteness when it stands alone (21b):

> (21) a. ?*Homer [$_V$ discussed]. (It was revealing.)
>   b. Homer's [$_N$ discussion] was revealing.

With nouns, then, we apparently need to be able to talk about **nonobligatory complements** or **optional arguments**.

Adjuncts in NP

Given the existence of noun complements, it is natural to expect nominal adjuncts as well. Consider the pairs in (22)–(24). Notice once again that the relation between the verbs and the boldfaced elements in the (a) examples parallels the relation between the nouns and the boldfaced elements in the (b) examples:

> (22) a. Homer [$_V$ discussed] his options **in the meeting.**
>   b. Homer's [$_N$ discussion] of his options **in the meeting**
> (23) a. Homer and Marge [$_V$ argued] about their vacation **on Thursday.**
>   b. Homer and Marge's [$_N$ argument] about their vacation **on Thursday**
> (24) a. Lisa **frivolously** [$_V$ claimed] that she had been abducted by aliens.
>   b. Lisa's **frivolous** [$_N$ claim] that she had been abducted by aliens

We classified the boldfaced elements in the (a) examples as verbal adjuncts: elements that provide additional but nonessential information about the action or state described by the verb. The boldfaced items in the (b) examples seem to perform the same function. Thus, the PP *in the meeting* describes the location of the action—the discussing—in (22a); and it appears to do the very same thing in (22b). The PP *on Thursday* describes the time of the argument in (23a); and it appears to do the same thing in (23b). Finally, the adverb *frivolously* describes the manner of action in (24a), and the corresponding adjective *frivolous* performs the same function in (24b). If the boldfaced elements are (verbal) adjuncts in the first case, it makes sense to analyze them as (nominal) adjuncts in the second case.

Attachment of Adjuncts

Verb complements occur under VP as sisters to V, and we have now seen that noun complements occur under N′ as sisters to N. VP and N′ are analogous:

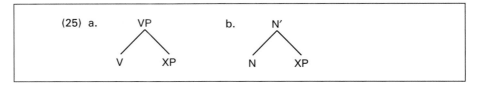

This gives us a simple idea for the attachment of noun adjuncts. Since verbal adjuncts occur under VP as (leading or trailing) sisters to VP, by parallelism, we would expect noun adjuncts to occur under N′ as (leading or trailing) sisters to N′:

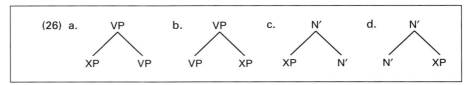

Under this idea, the VP *discussed his options in the meeting* and the N′ *discussion of his options in the meeting* would receive the very similar tree structures shown in (27):

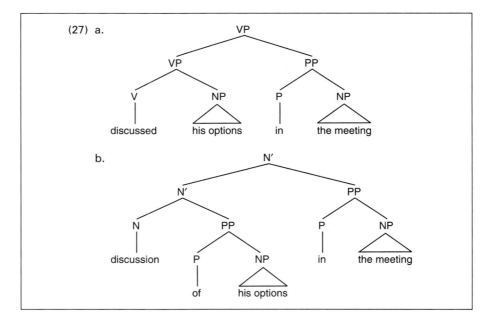

There is evidence that these structures are correct. One of our arguments for the VP-adjoined structure was the fact that the proform *do* can either include adjuncts in the material it replaces (28a), or exclude them (28b):

(28) a. He shouldn't have discussed his options in the meeting, but he [$_{VP}$ **did**].
(*did* = discuss his options in the meeting)

b. He discusses his options in the meetings, but he never [$_{VP}$ [$_{VP}$ **does**] in the cafeteria].
(*does* = discuss his options)

Do can replace either the larger VP or the smaller one.

We captured this behavior with the VP-over-VP adjunction structure shown in (27a): *do* can replace either the larger VP or the smaller one.

The same general phenomenon also occurs in nominals with the proform *one*. The latter can either include noun adjuncts in the material it replaces (29a), or exclude them (29b):

(29) a. This discussion of his options in the meeting helped more than that [$_{N'}$ **one**].
(*one* = discussion of his options in the meeting)

b. The discussion of his options in the meeting helped more than the [$_{N'}$ [$_{N'}$ **one**] in the cafeteria].
(*one* = discussion of his options)

Once again, we can capture this with the N'-over-N' adjunction structure shown in (27b): *one* can replace either the larger N' or the smaller one.

These proposals entail an important difference in structure between examples like (30a) and (30b), even though they both have a single PP following N:

(30) a. the discussion [$_{PP}$ of his options]
b. the discussion [$_{PP}$ in the meeting]

In the first case, PP is a complement and attaches as a sister of N. In the second case, PP is an adjunct and attaches as a sister of N':

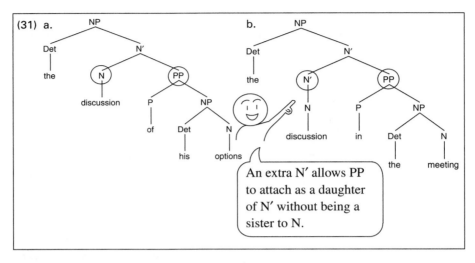

(31) a. [tree diagram for "the discussion of his options"]
b. [tree diagram for "the discussion in the meeting"]

An extra N′ allows PP to attach as a daughter of N′ without being a sister to N.

In the second case, there is an extra N′.

Order of Complements and Adjuncts

Our account of noun complements and adjuncts correctly predicts the mutual ordering of these elements, as shown in (32) and (33):

(32) a.   Homer's [$_N$ discussion] of his options in the meeting
     b.   ?*Homer's [$_N$ discussion] in the meeting of his options
(33) a.   Homer and Marge's [$_N$ argument] about their vacation on Thursday
     b.   ?*Homer and Marge's [$_N$ argument] on Thursday about their vacation

In each pair, the (a) example is more natural than the (b) example, unless special intonation is imposed. The generalization is clearly that complement PPs occur to the left of adjunct PPs.

As with verbal complements and adjuncts, our tree structures imply this result. Complements occur within the smallest N′ as sisters of N, whereas adjuncts occur farther out, as sisters of N′. When both occur to the right of N, therefore, the complement will occur closer to N than the adjunct. That is, it will occur before (to the left of) the adjunct:

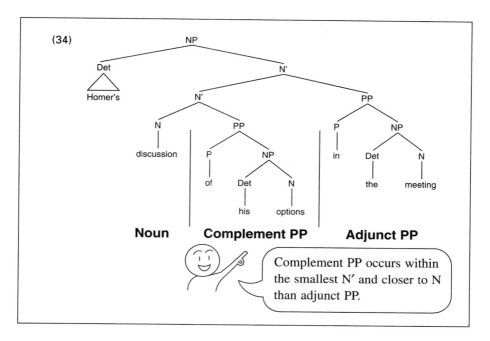

(34)

Noun   Complement PP   Adjunct PP

Complement PP occurs within the smallest N′ and closer to N than adjunct PP.

PRO in NP

A final parallel between sentences and nominals is shown in (35)–(37):

(35) a. [_CP_ For Homer to lose his driver's license] would be inconvenient.

  b. [_CP_ _____ to lose one's driver's license] would be inconvenient.

(36) a. [_NP_ Homer's losing (of) his driver's license] was inconvenient.

  b. [_NP_ _____ losing (of) one's driver's license] is inconvenient.

(37) a. [_NP_ Homer's loss of his driver's license] was inconvenient.

  b. [_NP_ _____ loss of one's driver's license] is inconvenient.

We saw that nonfinite clauses allow "missing subjects" in certain cases. We analyzed this phenomenon in terms of an inaudible subject, *PRO*, which, in cases like (35b), has the approximate meaning of 'one' (cf. *For one to lose one's driver's license would be inconvenient*):

(38) [_CP_ **PRO** to lose one's driver's license] would be inconvenient.

A natural extension of this proposal is to suggest that gerundive and derived nominals like (35b) and (37b) also contain an inaudible *PRO* subject in the position where a possessive NP would go:

(39) a. [~NP~ **PRO** losing (of) one's driver's license] is inconvenient.
b. [~NP~ **PRO** loss of one's driver's license] is inconvenient.

A Puzzle about Reflexives

The *PRO*-in-NP proposal receives interesting support from examples like (40a), which are problematic for our principles of reflexive licensing if we assume a tree like (40b). Here, *Lisa* is the apparent antecedent of *herself*, but it neither precedes nor c-commands the reflexive!

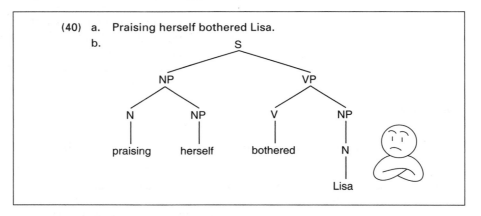

(40) a. Praising herself bothered Lisa.

This goes against what our principles require; hence, examples like (40a) raise a serious puzzle for our analysis of reflexives.

PRO Saves the Day!

The linguist John Ross found a clever solution to this problem involving (the equivalent of) *PRO*. Suppose, Ross said, that gerunds like (40a) contain an inaudible subject, so that the analysis of *Praising herself bothered Lisa* is similar to (41a,b), which contain overt possessives:

(41) a. Lisa's praising herself bothered Lisa.
b. Her praising herself bothered Lisa.

Under this idea, *Praising herself bothered Lisa* has the structure in (42):

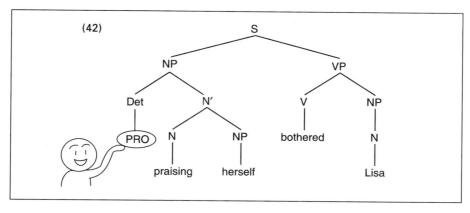

Notice now that instead of requiring *Lisa* to be the antecedent of *herself*, we can turn this job over to *PRO*, equivalent to the overt pronoun *her* in (41b). From its high, subjectlike position in NP, *PRO* both precedes and c-commands the reflexive *herself*. The only extra stipulation we must make is that *PRO* refer to the same thing as *Lisa* (i.e., that they **corefer**). Then the link between *Lisa* and *herself* is established; *herself* corefers with *PRO*, which in turn corefers with *Lisa*:

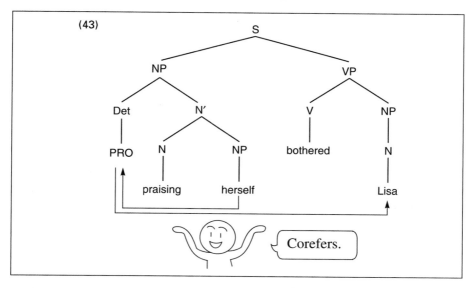

So by assuming *PRO*-in-NP, the problem for reflexive licensing raised by (41a) is neatly solved.

X-Bar Theory

Review

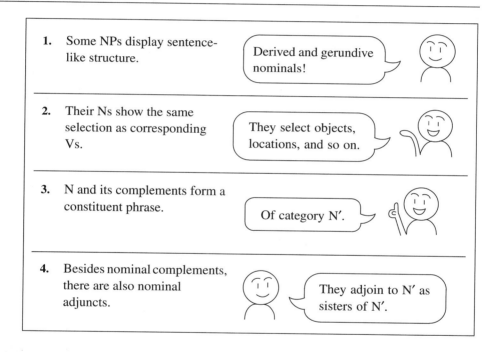

1. Some NPs display sentence-like structure.

   Derived and gerundive nominals!

2. Their Ns show the same selection as corresponding Vs.

   They select objects, locations, and so on.

3. N and its complements form a constituent phrase.

   Of category N′.

4. Besides nominal complements, there are also nominal adjuncts.

   They adjoin to N′ as sisters of N′.

More on NP - TP

The parallels we have uncovered between nominals and sentences are striking, but at this point the two categories still differ in an important way. Currently, the NP *Homer's discussion of his options* has the branched structure in (1a), containing an N′. By contrast, the TP *Homer discussed his options* has a flat structure with no parallel constituent (1b):

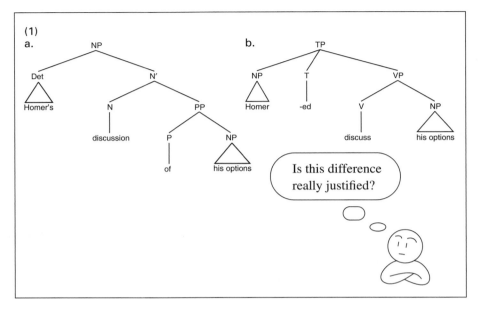

(1)

a. [NP [Det Homer's] [N' [N discussion] [PP [P of] [NP his options]]]]

b. [TP [NP Homer] [T -ed] [VP [V discuss] [NP his options]]]

Is this difference really justified?

Consider the examples in (2a–c):

(2) a. Bart can't drive a car and may have an accident.
     b. Homer can drive a car and Marge Ø too.
     c. Marge wants Lisa to attend college and to study music.

On reflection, you'll see that these data actually do suggest a structure in which T (*can('t)*, *may*, *to*) forms a constituent with its following VP (*drive a car*, *have an accident*, *attend college*, etc.):

Constituent!

EXERCISE   Construct a formal argument that the strings *can('t) drive a car*, *may have an accident*, and *to attend college* are constituents in (2a–c).

Assuming this branching structure, how should we label this new phrase? Recalling that TP inherits its features from T and that features pass from heads to phrases of the same category, a natural label for this new constituent is T′—a tense projection bigger than a T and smaller than a full TP:

With these changes, the last major difference between nominal and sentential structure disappears, and the two become very close indeed.

The Structure of PP

Having found a common structural pattern in NPs and TPs, we may immediately ask whether it is unique to them or whether it generalizes even further, to other phrases. A number of linguists have argued that it does. We will illustrate with PPs, borrowing from work by the linguist Ray Jackendoff (1977), who was the first to explore this question in detail.

We have seen that English verbs and nouns occur in forms taking no complement (intransitive), an NP/PP complement, or a CP complement:

(3) a. Homer **protested**.   (intransitive)
    b. Homer **protested** his innocence.   (NP complement)
    c. Homer **protested** that he was innocent.   (CP complement)
(4) a. Homer's **belief**   (intransitive)
    b. Homer's **belief** in Bart's innocence   (PP complement)
    c. Homer's **belief** that Bart was innocent   (CP complement)

Now examine the PPs in (5):

(5) a. Homer lived in Holyoke [**before**].
    b. Homer lived in Holyoke [**before** Lisa's birth].
    c. Homer lived in Holyoke [**before** Lisa was born].

Arguably, we also have here a case of a P (*before*) that selects either no complement (5a), an NP (5b), or a CP/TP (5c). It is easy to show by familiar arguments that the bracketed phrases are indeed constituents of category PP.

 EXERCISE   Give the relevant arguments for the constituency and the PP status of the bracketed items in (5).

Introducing Measure Phrases

Continuing now, observe the more complex PP examples in (6), containing an additional **measure phrase** (**MP**) item (*two years*), which specifies length of time:

(6) a. Homer lived in Holyoke **two years** before.
     b. Homer lived in Holyoke **two years** before Lisa's birth.
     c. Homer lived in Holyoke **two years** before Lisa was born.

Measure phrases!

The data in (7) argue that the measure phrase forms a larger constituent with the preposition and its complements:

(7) a. Homer moved to Springfield **one year after Lisa's birth** and **two years before Bart's birth**.
     b. **Seven miles from Holyoke** lived an old man.

The data in (8) furthermore suggest that the category of this larger constituent is PP:

(8) a. Homer put the rattle [$_{PP}$ **near Maggie**].
     b. Homer put the rattle **three inches nearer (to) Maggie**.
     c. The vase fell **three feet off the table** and **onto the floor**.

Finally, the data in (9) argue that, within the larger PP, the preposition and its complements form a phrase that excludes the measure phrase element:

(9) a. Homer moved to Springfield two years **after Moe** and **after Barney**.
     b. The car rolled three hundred feet **down the road** and **up the hill**.

The Category P′

Taking all the facts together, what picture do we get? Which of the following three structures (if any) is compatible with all our data about complex PPs: the tree in (10), (11), or (12)?

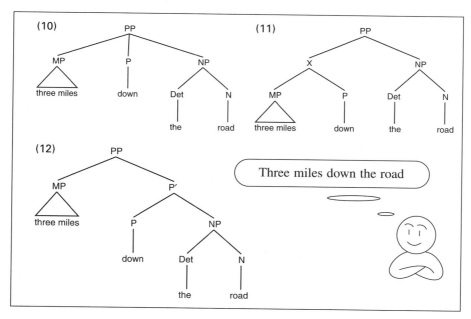

On reflection, the correct answer is clearly Tree (12). Tree (12)—and *only* Tree (12)—is compatible with all the facts cited above. Note in particular that since *three miles down the road* is a locative PP that inherits its locative features from P, and since features pass from heads to phrases of the same category, the final structure of PP must include an intermediate projection of P that is larger than a preposition but smaller than a full PP. We label it *P′*.

So PP shows the very same structural pattern as NP and TP!

EXERCISE   Use the data in (7)–(9) to construct a formal four-
                           part argument for the structure in Tree (12).

Abstracting a Common Shape

Generalizing over our results, we can abstract a common shape from the phrases
we have examined. In each case, the pattern is as shown here:

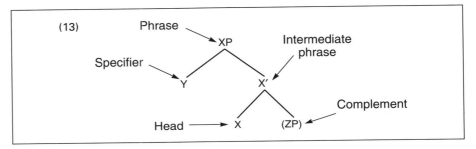

For each phrase XP, there is a **specifier** element (Y)—either a Det, an NP, or an
MP, depending on X. And there is an intermediate phrase X', consisting of the
head (X) followed by its complements (ZP), if any.

Constraining Phrase Structure Rules

The existence of this pattern is striking and provocative, and suggests an intriguing idea first advanced by Chomsky (1970).

Our earlier discussions have revealed a number of patterns in our phrase
structure (PS) rules—for example, the fact that a head and its complements group
together in a phrase projected from the head. Nonetheless, our tacit assumption
has been that a grammar can contain pretty much any PS rules it wants or needs.

Suppose this is not so, however. Specifically, suppose that these conditions
held instead:

- The kinds of PS rules available to a grammar are highly constrained.
- The common shape abstracted above represents a "template" for
  possible PS rules.

If these assumptions were correct, then only PS rules conforming to the schemata in (14) would be legitimate:

> (14) a. XP → Spec X′
>   (where Spec is a category whose nature depends on X)
>   b. X′ → X ZP*
>   (where ZP* means "zero or more phrases," possibly of different category)

For example, rules like (15)–(17)—the familiar ones for which we have already found evidence—would be allowed. But rules like (18a–d) would be disallowed, since they do not conform to either (14a) or (14b):

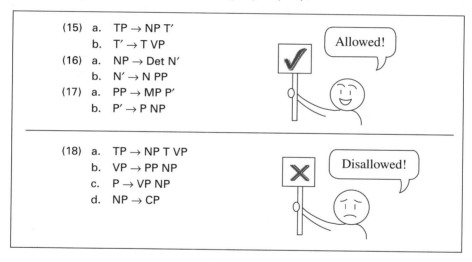

> (15) a. TP → NP T′
>   b. T′ → T VP
> (16) a. NP → Det N′
>   b. N′ → N PP
> (17) a. PP → MP P′
>   b. P′ → P NP

Allowed!

> (18) a. TP → NP T VP
>   b. VP → PP NP
>   c. P → VP NP
>   d. NP → CP

Disallowed!

More broadly, if these assumptions are correct, then the recurring patterns we find in English phrase structure are no accident. Instead, they follow from something "deep": the existence of an underlying scheme or template for PS rules. The proposal that such a template exists is called the **X-Bar Hypothesis**, in honor of the X variables and the prime or bar symbol " ′ " that appear in (14). The theory that attempts to develop this idea is called **X-Bar Theory**, and (14a,b) are called **X-bar rules**.

Powerful Implications!

The X-Bar Hypothesis is an attractive idea simply for the account it provides of patterns shared across English phrases. But in fact its attractions are much greater.

The X-Bar Hypothesis also has some tantalizing implications about how grammars are acquired, and how they vary.

Learning by Template

If children came equipped with a constraining X-bar template, then their task in figuring out the phrase structure of their language would be greatly simplified. In effect, they would "know," in advance, that only structures conforming to a limited range would be possible. They would not conjecture, or need to find evidence against, rules like (18a–d). They would simply know that such rules are impossible given that they don't match the X-bar scheme.

Putting things differently, if children approach the task of language learning equipped with X-bar rules, the task of mastering their language then reduces to discovering which specific PS rules conforming to X-bar theory their grammar contains. Much of this may be easy. Having identified a certain item as a T, they would presumably know that their grammar contains the rules in (15), which project Ts. Having identified a certain item as a P, they would know that their grammar contains the rules in (17), which project Ps. And so on.

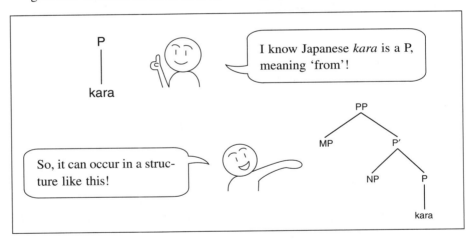

The child might have to discover what kind of specifiers his or her grammar allows for a particular category of phrase (Det, NP, MP, etc.), or how many complements a given category can have (0, 1, 2, etc.). But these things could presumably be determined by direct observation of relatively simple data.

This picture seems to go some distance toward explaining the striking facts of language acquisition: that it occurs quickly, without significant instruction, and in the face of defective data. Equipped with X-bar templates, children would already know the core shape of their phrase structure, and the residue would appear to be learnable on the basis of simple examples of a sort the child would be quite likely to hear. Much defective data, at least as far as phrase structure is concerned, would presumably be screened out by X-bar constraints.

Variation by Template

The X-Bar Hypothesis also suggests a powerful explanation for the fact that when languages differ in phrase structure, they differ in systematic ways. Compare the English examples in (19) with the corresponding Japanese examples in (20), whose patterns are representative for the language:

(19) a. Homer may leave.
      b. Homer may visit Marge.
      c. Homer may give an apple to Marge.

(20) a. Taroo-wa   deru   daroo.
          Taroo-TOP   depart   may

      b. Taroo-wa   Hanako-o   tazuneru daroo.
          Taroo-TOP   Hanako-ACC   visit   may

      c. Taroo-wa   ringo-o   Hanako-ni   ageru daroo.
          Taroo-TOP   apple-ACC   Hanako-DAT   give may

If you contrast the word orders in the two sets, you will observe the following things (among others):

- Whereas T *precedes* the verb plus its complements in English, T *follows* the verb plus its complements in Japanese.

- Whereas V *precedes* its complements in English, V *follows* its complements in Japanese.

- Whereas P *precedes* its object in English (*to Mary*), P *follows* its object in Japanese (*Hanako-ni*).

If you further contrast tree diagrams for the phrases in (19) and (20), the picture is quite striking:

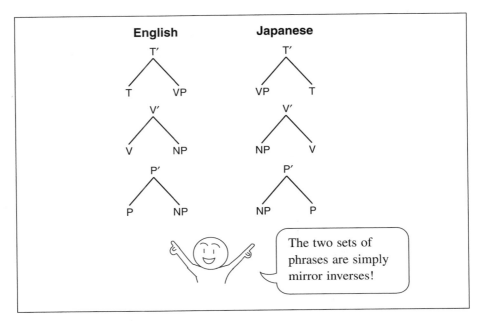

Notice now that all of this would be accounted for under these two simple assumptions:

- All languages follow an X-bar template.
- Across languages, the rule for X′ is allowed to vary in the order of head and complements.

If all languages follow an X-bar template, then within a given language, all phrases will show the same pattern. Each language will be systematic in this way. And if X-bar templates are allowed to vary in the order of head (X) and complements (ZP*), then we will expect to see two basic templates:

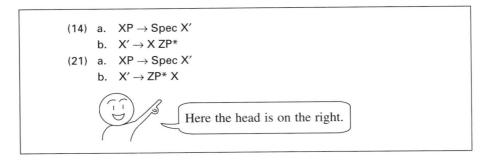

A language following the first template will have all of its heads on the left (14); a language following the second template will have all of its heads on the right (21).

This is exactly the kind of variation we see between English and Japanese. Furthermore, linguists have found that this kind of behavior is fully systematic for other languages like them. If a language is like English in that V precedes its complements, then it is highly likely that P will also precede its object, and T will precede V. French and Spanish, for example, show the English pattern. If a language is like Japanese in that V follows its complements, then it is highly likely that P will also follow its object, and T will follow V. Hindi and Korean show the Japanese pattern.

These kinds of crosslinguistic patterns are sometimes called **Greenbergian universals**, in honor of the linguist Joseph Greenberg, who studied them extensively and drew attention to their importance. The X-Bar Hypothesis offers a plausible account of these universals.

Simple Rules versus Complex Structures

The X-Bar Hypothesis clearly has many virtues, but notice that it also makes the analysis of previously simple cases more complex. Consider, for example, NPs like *the man* and *Homer*. Under the single X-bar template, *the man* gets a structure like (22a), with a nonbranching N′ node, and *Homer* gets a structure like (22b), with an empty Det and a nonbranching N′ node:

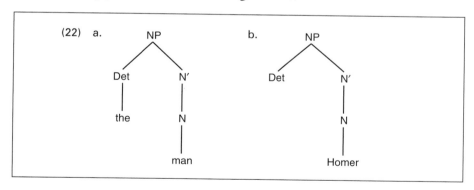

These contrast with the simpler structures in (23a,b) that we assigned earlier:

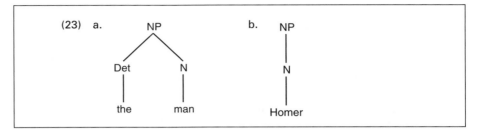

At this point, we could either leave our theory as is and assume that the newer, more complex structures are indeed correct, or we could enrich our X-bar rules to permit the original, simpler structures—for example, by adding templates like this:

(24) a.   XP → Spec X
      b.   XP → X

The first allows us to dispense with X′ when no complements are present. The second allows us to dispense with both Spec and X′ in a phrase containing no specifiers or complements. For concreteness, we will adopt the second proposal, allowing us to stick to the simpler trees. But we will return to this issue in the exercises.

EXERCISES

1. Give an English sentence illustrating each of the following. In each case, give an example involving a complement clause:

   A. An embedded finite declarative

   B. An embedded infinitival constituent interrogative

   C. A main finite polarity interrogative containing an embedded infinitival constituent interrogative

   D. A main finite declarative containing an embedded finite interrogative containing an embedded infinitival interrogative

2. Here is a set of phrase structure rules allowing various types of complement sentences to be produced:

   (1) a. S → NP VP

        b. NP → N

        c. VP → V

        d. VP → V CP

        e. VP → V NP CP

        f. CP → C S

   Here also is a list of sentences:

   (2) a. Bart asked Homer when Lisa left.

        b. Bart asked Homer whether Lisa left.

        c. Bart asked Homer whether Marge said that Lisa left.

        d. Bart asked if Lisa left.

        e. Bart asked when Lisa left.

        f. Bart asked where Lisa went.

        g. Bart believes Lisa left.

        h. Bart believes that Lisa left.

        i. Bart knows Lisa left.

    j.   Bart knows if Lisa left.

    k.   Bart knows that Lisa left.

    l.   Bart knows whether Lisa left.

    m. Bart said Lisa left.

    n.   Bart said that Lisa left.

    o.   Bart told Homer that Marge wondered if Lisa left.

    p.   Bart wonders if Lisa left.

    q.   Bart wonders whether Lisa left.

    r.   Lisa left.

    s.   Bart told Homer that Lisa left.

    t.   Bart told Homer when Lisa left.

A.   Create a lexicon that will interact with the rules in (1) to generate trees for *all* the sentences in this list. (Note: Do not add any new rules in doing this exercise.)

B.   Check to see that your lexicon *doesn't* produce ungrammatical outputs like these:

(3) a.   *Bart asked that Lisa left.

     b.   *Bart asked Lisa left.

     c.   *Bart believes whether Lisa left.

     d.   *Bart believes when Lisa left.

     e.   *Bart wonders that Lisa left.

     f.   *Bart wonders Lisa left.

     g.   *Bart told Homer that Marge wondered that Lisa left.

     h.   *That Lisa left.

     i.   *Whether Lisa left.

(To be thorough, you should check your grammar against additional ungrammatical sentences of your own.)

2. Consider the rules and lexical entries below:

  (1) *Rules*

     a.   S → NP VP

     b.   VP → V NP

     c.   VP → V CP

d. VP → V NP CP

e. CP → C S

(2) *Lexical entries*

a. *that,* C, [+D]

b. *whether,* C, [+Q]

c. *tell,* V, [+ __ NP CP], [+ __ NP CP]
    [+D]   [+Q]

d. *ask,* V, [+ __ CP]
    [+Q]

e. *speak,* V, [+ __ NP]

Using these rules and lexical entries (together with any of the other familiar rules and lexical entries we've been assuming all along), give a phrase marker for the following sentence:

(3) Homer told Marge that Bart asked whether Lisa speaks Turkish.

3. Here is a set of phrase structure rules allowing various types of complement sentences to be produced:

(1) a. TP → NP T′

b. T′ → T VP

c. NP → N

d. VP → V

e. VP → V NP

f. VP → V CP

g. VP → V NP CP

h. CP → C TP

Here also is a list of sentences:

(2) a. Lisa hopes that Bart will win.

b. Lisa hopes for Bart to win.

c. Lisa thinks that Bart should win.

d. Lisa wonders if Bart will win.

e. Lisa wonders whether Bart will win.

f. Lisa wonders whether to win.

g. Lisa wonders how to win.

      h.   Lisa knows that Bart may win.

      i.   Lisa knows if Bart can win.

      j.   Lisa knows whether Bart can win.

      k.   Lisa knows why Bart can win.

      l.   Lisa persuaded Bart that he could win.

      m.   Lisa persuaded Bart to win.

      n.   Lisa persuaded Bart that he might win.

      o.   Lisa expects that Bart will win.

      p.   Lisa expects Bart to win.

      q.   Lisa expects for Bart to win.

      r.   Lisa expects to win.

A.   Create a lexicon that will interact with the rules in (1) to generate trees for *all* the sentences in this list. (Note: Do not add any new rules in doing this exercise.)

B.   Check to see that your lexicon *doesn't* produce ungrammatical sentences like these:

(3) a.   *Lisa hopes whether Bart will win.

      b.   *Lisa hopes whether Bart to win.

      c.   *Lisa thinks that Bart to win.

      d.   *Lisa thinks for Bart to win.

      e.   *Lisa wonders if to win.

      f.   *Lisa knows for Bart to win.

      g.   *Lisa persuaded Bart for him to win.

      h.   *Lisa persuaded Bart whether he could win.

      i.   *Lisa persuaded Bart if he could win.

C.   Consider the following additional sentences:

(4) a.   Lisa believes that Bart likes candy.

      b.   Lisa believes Bart to like candy.

      c.   *Lisa believes for Bart to like candy.

      d.   *Lisa believes to like candy.

Extend your lexicon so that your grammar now generates (4a,b). Does it generate (4c,d) as well? If it does, revise your lexicon so that it does not.

4. Give a tree diagram for each of the following sentences. Be sure to diagram them according to the view of the structure of complement clauses and sentences that we reached at the end of Unit 22.

   (1) Homer may want Bart to admit that he skipped school on Friday.

   (2) Marge quickly asked whether Homer ever said that Lisa wanted to visit Paris next year. (Note: In this example, *quickly* and *ever* are adverbs.)

   (3) Marge expects to persuade Homer to ask Burns to give him a raise.

   (4) The recent discussion of where to eat dinner showed Homer to be seriously confused about food.

5. Sentence (1) is **semantically ambiguous**, having two distinct readings. It is also **structurally ambiguous** under the rules we have assumed, and has two distinct trees.

   (1) Marge told us that Bart left yesterday.

   A. Give paraphrases for each of the two readings, making sure that your paraphrases are themselves unambiguous.

   B. Give the two trees corresponding to the two readings.

6. Look at the following facts concerning the English verbs *prefer* and *coax*, which both show the V-NP-*to*-VP form. Assume the judgments given.

   (1) a. Bart preferred for Lisa to leave.

        b. Bart preferred for there to be a PTA meeting.

        c. Bart preferred for the cat to get out of the bag.
            (both literal and idiomatic meaning)

   (2) a. Bart coaxed Lisa to leave.

        b. ?*Bart coaxed there to be a PTA meeting.

        c. Bart coaxed the cat to get out of the bag.
            (literal meaning only)

   Now do the following:

   A. Explain how many elements are involved in typical situations of *preferring* and *coaxing*.

   B. Give a phrase marker for *Bart preferred for Lisa to leave.*

   C. Give a phrase marker for *Bart coaxed Lisa to leave.*

   D. Consider these additional facts:

(3) a.   For Lisa to leave at 3:00 p.m. is what Bart preferred.

b.   ?*For Lisa to leave at 3:00 p.m. is what Bart coaxed.

Explain how these data support the trees that you have given above.

7. Consider these two phrase markers, noting carefully the difference between the two structures:

(1)

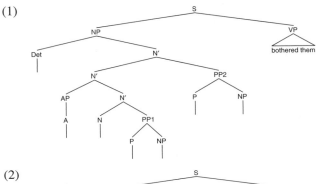

(2)

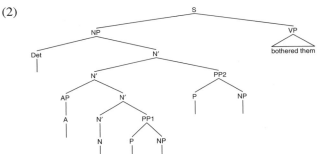

A.   Complete the two phrase markers by inserting appropriate terminal elements (words!).

B.   Now complete the following statements:

In Tree (1), PP1 is a(n) _____ . (complement, adjunct)

In Tree (2), PP1 is a(n) _____ . (complement, adjunct)

C.   Consider these two sentences (from Radford 1988), and assume the judgments given:

(3) a.   The lack of any discipline in some schools bothered them.

b.   *The lack of discipline in any schools bothered them.

Thinking about the difference in structure between complements and adjuncts, and our principle governing negative polarity items, we can account for this contrast. How? Draw phrase markers for (3a) and (3b) to help you see the solution. (Hint: *Lack* is a negative item.)

D.   Assume that (4) (from Radford 1988) is well-formed.

(4)   The lack of teachers with any qualifications bothered them.

Given your account of (3a,b), explain why this is possible.

8. Observe the NP in (1) and its meaning. Thinking carefully, you will see that (1) is ambiguous, having two different meanings:

(1)   [NP The French leader] arrived today.

    a.   'The leader who is French arrived today.'

    b.   'The leader of the French arrived today.'

On reading (a), the person must be French, but it is not necessary that he or she *lead* the French. On reading (b), the person must lead the French, but it is not necessary that he or she *be* French.

Now compare example (2):

(2)   [NP The English French leader] arrived today.

Interestingly, this example can only refer to the leader of the French who is English; it cannot refer to the leader of the English who is French.

Using what you know about the syntax of complements and adjuncts, propose structures for (1) and (2) that explain the following things:

A.   Why (1) is ambiguous, and

B.   Why (2) has exactly the reading that it has (namely, why it means 'The leader of the French who is English' and not 'The leader of the English who is French').

In working out your answer, you might want to consider the following additional data:

(3)   a.   the leader who is French   (unambiguous; reading (a))

    b.   the leader of the French   (unambiguous; reading (b))

    c.   *the leader [of the French] [of the English]

    d.   the English leader of the French (unambiguous; equivalent to (2))

    e.   the leader [of the French] [who is English]

                   (unambiguous; equivalent to (2))

    f.   *the leader [who is English] [of the French]

                    (under normal intonation)

PART VII Expanding and Constraining the Theory

As we develop a scientific theory, circumstances will inevitably arise where we wish to expand the machinery available to us for analysis. We have already seen this in the case of lexical items. Initially, our sole technical device was the (context-free) phrase structure rule, and we introduced lexical items by this means. Later, we introduced the idea of a lexicon, consisting of lexical items with subcategory features. These features could contain features themselves.

Lexical rule: Vd → *put*
Lexical entry: *put*, V, [+ __ NP PP]
                              [+loc]

A theory with phrase structure rules plus lexical items is more "powerful" than one with phrase structure rules alone, in the sense that a wider class of languages can be described by the first than by the second. This is positive from one perspective, but negative from another.

On the one hand, linguistic theory must be capable of describing accurately and adequately all of the world's languages. Chomsky refers to this as the requirement of **descriptive adequacy**. The apparent richness and variety in natural language grammars would seem to demand a correspondingly rich and varied class of technical devices in order to pass the test of descriptive adequacy.

On the other hand, all natural languages must be acquired by children, presumably from a developmental starting point that is constant across the species. Another task of linguistic theory is to explain how this is possible. Chomsky refers to this as the requirement of **explanatory adequacy**. As we have seen, the nature of language acquisition—the fact that it is untutored and occurs rapidly in the face of impoverished input—suggests the presence of a Universal Grammar that sharply constrains the space of possible grammars in which children must search for the one that matches the language of their environment. This would seem to imply very limited possibilities in variation at the level of Universal Grammar.

As Chomsky has emphasized, descriptive and explanatory adequacy appear to conflict:

There is a serious tension between these two research tasks. The search for descriptive adequacy seems to lead to ever greater complexity and variety of rule systems, while the search for explanatory adequacy requires that language structure must be invariant, except at the margins.
—*New Horizons in the Study of Language and Mind*, p. 7

Nonetheless, we know that this conflict must only be apparent. Our shared linguistic mechanism must be compatible with apparently wide variation. Interestingly, analogies from other domains suggest how this tension might be resolved.

Sifakas, a group of lemuriform primates (genus *Propithecus*) living on the island of Madagascar, show remarkable variation in pelage (coat coloration) and facial patterning, and this variation is sufficient to separate them into distinct species. Sifakas identify each other by these markings and do not associate or interbreed with animals that exhibit different patterning. Nevertheless, sifakas are, to a very high order of approximation, genetically identical. For all intents and purposes, they share the same DNA and are in fact interfertile. How is this possible? How is surface variation reconciled with genetic uniformity?

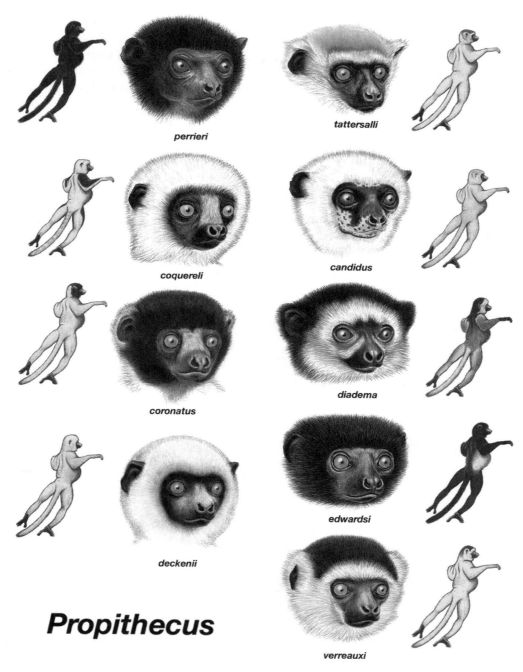

perrieri

tattersalli

coquereli

candidus

coronatus

diadema

deckenii

edwardsi

verreauxi

Propithecus

Courtesy of Stephen D. Nash/Conservation International

Biologists have determined that very small and highly limited variations in the otherwise constant sifaka genome, interacting with other developmental factors, combine to produce the sharply different coat and facial patterns that we observe. These phenotypic differences, though superficial from a genetic point of view, are nonetheless enough to isolate sifaka species from each other behaviorally. Small changes, with cascade effects, produce large differences.

It is attractive to think that human linguistic variation might follow a similar model. Suppose that Universal Grammar, although largely fixed for the species, allows for a very limited degree of variation, and that this variation can interact in rich ways with other aspects of the grammar. Then small changes with cascade effects might indeed yield the range of "superficial" variation that we observe. In this final part, we will explore a class of phenomena illustrating this view. We will see that what we have called "dislocation" points toward the presence of a new kind of device in the grammar: movement. Investigating this device, we will see that it is powerful, but also powerfully constrained, apparently by universal principles. Finally, we will also see that, although universal, these constraints allow for limited variation that nonetheless yields the rich array of surface differences exhibited across natural languages.

Interrogatives and Movement

Review

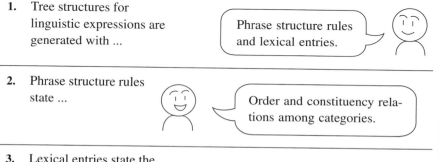

1. Tree structures for linguistic expressions are generated with ...

    Phrase structure rules and lexical entries.

2. Phrase structure rules state ...

    Order and constituency relations among categories.

3. Lexical entries state the specific properties of members of a given category.

    The properties of specific verbs, determiners, and so on.

The Problem of Constituent Interrogatives

In Unit 19, we looked at embedded constituent interrogatives like (1a–e):

(1) a. I wonder [CP **who** gave SLH to Lisa at the party yesterday].
     b. I asked [CP **what** Bart gave to Lisa at the party yesterday].
     c. I know [CP **to whom** Bart gave SLH at the party yesterday].
     d. I wonder [CP **where** Bart gave SLH to Lisa yesterday].
     e. I inquired [CP **when** Bart gave SLH to Lisa at the party].

Each example has a clause-initial question word or question phrase. In English, these words and phrases typically contain the sequence *wh-* (*who, what, whom, to whom, where,* etc.) and so are sometimes called ***wh*-words** or ***wh*-phrases**.

Now consider the status of the CP-initial *wh*-elements. How should these be analyzed? One simple idea would be to treat them as interrogative complementizers, just like *whether* and *if*. The structure of the embedded CP in (1e) would look like this (where the triangles abbreviate irrelevant structure):

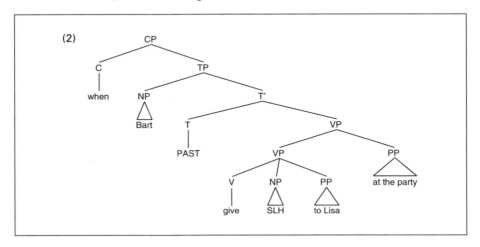

This view has attractions. *Inquire* selects a [+Q] complement. If question words like *what* and *when* are also [+Q] (which seems reasonable) and are analyzed as Cs, then selection works out fine. The [+Q] feature carried by *when* percolates from C to CP, where it is selected by *inquire*:

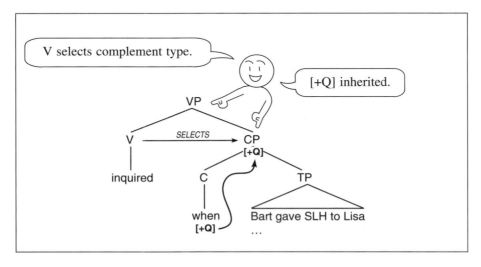

Nonetheless, even though the complementizer analysis is simple and attractive in some ways, it encounters serious problems.

The Category of *Wh*-Elements

The analysis embodied in (2) classifies *when* and all other *wh*-words and *wh*-phrases as complementizers—items of category C. But this seems doubtful. *When* and *where* show obvious morphological and semantic parallels to the non-*wh* proforms *then* and *there*, items that we analyzed as PPs. Given this, it seems natural to analyze *when* and *where* as PPs too (3a,b). Consider also *wh*-forms like *which person* and *to whom*, which plainly resemble NPs and PPs, respectively. Again, it is natural to put them in those categories (3c,d):

(3) a. [PP when] ≈ [PP then]
     b. [PP where] ≈ [PP there]
     c. [NP which person] ≈ [NP that person]
     d. [PP to whom] ≈ [PP to her]

A categorial relation between *wh*-items and non-*wh*-items occurs in another context as well. Consider (4a–g), focusing on the question items and the words and phrases used to answer them:

(4)	Question	Answer
a.	**Who** left?	[NP **Bart**]. / [NP **The boy**] left.
b.	**What** broke?	[NP **That**]. / [NP **Marge's vase**] broke.
c.	**Which vase** broke?	[NP **That one**]. / [NP **That vase**] broke.
d.	**To whom** did Bart give a present?	[PP **To Lisa**]. / Bart gave a present [PP **to Lisa**].
e.	**When** did Bart arrive?	[PP **At 5:00 p.m.**]. / He arrived [PP **at 5:00 p.m.**].
f.	**Where** did Bart arrive?	[PP **In Springfield**]. / He arrived [PP **there**].
g.	**How** did Bart behave?	[AdvP **Rudely**]. / Bart behaved [AdvP **rudely**].

In each case, there appears to be a stable relation between the question word used to ask a question and the category of the phrase used to answer it. When we answer *who*-, *what*-, and *which*-questions, we do so with a noun phrase (4a–c). We answer questions like (4d) with a PP that repeats the preposition and substitutes some NP inside. We answer *when*- and *where*-questions with temporal and locative PPs, respectively (4e,f). And we answer *how*-questions with a manner adverb (4g).

The relation between an answer word and a *wh*-form appears to be somewhat like the relation between an antecedent and an associated proform (5a–c). Recall our principle that proforms refer back to items of the same category (5d):

(5) a. [NP **Bart**] left.   [NP **He**] was angry.
     b. Bart arrived [PP **at 5:00 p.m.**].   It was already dark [PP **then**].
     c. Bart lives in [PP **in Springfield**]. He was born [PP **there**].
     d. ... [XP α] ...   ... [XP **proform**] ...

A natural idea is to view (4) and (5) as analogous. Just as proforms come in different categories and refer back to items of the same category, so *wh*-forms come in different categories and are answered with items of the same category (6):

(6) Q: [XP **WH-proform**] ... ?   A: ... [XP α] ...

But note that this proposal can only be made in an account that separates *wh*-items into different categories in the first place. It won't be possible in an analysis like that in (2), which lumps all *wh*-forms together as Cs.

"Gaps" and Selection

Another serious problem for the complementizer analysis arises with examples (1a–c) (repeated below). Notice that in all of these cases, the material following the *wh*-word constitutes a sentence fragment; in each instance, there is a **gap**:

(1) a. I wonder [CP **who** gave SLH to Lisa at the party yesterday].
     b. I asked [CP **what** Bart gave to Lisa at the party yesterday].
     c. I know [CP to **whom** Bart gave SLH at the party yesterday].

In the string following *who* in (1a), the subject is missing from TP (7a). In the string following *what* in (1b), the direct object is missing from its expected VP position between *gave* and *to Lisa* (7b). And in the string following *to whom* in (1c), the dative PP is missing that would normally occur after *gave SLH* (7c):

(7) a. [CP **who**   [TP ___ gave SLH to Lisa at the party yesterday]]
     b. [CP **what**   [TP Bart gave ___ to Lisa at the party yesterday]]
     c. [CP **to whom** [TP Bart gave SLH ___ at the party yesterday]]

Missing elements like these raise a basic question for selection. Consider a simple tree for (1b), analogous to that given in (2):

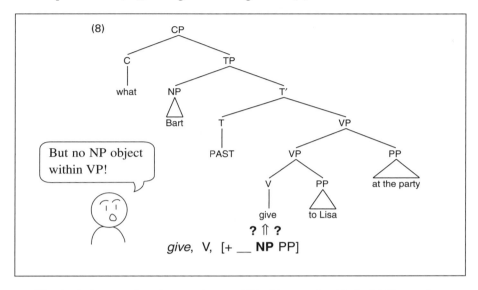

The lexical entry for *give* requires an NP object and a (dative) PP complement. Furthermore, these complements should occur as sisters to their selecting V head. But in Tree (8), *give* has no NP object within VP. Its selectional requirements are not satisfied. This structure sharply violates our principle relating complement selection to structure. Trees for (1a) and (1c) encounter the same problem.

Wh-Movement

Putting aside the idea that *wh*-words and *wh*-phrases are simple complementizers, let us reconsider the general relation between constituent interrogatives like (9a–d) and a corresponding declarative (10):

(9) a. I know [CP **who** gave SLH to Lisa at the party].
     b. I know [CP **what** Bart gave to Lisa at the party].
     c. I know [CP **to whom** Bart gave SLH at the party].
     d. I know [CP **where** Bart gave SLH to Lisa].
(10) I know [that **Bart** gave **SLH to Lisa at the party**].

Figuratively speaking, one might describe (9a–d) as formed from (10) by "questioning one of its constituents"—specifically, by replacing one of the boldfaced strings in (10) with an appropriate *wh*-item of matching category and by moving it to the front of the sentence. On this view, (9a) is formed by questioning the embedded subject with *who* (11a). (9b) is formed by questioning the embedded object with *what* (11b). (9c) is formed by questioning the PP with *to whom* (11c). And so on.

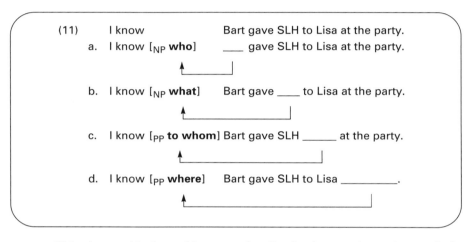

(11)   I know   Bart gave SLH to Lisa at the party.
    a. I know [NP **who**]   ____ gave SLH to Lisa at the party.

    b. I know [NP **what**]   Bart gave ____ to Lisa at the party.

    c. I know [PP **to whom**] Bart gave SLH _____ at the party.

    d. I know [PP **where**]   Bart gave SLH to Lisa _____.

This view avoids the problems noted earlier for the complementizer analysis. (11a–d) do not take *wh*-items to be Cs; rather, *wh*-forms come in different categories depending on where they originate: NP position, PP-complement position, and so on. Furthermore, assuming that an answer occurs in the position of the gap left by *wh*-, this view also explains why the two must match in category:

(12) a. [NP **Who**]   _____ gave SLH to Lisa at the party?
      b.   [NP **Bart**] gave SLH to Lisa at the party.
(13) a. [NP **What**]   did Bart give _____ to Lisa at the party?
      b.   Bart gave [NP **SLH**] to Lisa at the party.
(14) a. [PP **To whom**] did Bart give SLH _____ at the party?
      b.   Bart gave SLH [PP **to Lisa**] at the party.
(15) a. [PP **Where**]   did Bart give SLH to Lisa _____?
      b.   Bart gave SLH to Lisa [PP **at the party**].

Wh- and its answer match in category because they occur in the same position.

Finally, the analysis also avoids the selection problem noted in (9). Since the *wh*-phrase originates in a sentence-internal position, it can satisfy selectional requirements in this position before movement. Thus, the tree for (1b) is not (8), but (16):

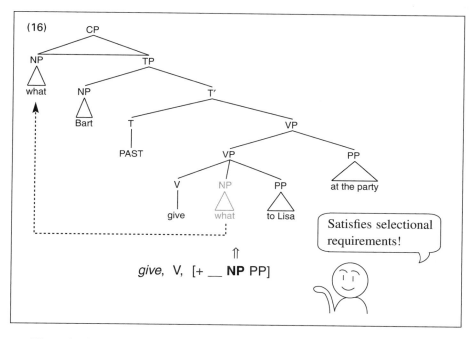

The selectional requirements of *give* are met here, and there is no violation of principles relating selection to complement attachment. *Give*'s need for an NP object is satisfied by *what*, which subsequently raises to a clause-initial site.

Further Evidence for Movement

The "movement" analysis of constituent interrogatives postulates that *wh*-items are initially at one place in a tree and later at another. Put another way, it claims that *wh*-items are always associated with at least *two* positions: where they are "heard" (clause-initial position) and where they originate (inside the sentence). There is a variety of interesting evidence showing that *wh*-words and *wh*-phrases indeed have this "dual position" status.

To-Contraction

English examples with *want* and an infinitival complement can undergo a contraction process that converts *want* + *to* into *wanna* (17a,b). "*To*-contraction" requires a *PRO* subject in the infinitive; an overt subject blocks contraction (18a,b):

---

(17) a.   I want [PRO to visit Homer].
     b.   I wanna visit Homer.
(18) a.   I want [Lisa to visit Homer].
     b.   *I wanna Lisa visit Homer.

Contraction doesn't generally affect the interpretation of the result: (17a,b) mean exactly the same thing. However, observe the following pair of examples (due to the linguist Larry Horn):

---

(19) a.   Who do you want to succeed?
     b.   Who do you wanna succeed?

Unlike in the previous case, for many speakers there is a shift of meaning between (19a) and (19b). In particular, (19a) is ambiguous in a way that (19b) is not.

There are in fact two verbs *succeed* in English. One is intransitive; it takes only a subject (20a). The other *succeed* is transitive; it takes a subject (20b):

---

(20) a.   I really hope Bart succeeds.
        (cf. *I really hope Bart is a success.*)
     b.   I really hope Charles succeeds Lizzie.
        (cf. *I really hope Charles follows Lizzie in the royal succession.*)

Sentence (19a) is ambiguous; *succeed* can be understood either intransitively (21a) or transitively (21b). In contrast, (19b) has only the second reading. It can only be understood with the transitive sense of *succeed* (21b):

(21) a. 'Who is the person such that you want him or her to be a success?'
      b. 'Who is the person such that you want to succeed him or her?'

This result appears mysterious. Why should one of the two readings of (19a) be lost in the contracted form? And why that particular reading?

Notice something very interesting about the position with which *who* is associated in the two readings. In the reading that is retained under contraction, *who* is associated with the embedded object—a position that does not fall between the contracted elements:

(22) Who (do) you want [to succeed ___]?

'Who is the person such that you want to succeed **him or her**?'

In the reading that is lost under contraction, *who* is associated with the embedded subject—a position lying between *want* and *to*:

(23) Who (do) you want [___ to succeed]?

'Who is the person such that you want **him or her** to be a success?'

Essentially, then, the situation seems to be this: even though *who* appears in clause-initial position in (19a), it *behaves* as though it were in its sentence-internal site prior to movement! When that site occurs after *want*, as in (22), no problem occurs for contraction (24a). However, when the site occurs between *want* and *to*, as in (23), the result is just as if *who* itself were standing there. Since an overt subject blocks contraction (18a,b), and *who* is overt, the result is blocked contraction (24b).

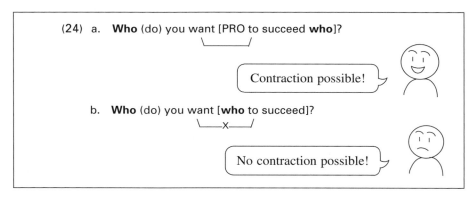

(24) a. **Who** (do) you want [PRO to succeed **who**]?

Contraction possible!

b. **Who** (do) you want [**who** to succeed]?

No contraction possible!

Thus, the facts of *to*-contraction give important evidence for the dual-position status of *wh-*.

An Unexpected Restriction on Reflexives

Consider the sentences in (25), involving reflexives in an embedded clause:

(25) a.   Bart expects [**Milhouse** to vote for **himself**].
    b.   *__Bart__ expects [Milhouse to vote for **himself**].
         (cf. ***Bart*** *expects Milhouse to vote for **him**.*)
    c.   *__Bart__ expects [the girls to vote for **himself**].
         (cf. ***Bart*** *expects the girls to vote for **him**.*)

In (25a,b), the reflexive *himself* shows an interesting "locality constraint": even though both *Bart* and *Milhouse* precede and c-command the reflexive, *himself* must be understood as referring to the "closer" NP *Milhouse*, not to *Bart*. (25c) shows that even when the embedded subject is not a suitable antecedent, a relationship between *himself* and the more distant NP *Bart* is disallowed. The sentence simply fails in this case.

Example (26a) might appear to violate this constraint at first since *himself* in this case *can* be understood as referring to *Bart*. Recall, however, that "subjectless" infinitives like this actually contain a covert *PRO* subject that is understood as referring back to the matrix subject (26b). The presence of *PRO* allows us to maintain the claim that *himself* takes only a local antecedent. *Himself* refers locally back to *PRO*, which in turn refers back to *Bart* (26c):

(26) a. **Bart** expects [to vote for **himself**].
    b. **Bart** expects [**PRO** to win].
    c. **Bart** expects [**PRO** to vote for himself].

With these points in mind, consider (27):

(27) *Which girls does **Bart** expect [to vote for **himself**]?
    (cf. *Which girls does **Bart** expect to vote for **him**?*)

Note carefully that the portion of the string to the right of *does* in (27) matches (26a). In both cases, no overt embedded subject intervenes between *Bart* and *himself*. Surprisingly, however, (27) does not behave like (26a) with respect to the reflexive. Instead, it behaves like (25c)! *Himself* cannot take *Bart* as its antecedent, and the sentence is ungrammatical. Why is this?

Once again, the dual-position status of *wh-* provides an explanation. On the movement analysis, the *wh*-phrase in (27) is associated with a sentence-internal position—specifically, with the subject position of the embedded clause:

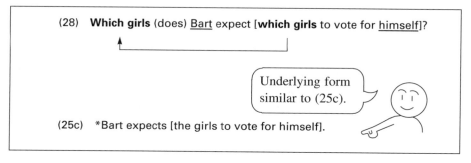

(28) **Which girls** (does) <u>Bart</u> expect [**which girls** to vote for <u>himself</u>]?

Underlying form similar to (25c).

(25c) *Bart expects [the girls to vote for himself].

Underlyingly, then, the embedded clause in (27) has an overt subject, and the situation is really no different from that in (25c). In both cases, *himself* fails to find a local antecedent within its clause.

Under the movement account, then, with *wh-* being generated in one place and moving to another, we can explain the otherwise peculiar fact that although (27) looks like (26a), it behaves like (25c). Under the movement theory, (27) actually has an underlying form like that of (25c).

An Unexpected Freedom for Reflexives

As a final piece of evidence, consider a class of apparent counterexamples to our principles governing reflexives:

> (29)   Which picture of **himself** does Lisa think that **Bart** will prefer?

We saw that reflexives had to be preceded and c-commanded by their antecedents. But (29) presents a very direct challenge to this proposal. In the structure for this sentence, the reflexive occurs inside a *wh*-phrase that is attached in the main clause roughly as follows:

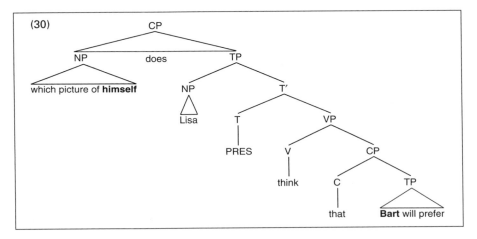

As we see, *Bart*, the understood antecedent of *himself*, occurs both lower than the reflexive and following it in the tree. How is it, then, that (29) is well-formed?

In fact, it seems we can keep our original ideas about reflexives intact if we take seriously the idea that the *wh*-phrase is associated with a sentence-internal site. Observe that the clause-initial *wh*-phrase *which picture of himself* is linked with the object position of *prefer* in the embedded clause. So we are dealing with a situation like this:

> (31)   [Which picture of **himself**] (does) Lisa think **Bart** will prefer ___ ?
>
>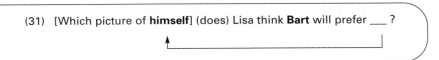

Consider also that noninterrogative cases like (32) encounter no problem with the reflexive. *Himself* takes *Bart* as its antecedent in the usual way:

(32)   Lisa thinks **Bart** will prefer [that picture of **himself**].

Taking these points together, then, it seems we want to say something like this: in structure (30), the antecedence possibilities for *himself* are not limited to the sentence-initial position *to which* the *wh*-phrase has moved. In addition, they can be determined by the position *from which* it has moved.

(33)   [**Which picture of himself**] (does)
        Lisa think <u>Bart</u> will prefer [**which picture of <u>himself</u>**]?

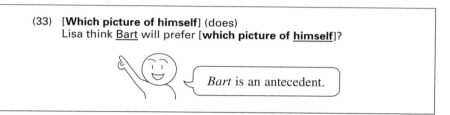

Bart is an antecedent.

In this low position, *himself* is in a suitable position to take *Bart* as its antecedent. Once again, this proposal requires us to adopt the movement view of *wh*-interrogatives.

More on *Wh*-Movement

Review

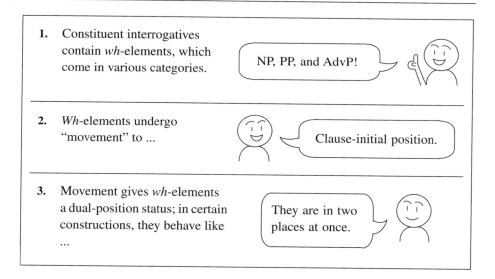

1. Constituent interrogatives contain *wh*-elements, which come in various categories.

   NP, PP, and AdvP!

2. *Wh*-elements undergo "movement" to ...

   Clause-initial position.

3. Movement gives *wh*-elements a dual-position status; in certain constructions, they behave like ...

   They are in two places at once.

Movement in General

Having motivated a movement account of constituent questions, let us now examine the details of *wh*-movement more closely. When we have constructed a tree, and it undergoes *wh*-movement, what exactly does the tree look like afterward?

Origins and Destinations

Thinking in general terms, all movement involves an origin and a destination. When we consider the effects of moving any object, we can ask these questions:

- What occurs at the *origin*, the position the element moves from?
- What occurs at the *destination*, the position the element moves to?

When you displace an object, there are always two general possibilities for the original position: either it will show the traces of the moved object, or it will not. For example, think about moving an egg out of an egg carton versus a bowl of eggs. An egg carton is a structured container. When you extract an egg from it, extraction leaves a "space" or gap in the place where the egg was. In contrast, a bowl of eggs is an unstructured collection. When you move an egg, the other eggs fill in the vacant space. No trace of movement remains. We'll call the first **gapped movement**, and the second **nongapped movement**.

When you displace an object, there are also two general possibilities for the destination: either you move to a designated site, or you don't. Think of parking a car, for instance. You might park in a painted parking space or stall; alternatively, you might simply stop along the roadside. Likewise, in moving a boat, you might tie up at a slip or mooring, or you might simply drop anchor in shallow water. We'll call the first **targeted movement**, and the second **nontargeted movement**.

Wh-Movement as Gapped Movement

For *wh*-movement, whether it's gapped or nongapped amounts to the choice illustrated below. Suppose we start with a VP containing the *wh*-NP *what* (1). When *what* is moved, does it leave an NP "trace" in VP, like the space in our egg carton (A), or does the NP position disappear, and do other VP-elements "fill in" the space, like eggs in a bowl (B)?

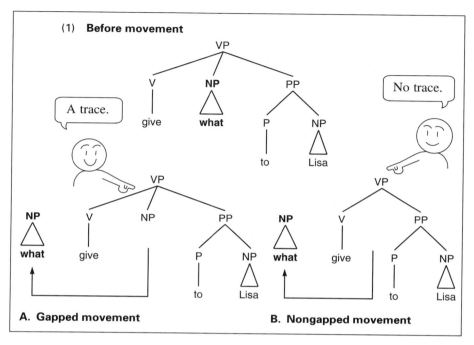

(1) **Before movement**

A. **Gapped movement**   B. **Nongapped movement**

In Unit 24, we considered evidence supporting the dual-position status of *wh*-elements. We saw that the position left vacant by *wh*-movement blocks *to*-contraction (2a), blocks antecedent-reflexive relations (2b), and enables antecedent-reflexive relations in certain cases where the reflexive has been displaced (2c):

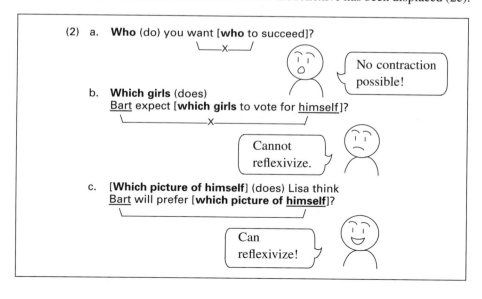

These results also support the view that *wh*-movement is gapped movement. With each of these phenomena, we seem to need to refer to the original position of *wh*- as though it still remained syntactically "active" even after movement. This strongly suggests a gapped movement analysis.

Wh-Movement as Targeted Movement

There is also evidence bearing on the question of whether *wh*-movement in English is targeted or nontargeted. Along with standard *wh*-questions involving a single *wh*-word or *wh*-phrase, English permits so-called multiple *wh*-interrogatives in which more than one *wh*-element occurs:

(3) a. **Who** bought **what**?
    b. I know [**who** bought **what**].
(4) a. **What** did Bart give **to whom**?
    b. I know [**what** Bart gave **to whom**].
(5) a. **Who** gave **what to whom**?
    b. I know [**who** gave **what to whom**].

Questions like these can be difficult to process. However, on reflection their sense is clear enough. Whereas a constituent question with a single *wh*-word requests a single thing as answer, a constituent question with multiple *wh*-words requests pairs, triples, quadruples (etc.) of things as answers. Thus, (3a) asks for pairs of people and things such that the first bought the second. It might be answered, "Bart bought a record," "Lisa bought a book," with emphasis on the subject and object. Similarly, (5a) asks for triples of people and things such that the first gave the second to the third. It might be answered, "Marge gave a record to Bart," "Homer gave a book to Lisa." And so on.

Notice that in multiple *wh*-questions, only one *wh*-phrase can occur initially. We cannot form multiple *wh*-questions as shown in (6)–(8):

(6) a. *****Who what** bought?
    b. *****I know [**who what** bought].
(7) a. *****What to whom** Bart gave?
    b. *****I know [**what to whom** Bart gave].
(8) a. *****Who what to whom** gave?
    b. *****Who what** gave **to whom**?
    c. *****I know [**who what to whom** gave].

Under our movement picture, this means that only one *wh-* may move forward:

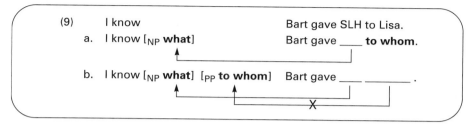

Suppose now that *wh-*words are assigned their own special "parking spot" in English: a position [?] at the beginning of the clause where they, and only they, must land. Then just as we get only one car in a parking space, we will get only one *wh-* at the beginning of a clause. With only one space to land in, *wh-* will "occupy" the space as soon as it moves in, blocking other occupants:

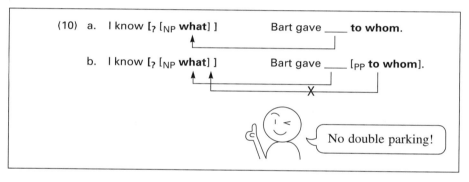

Thus, if we analyze *wh-*movement as targeted movement, we get a grasp on why only one *wh-* appears clause-initially in a multiple *wh-*interrogative.

Movement in CP

Accepting this line of reasoning, what precisely is the designated position **?** that *wh-*items move to? At this point, all we know is that it lies somewhere at the beginning of the clause:

(11) know [**?** [TP Bart PAST [VP gave **what** to Lisa]]]

A Hint from Middle English!

There is interesting evidence from the history of English pointing toward an answer. In Modern English (MoE), forms like (12a–c), in which *wh-* and a complementizer cooccur, are unacceptable:

> (12) a.   *I know **who that** gave SLH to Lisa.
>   b.   *I know **that who** gave SLH to Lisa.
>   c.   *I know **who whether** gave SLH to Lisa.

Interestingly, however, such constructions were apparently quite acceptable in the immediately preceding period of Middle English (ME). Below are some fourteenth-century examples (Allen 1980, pp. 256–257):

> (13) a.   Tel me **what that** ye seken.
>   (Tell me what that you seek.)
>   b.   ... dat noman wist **who dat** hade de better partie.
>   (... that no one knew who that had the better part.)
>   c.   And wyted wel **haus det** hi byed.
>   (And know well whose that they are.)
>   d.   Dan asked he here, **why dat** hyt was dat she suffred swyche peyne.
>   (Then he asked her why that it was that she suffered such pain.)

Observe that *wh-* and *that* coexist peacefully here. This fact suggests that question movement in ME targeted some position to the left of the complementizer.

Articulated CP

Historical data typically involve many unknowns, and when we are working with unknowns, it's usually best to be conservative in our assumptions. Thus, in thinking about ME versus MoE, it is reasonable to *start* from the view that the syntactic differences between the two were minimal.

Suppose, then, that ME and MoE did not differ in their destination for *wh-*. The facts of (13) then suggest that this site lies somewhere to the left of C, but still within the complement clause. The approximate structure of *know what Bart gave to Lisa* thus looks like this:

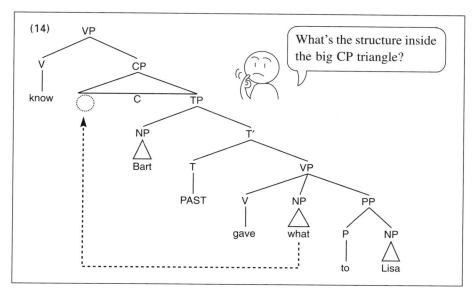

Evidently, to execute this idea we must assume a richer, more articulated structure for CP. What can we say about the structure inside the triangle?

C′

In the tree in (14), there are three main items under CP: *what*, C, and TP. As usual when we have three elements, there are three different ways of grouping them:

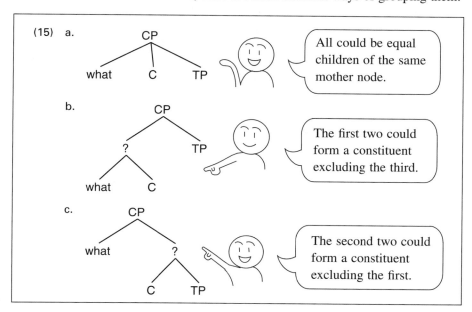

Ellipsis offers potential evidence in favor of the third structure. Observe that it's not generally possible to elide a sentence (TP) after a complementizer:[1]

> (16) a.   *Marge THOUGHT that Lisa was going, but
>   she didn't KNOW **that** Ø. (Ø = *Lisa was going*)
>
>   b.   *Marge asked whether Lisa was going, but
>   Homer didn't know **if/whether** Ø. (Ø = *Lisa was going*)

However, ellipsis *is* possible after a *wh*-phrase in so-called **sluicing constructions** (17a–c).

> (17) a.   Marge said that someone met Lisa, but
>   she didn't know **who** Ø. (Ø = *met Lisa*)
>
>   b.   Marge knew that Homer ate something in the refrigerator,
>   but she didn't know **what** Ø. (Ø = *Homer ate*)
>
>   c.   Burns knew that Smithers left sometime, but
>   he didn't know **when** Ø. (Ø = *Smithers left*)

The data in (16) and (17) look somewhat contradictory at first; in one case it's forbidden to elide a sentence after a CP-initial element, while in the other case it's okay. Note however that structure (15c) would allow us to distinguish the two cases. Suppose that TP-ellipsis is indeed forbidden, but that it is permissible to delete the phrase labeled "?" in (15c), made up of C + TP. Then the two cases can be separated. In (17), we will not be deleting TP; rather, we'll be deleting the **?**-phrase that follows *wh-*.

Adopting (15c), how should we label the intermediate node? Assuming that the larger phrase is CP and that C is its head, the intermediate phrase should be some projection of C. Proceeding as we did with TP and NP, we will label the node "C′". Note the resulting close parallelism between the three categories:

---

1. *That* in (16a) must be pronounced as [thut], to avoid confusion with demonstrative [thæt].

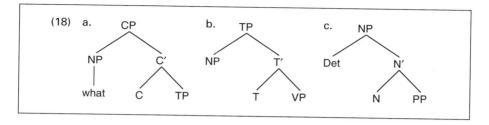

What Is in C Position?

In Tree (14), which shows movement into the articulated CP, the C position is unoccupied. On reflection, however, it seems we must assume that C is filled with a covert element (call it *WH*) that is [+Q].

The reason, once again, is selection. Under principles that we've consistently assumed, the features of an XP percolate up from its X head. An element in specifier position may agree with X, but X must itself bear features if XP is to possess them. In the present case, this means that if a constituent interrogative CP is selected by a higher verb like *wonder* or *inquire*, then that CP must be headed by a [+Q] element. The *wh*-phrase in specifier position may also carry [+Q] and agree, but there must be an independent head of CP (*WH*) to provide the [+Q] feature:

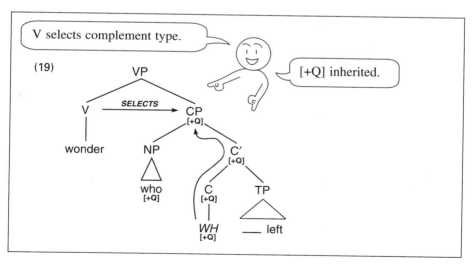

Hence, it seems we must assume a covert [+Q] complementizer in constituent interrogatives.

Matrix Interrogatives

Main clause or **matrix** constituent interrogatives, which we have not considered so far, provide additional support for the articulated CP structure.

Matrix and embedded constituent interrogatives look similar in one set of cases, namely, when the subject is questioned:

(20) a. **Who** drank the beer?
      b. Homer wonders [**who** drank the beer].

However, whenever anything *other* than the subject is questioned, matrix and embedded forms diverge. In matrix interrogatives with a modal, the modal gets fronted along with the *wh*-phrase. This doesn't happen in the embedded form. Compare (21a,b):

(21)   Homer **will** drink beer.
      a. **What will** Homer   drink ___ ?
      b. Marge wonders [**what** Homer **will** drink].
          (cf. *Marge wonders [what will Homer drink].)

In matrix forms with a tensed verb, a tensed version of the verb *do* gets fronted along with the *wh*-phrase and the main verb appears untensed. Again, this doesn't happen in the embedded form. Compare (22a,b):

(22)   Homer **drank** beer.
      a. What **did** Homer **drink** ___ ?
      b. Marge wonders [**what** Homer drank].
          (cf. *Marge wonders [what did Homer drink].)

Observe now that under the articulated-CP analysis, there are *two* positions open above TP in an interrogative: a *wh*-position (circled in (23a)) and a head position (C). A very simple idea is to analyze matrix interrogatives like (21a) and (22a) as undergoing "double movement," with the *wh*-phrase raising to the *wh*-position and the T element raising to C. This will derive the correct word order (23b):

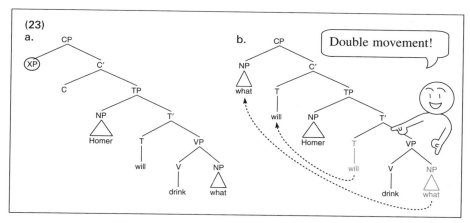

In the case of (22b), we could say that when the tense is raised away from its corresponding main verb, it gets "spelled out" by means of the "dummy verb" *do*. Specifically, a raised PAST is spelled out as *did*:

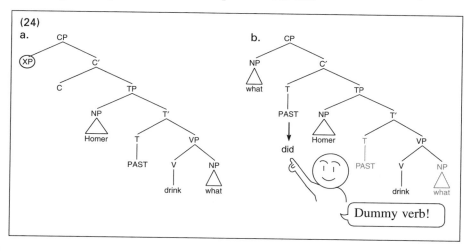

Thus, our articulated structure for CP provides a natural way of understanding some additional complexities involved with matrix constituent interrogatives.

Constraints on Movement I

Review

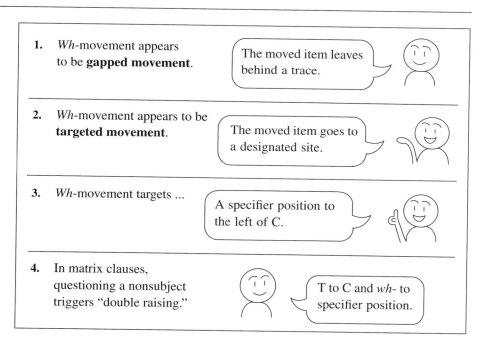

1. *Wh*-movement appears to be **gapped movement**.

   The moved item leaves behind a trace.

2. *Wh*-movement appears to be **targeted movement**.

   The moved item goes to a designated site.

3. *Wh*-movement targets ...

   A specifier position to the left of C.

4. In matrix clauses, questioning a nonsubject triggers "double raising."

   T to C and *wh*- to specifier position.

"Long-Distance" Movement

The cases of *wh*-movement we have examined so far all involve "short" *wh*-movement from within a sentence (TP) to the CP immediately above it:

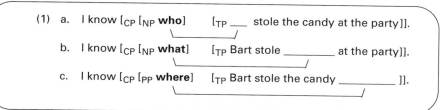

(1) a. I know [CP [NP **who**]   [TP ___ stole the candy at the party]].

     b. I know [CP [NP **what**]   [TP Bart stole _____ at the party]].

     c. I know [CP [PP **where**]   [TP Bart stole the candy _____]].

But English (and many other languages) allow "long" movement across much greater distances. Consider (2a), for instance. If you reflect on the meaning of the embedded question, you'll see that the *wh*-word *what* appearing after *know* originates far down inside a whole series of embedded CPs: it starts out as the object of *steal* (2b):

> (2) a.   I know what Marge believes (that) Lisa said (that) Bart stole.
>   b.   I know [_{CP} what Marge believes [_{CP} (that) Lisa said [_{CP} (that) Bart stole ___]]].

> **? QUESTION**   How exactly does *what* get from the trace position to the highest embedded CP?

The most obvious idea is that it moves directly from the trace position to the site where we actually "hear it," something like this:

> (3)   I know [_{CP} **what** Marge believes [_{CP} (that) Lisa said [_{CP} (that) Bart stole __]]].

On this view, *wh*-items leap over the material intervening between their "launching" and "landing" sites, and we therefore wouldn't expect this material to affect the well-formedness of the sentence. Perhaps surprisingly, however, intervening material and its structure *do* seem to matter. They do affect well-formedness!

Complex NPs

Consider the examples in (4)–(6):

> (4) a.   I know that Lisa believes that Bart stole the candy.
>   b.   I know **what** Lisa believes that Bart stole ___ .
> (5) a.   I know that Lisa believes the claim that Bart stole the candy.
>   b.   *I know **what** Lisa believes the claim that Bart stole ___ .
> (6) a.   I wonder **which candy** Bart denies that he stole ___ .
>   b.   *I wonder **which candy** Bart denies the insinuation that he stole ___ .

If you examine the trees for these examples, you'll see a pattern. In each case, movement out of a structure like (7) is okay:

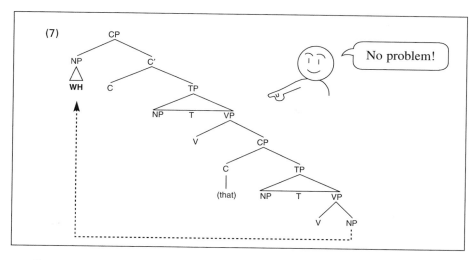

But we encounter trouble with (8):

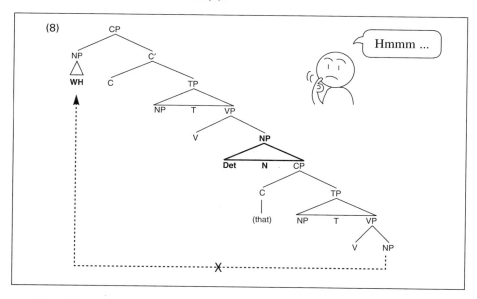

The difference is that in (8), but not in (7), there is intervening NP structure. This somehow seems to interfere with movement out of the lower TP.

Sentential Subjects

Let's look at another case of "blocked movement." There are sentences of English whose subjects are themselves sentences:

(9) a. [That the fuel rods were lost] bothered Mr. Burns.
    b. [That Bart got an A on his spelling test] surprised everyone.
    c. [That Lisa plays saxophone] is well-known.

Plausibly, these have a structure like (10), with a CP in subject position (ignoring the X-bar violation for now):

Observe now what happens when we try to form a constituent interrogative from (9a–c) by questioning something inside the sentential subject:

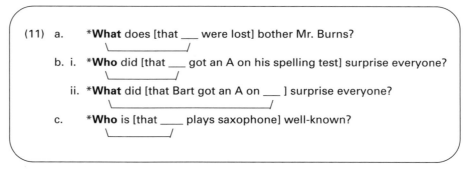

The resulting sentences are very bad. Evidently, sentential subjects also constitute some sort of barrier to movement:

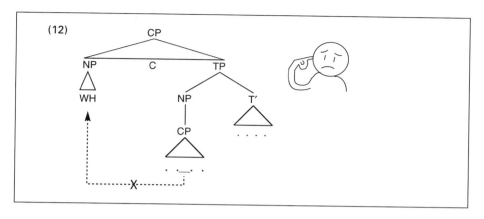

(12)

Wh-Islands

Finally, reconsider familiar embedded interrogatives:

(13) a. Marge wondered [CP **who** stole the candy at the party].
      b. Marge asked Homer [CP **what** Bart did at the party].
      c. Lisa wonders [CP **where** Bart hid the candy].

We can form questions from (13a–c) by questioning material from the *matrix* clause:

(14) a. Who ___ wondered [CP **who** stole the candy at the party]?
      b. Who did Marge ask ___ [CP **what** Bart did at the party]?
      c. Who ___ wonders [CP **where** Bart hid the candy]?

But note that when we try to question material from the *embedded* interrogative clause—that is, when we attempt *wh*-movement out of the bracketed portion in (13)—the result is very bad:

(15) a. ****What** does Marge wonder [CP **who** stole ___ at the party]?
      b. ****Who** did Marge ask Homer [CP **what** ___ did at the party]?
      c. ****What** does Lisa wonder [CP **where** Bart hid ___]?

Thus, we have yet another problematic structure for movement—configurations of this kind:

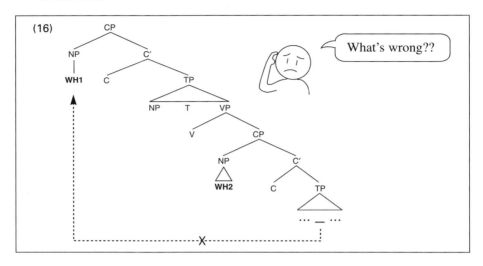

(16)

Stepwise Movement

These results are puzzling if *wh*-movement raises a question phrase directly from trace position to surface position in one fell swoop. As noted, under this idea we don't expect intervening material to affect well-formedness. So what *is* going on here? How are we to understand these limitations? What is causing them?

To get a hint, consider the problematic movement structures again, specifically, the examples in (15). These were cases where we tried to move a *wh*-phrase out of a CP whose specifier was already occupied by a *wh*-phrase. Does this suggest anything? Recall our conclusion from the last unit that *wh*-movement is *targeted* movement, and that its target is precisely the specifier of CP (hereafter, **CP Spec**).

Suppose we said that instead of moving directly from trace to surface position in one long jump, *wh*-words "climb the tree" in little jumps, moving from CP Spec to CP Spec. On this idea, a sentence like (17a) would not have the "long-distance movement" derivation in (17b). Rather, it would have the "stepwise movement" derivation in (17c):

(17) a. Who do you think (that) Marge believes (that) Lisa kissed ____ ?

b.

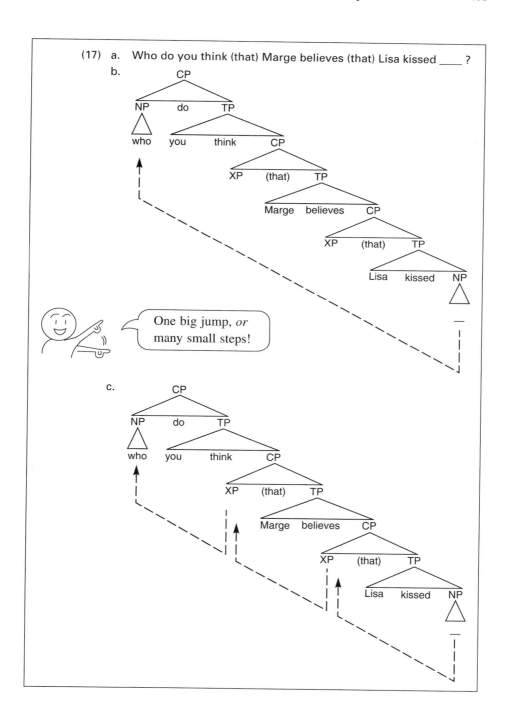

One big jump, *or* many small steps!

c.

In (17c), *wh-* moves incrementally upward.

How does this help with our indirect question examples? Well, notice that in (16) movement of WH1 to the lower CP Spec is blocked by the presence of WH2. The latter already occupies the only available target position in CP. Supposing then that *wh*-movement *must* go from CP Spec to CP Spec position, an indirect question will create an "island" for further movement. Once *wh-* moves into CP Spec, the only "escape hatch" from the sentence will be blocked for further movement.

A Problem

This idea looks pretty slick, but does it really work? Here is an apparent problem that you might have just noticed. Reconsider (15a):

(15a)   *What does Marge wonder who stole ___ at the party?

We said this was bad because *what* cannot go through the lower CP Spec, which is plugged by *who*. But isn't there another derivation for (15a) that is okay?

Suppose we start with (18):

(18)   [$_{CP2}$ Marge wonder [$_{CP1}$ **who** stole **what** at the party]]

First, we move *what* to the *lower* CP Spec:

(19)   [$_{CP2}$ Marge wonder [$_{CP1}$ **what who** stole ____ at the party]]

Then we move *what* into the *upper* CP Spec:

(20)   [$_{CP2}$ **What** does Marge wonder [$_{CP1}$ ____ **who** stole ____ at the party]]?

Finally, we move *who* into the lower CP:

(21)   [$_{CP2}$ **What** does Marge wonder [$_{CP1}$ **who** ____ stole ____ at the party]]?

There are no obvious problems with this derivation. Both *wh*'s move only to CP Spec positions, and the lower CP Spec is unplugged at the point where *who* finally gets around to moving in. Nonetheless, we must find some principled way of ruling out derivations like (18)–(21); otherwise, our account of why (15a) is bad will fail.

The Principle of the Strict Cycle

As it turns out, there is a special aspect of the derivation in (18)–(21) that we might want to exclude. Reflect on the way we moved the *wh*-words around in getting the problematic result. First we did movement in the smaller, inner clause (CP1). Then we did movement in the larger, outer clause (CP2). Then we went back to the inner clause (CP1) and did movement again.

This kind of derivation violates a natural principle that has been found to apply in a number of areas of linguistics (including morphology and phonology)—what we might call the **Principle of the Strict Cycle**. We will formulate the idea like this:

> **Principle of the Strict Cycle**
> Suppose rule R can apply in syntactic domains D and D′, where D is a subdomain of D′. Then if R has applied in D′, it cannot later apply in D.

In other words, suppose you have a rule R that applies in some syntactic domain D, which is part of some larger domain D′, where R can also apply. Then if you apply R in D, and later apply it in D′, you are not permitted to go back down into the subdomain D and apply R again.

Let's see how the Principle of the Strict Cycle applies in our problem case. Consider the (simplified) tree in (22):

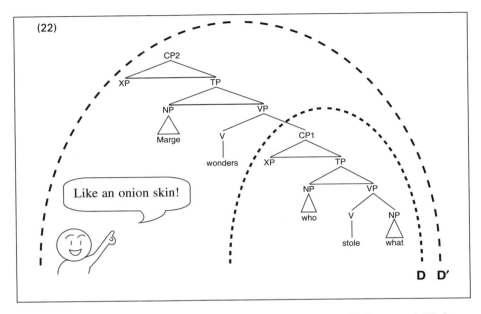

(22)

Like an onion skin!

We have said that *wh*-movement goes from CP Spec to CP Spec, and CP Specs occur in the category CP. Thus, CP is clearly the domain in which *wh*-movement applies. What the Principle of the Strict Cycle says with respect to (22) is therefore this: You are allowed to apply *wh*-movement in domain D (CP1), and subsequently in domain D′ (CP2). But once you go to the larger, more inclusive domain D′, there is no going back down into the smaller D to apply *wh*-movement in D.

But this is exactly what we have done in the derivation (18)–(21). (Look back at Steps (20) and (21)!) Thus, the Principle of the Strict Cycle guarantees that when CPs are layered like an onion, as in (22), we must apply relevant rules on a layer-by-layer basis. And once we move to an outer layer, inner layers become inaccessible.

Constraints on Movement II

Review

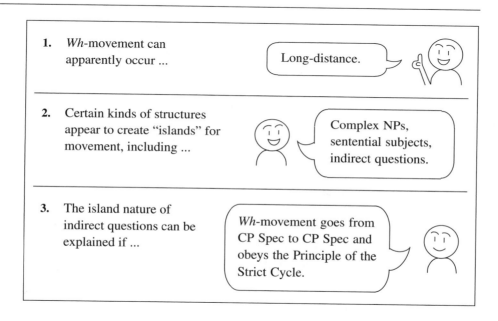

1. *Wh*-movement can apparently occur ...

   Long-distance.

2. Certain kinds of structures appear to create "islands" for movement, including ...

   Complex NPs, sentential subjects, indirect questions.

3. The island nature of indirect questions can be explained if ...

   Wh-movement goes from CP Spec to CP Spec and obeys the Principle of the Strict Cycle.

NP Domains

Our explanation for why indirect questions are islands for movement seems natural enough. But it's not clear that the idea will extend to other cases of blocked movement. In complex NP violations like (1a), and sentential subject violations like (1b), there does not appear to be any problem with a "plugged" CP Spec. Rather, the problem seems to lie in movement out of NPs:

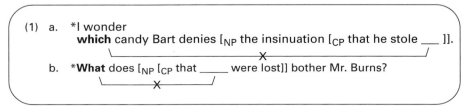

(1) a. *I wonder
which candy Bart denies [_{NP} the insinuation [_{CP} that he stole ___]].

  b. ***What** does [_{NP} [_{CP} that _____ were lost]] bother Mr. Burns?

(1a) and (1b) both have an NP node intervening between the target CP Spec position and the trace site. We might suspect that this shared feature has something to do with the impossibility of movement. But how can we relate this to what we've seen so far?

Movement and Complete Sentences

Let's approach this question by asking a more general one. We've seen that we can account for certain restrictions on *wh*-movement by assuming that it climbs CPs from Spec to Spec. But why should things be like this? Why should movement have this "local" character, where *wh*-phrases relocate in little hops, instead of big jumps?

It isn't obvious where such a constraint might come from; however, one idea might be that it reflects (at some level) the way the human language faculty computes and assigns interpretations to sentences. Spec-to-Spec movement might follow somehow from the "architecture" of this faculty.

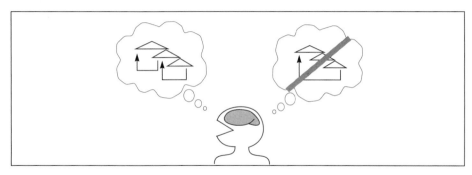

We know that the language faculty computes representations for sentences in "chunks," so that we derive the structure and meaning of a sentence via the structure and meaning of its parts, and how those parts go together. As we have seen, this idea explains why speakers can understand and assign structures to a potentially infinite set of sentences; they do so through knowledge of a constructive procedure of this kind.

"Complete Thoughts"

Among the chunks that are computed are sentencelike ones, domains like TP (S). These are widely viewed as having a privileged status. In traditional terms, sentences are the special grammatical objects that "express a complete thought," that can "stand on their own" as a piece of discourse, that can be true or false, and so on. Suppose this special status is enforced by a grammatical constraint; informally:

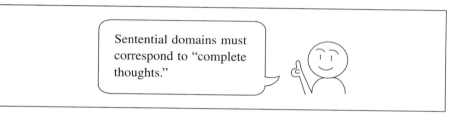

> Sentential domains must correspond to "complete thoughts."

Now compare the sentences in (2). In both examples, the smaller TP (indicated with brackets) is incomplete. It fails to "express a complete thought" because a part of it is missing: the locative PP required by *put*.

(2) a.   On the kitchen wall,
Marge claimed that [Bart put a picture of Elvira ___].   √
 b.   Marge claimed that [Bart put a picture of Elvira ___].   ×

Nonetheless, there is an important difference in the two cases. Although (2a) is incomplete in the smaller TP, it is complete in the larger one: the PP missing from the embedded TP is found in the matrix TP. We might put this by saying that although (2a) is locally incomplete, it is globally complete. By contrast, (2b) is both locally and globally incomplete: the required PP is simply nowhere to be found.

Marking the Edge

Given that (2a) is grammatical, it seems that local incompleteness is tolerated in language. Suppose we think of Spec-to-Spec movement as responsible for this fact. Specifically, suppose CP Spec—the left edge of the clause—represents a place where we can formally "register" or mark TP as containing missing elements. Suppose further that if such registration is made, we are excused from the requirement that the TP be complete. In effect, the grammar says, "Okay, this is a TP whose contents will be completed later, so let it pass."

To see how these ideas work, let's look at (3a) and its phrase marker (3b). The *wh*-word advances from CP Spec to CP Spec, each time leaving a trace (t). TP1 is incomplete in virtue of the *wh*-NP that has been moved out of it, but this fact is registered by the trace of *wh* in CP1 Spec, so the structure satisfies completeness. TP2 is incomplete for the same reason, but again this fact is registered by the *wh*-trace in CP2 Spec. Finally, TP3 is incomplete in virtue of the missing NP, but the missing item is present in CP3 Spec. So the sentence is now globally complete.

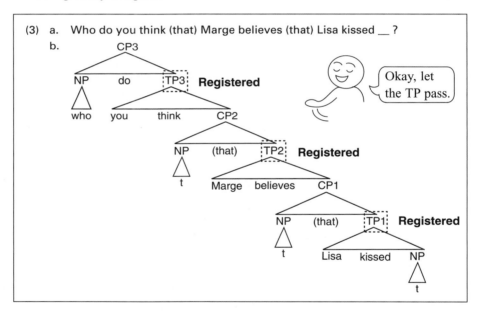

(3) a. Who do you think (that) Marge believes (that) Lisa kissed __ ?

Compare this with the case of *wh*-movement out of an embedded constituent interrogative: (4a) and its phrase marker (4b). The lower TP is an incomplete sentence, but its incompleteness is not registered in this case. No trace of *what* appears in the lower CP. Hence, this example is ruled out.

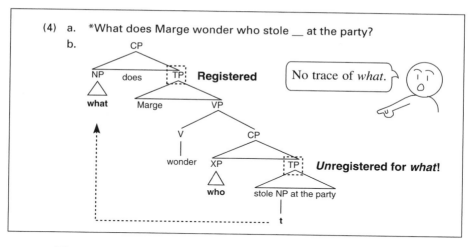

(4) a. *What does Marge wonder who stole ___ at the party?

b.

CP

NP does TP **Registered**   No trace of *what.*

what Marge VP

V CP

wonder XP TP **Unregistered for *what*!**

who stole NP at the party

t

Thus, the stepwise path of *wh*-words follows from the fact that, if the grammar is to have long-distance movement and still satisfy the completeness requirement, this must be achieved by a series of local movements that formally register the incompleteness of each intervening TP node.

Movement and Nominals

Let's now consider our other cases of blocked movement: movement from complex NPs and sentential subjects. We noted that these structures involve intervening NP material (1), and we speculated that this had something to do with their ill-formedness.

Assuming the picture of *wh*-movement sketched above, we can make a connection. Recall that TPs are not the only sentencelike domains. Some NPs have this character, too. Reconsider the close parallels between sentences like (5a,b) and NPs like (6a,b):

(5) a. Homer refused the offer.
    b. Mr. Burns destroyed the city.

(6) a. Homer's refusal of the offer
    b. Mr. Burns's destruction of the city

As we observed, the structure of these phrases is very similar. The examples in (5) have the form in (7a), and the examples in (6) have the form in (7b):

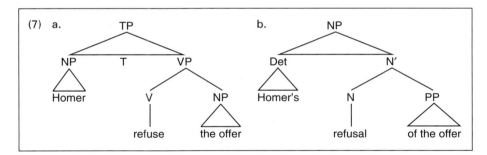

One fact about TPs and sentencelike NPs that *is* quite different, however, is that the former have an associated "supersentence" category CP, containing a Spec position XP (8a). There is no parallel "supernominal" category ?P with a Spec position XP that can be the target of *wh*-movement (8b):

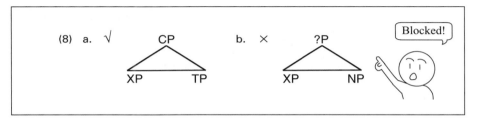

These points suggest a natural extension of our general approach to blocked movement. Given the sentencelike nature of NP nodes, assume that they too fall under the "completeness condition" discussed earlier. But given the fact that NPs have no higher "supercategory," there will be no parallel means of registering local incompleteness for them as we did for TP. This means that movement out of a sentencelike NP will always violate the completeness condition.

The Phase Principle

Let us collect these assumptions, stating them in an exact way. We will call the sentencelike nodes that require completeness **phases**. According to what we have seen, TP and some NP are phases in English. Now we will state the following condition on incomplete phases—phases containing a missing element:

> **The Phase Principle**
> An incomplete phase must be registered at its edge by a trace of the missing element or the element itself.

"The edge of a phase" is to be understood as the maximal projection immediately dominating that phase. Hence, the Phase Principle requires either of the situations shown in (9), where α is a phase, β is the category immediately dominating α, and [$_{XP}$ *wh/t*] is either the *wh*-item or its trace.

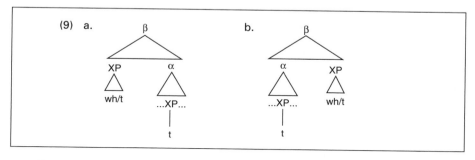

The Phase Principle will correctly account for the two cases of blocked movement from NPs introduced in Unit 26. Movement out of a complex NP will yield a violation, since the NP will constitute an incomplete phase whose incompleteness is not registered at its edge:

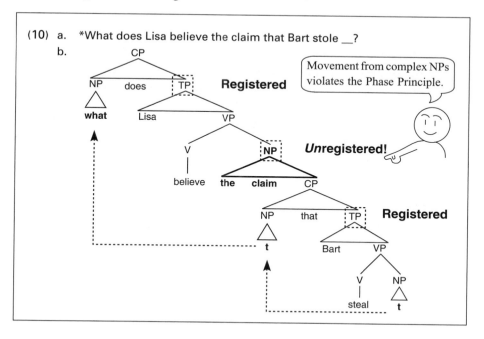

Movement out of a sentential subject will yield a violation for the same reason. Once again there will be an NP phase that contains missing material, but is not registered as such:

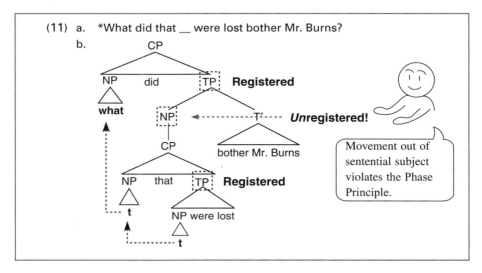

(11) a.   *What did that __ were lost bother Mr. Burns?
     b.

     Movement out of sentential subject violates the Phase Principle.

Summarizing, then, we see that the requirement that movement obey the Phase Principle formally captures our idea that certain domains in the clause must be complete, and, if not, then "registered" in an appropriate way. Assuming that being registered means having a trace at the phase edge, the Phase Principle forces movement to go stepwise from CP Spec to CP Spec if a *wh*-word or phrase is to be able to escape its clause of origin. Where no Spec is available, no movement will be possible.

Parametric Variation

Review

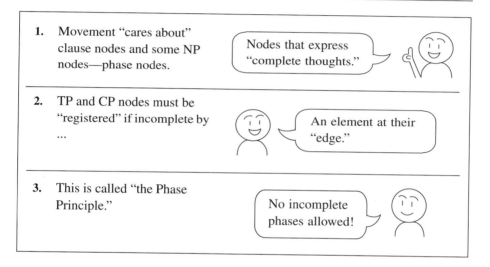

1. Movement "cares about" clause nodes and some NP nodes—phase nodes.

   Nodes that express "complete thoughts."

2. TP and CP nodes must be "registered" if incomplete by ...

   An element at their "edge."

3. This is called "the Phase Principle."

   No incomplete phases allowed!

Crosslinguistic Variation in Movement

We have observed various facts about movement in English, and we've explored ideas like the Phase Principle in attempting to account for them. Now consider the following simple question: Do the same facts hold in languages other than English? Do other languages behave the same way regarding what kinds of phrases move, and how far?

The question is important. A key goal of linguistic theory is to discover the general rules and principles arising out of the universal, genetically determined, human linguistic mechanism. The Phase Principle seems like a good candidate for a general principle of this kind, since we motivated it on very broad conceptual grounds. But how would we square such a principle with crosslinguistic variation, if it occurred? How could something universal allow for variation?

German

As a matter of fact, variation in movement patterns does occur. Consider Standard German, for example. In German, *wh*-movement is fully acceptable in simple clauses or in the matrix portion of sentences with embedding:

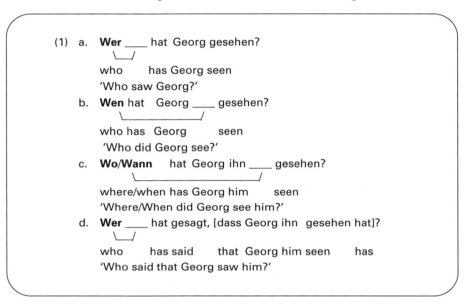

(1) a. **Wer** ____ hat Georg gesehen?

      who   has Georg seen

      'Who saw Georg?'

   b. **Wen** hat   Georg ____ gesehen?

      who has Georg   seen

      'Who did Georg see?'

   c. **Wo/Wann**   hat Georg ihn ____ gesehen?

      where/when has Georg him   seen

      'Where/When did Georg see him?'

   d. **Wer** ____ hat gesagt, [dass Georg ihn gesehen hat]?

      who   has said   that Georg him seen   has

      'Who said that Georg saw him?'

But movement out of a tensed sentence is considerably more problematic in Standard German:

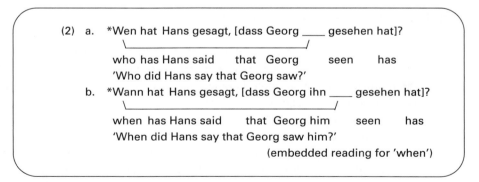

(2) a. *Wen hat Hans gesagt, [dass Georg ____ gesehen hat]?

      who has Hans said   that Georg   seen   has

      'Who did Hans say that Georg saw?'

   b. *Wann hat Hans gesagt, [dass Georg ihn ____ gesehen hat]?

      when has Hans said   that Georg him   seen   has

      'When did Hans say that Georg saw him?'

                       (embedded reading for 'when')

Thus, movements of a sort allowed in English are not allowed in German.

Italian

By contrast, certain movements that would be impossible in English appear to be fully grammatical in Italian. Compare (3a)/(4a), observed by the linguist Luigi Rizzi, with their English equivalents (3b)/(4b):

> (3) a. Il solo incarico che non sapevi [a chi avrebbero affidato t] e poi finito proprio a te.
>   b. *The only charge which you didn't know [to whom they would entrust t] has been entrusted exactly to you.
> (4) a. Tuo fratello, a cui mi domando [che storie abbiano raccontato t], era molto preoccupato.
>   b. *Your brother, to whom I wonder [what stories they told t], was very troubled.

Despite the nearly word-for-word matchup in the two sets of examples, the Italian cases are acceptable whereas the English ones are not. Nonetheless, it's not true that "anything goes" in Italian. *Wh*-extractions from complex NPs and sentential subjects are just as bad in Italian as they are in English.

"Parameterizing" Principles

One important move that linguists can make in accounting for variation like this is to try to "parameterize" their principles: to state them in a way that allows for a degree of variation, an idea due to Rizzi. To give a brief example, reconsider the Phase Principle:

> **The Phase Principle**
> An incomplete phase must be registered at its edge by a trace of the missing element or the element itself.

This principle requires incomplete phases to be registered. But notice that it doesn't actually say what a phase is. We have taken the view that sentences (TPs) and certain nominals (NPs) are phases, because they are both sentencelike. But are these the only possibilities? What about CPs, for instance? They are sentence-like, too. Could they also be phases, in place of, or perhaps in addition to, TPs?

Suppose we allow the definition of a phase to differ across languages. The principle itself would remain valid for all languages. However, an important aspect of it—the notion of phase—would take on the status of a "variable" or parameter. Its value would be allowed to change so that one language might have nodes X and Y as its phases, whereas another might have X and Z (partial over-lap), or another W and Z (nonoverlap).

CP and NP as Phase Nodes (Italian?)

As it turns out, a difference in our definition of phase will predict differences in movement possibilities under the Phase Principle, as noted by Rizzi. For example, reconsider the schematic diagram of movement from a *wh*-island (reproduced in (5)). If TP is a phase, then this movement violates our principle and is predicted to be bad: the lower TP is crossed with no registration at its edge:

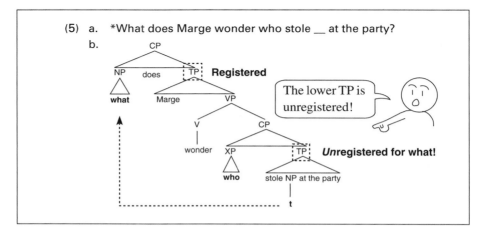

(5) a. *What does Marge wonder who stole __ at the party?

Suppose however that we replace TP with CP as our phase node. *Wh*- now leaves only *one* CP node below it in edge position (6):

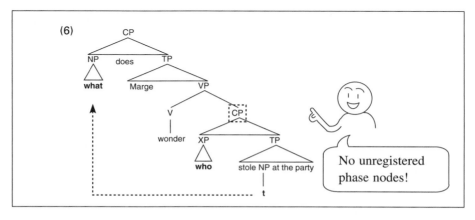

Suppose further that we can regard the high CP Spec position as registering the lower CP node. (Even though the upper CP does not dominate the lower CP immediately, there are no phase nodes between them.) Then, with TP rather than CP as a phase node, our prediction about movement out of *wh*-islands changes. With TP, movement is predicted to be unacceptable. With CP, it is predicted to be acceptable.

Continuing, consider the schematic diagram of movement from a complex NP (reproduced in (7)). Again if TP and NP are phase nodes, then this movement violates the Phase Principle: NP is crossed with no registration at its edge:

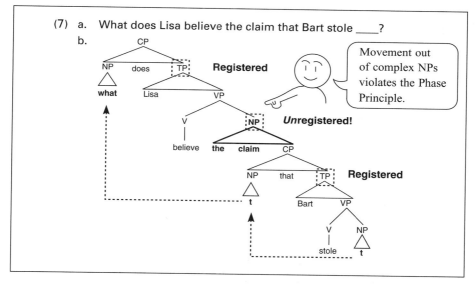

Suppose now that CP and NP were our phase nodes. Interestingly, we get the same result. *Wh-* crosses both CP and NP before achieving an edge position; this leaves the lower CP unregistered:

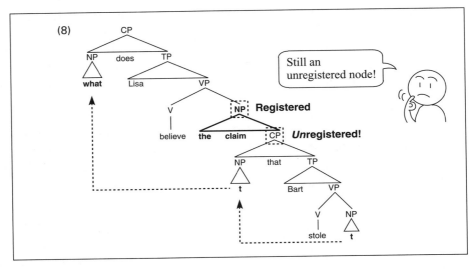

Hence, with CP and NP as phase nodes, movement from a complex NP is still predicted to be ungrammatical.

Finally, reconsider movement out of a sentential subject. With TP and NP as phase nodes, movement is blocked:

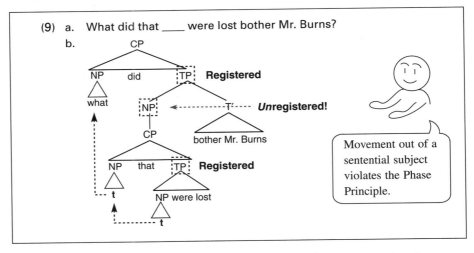

But with CP and NP as phase nodes, we get the same result! Again *wh-* crosses two phase nodes before landing in edge position (10), so it can register only one:

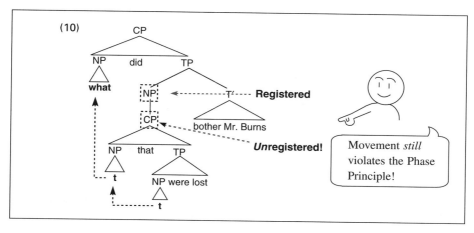

In summary, then, a language with CP and NP as its phase nodes would contrast with English in movement possibilities. Like English, it would disallow movement out of complex NPs and sentential subjects. But unlike English, it would permit movement from a *wh*-island. These are exactly the Italian facts. Italian disallows movement from complex NPs and sentential subjects, but allows it from *wh*-islands ((3) and (4)). Varying phase nodes would thus allow us to capture the English/Italian contrasts.

CP, TP, *and* NP as Phase Nodes (German?)

We can perform a similar thought experiment with the case where CP doesn't replace TP as a phase node, but rather is added to it. Such a language would have three phase nodes (CP, TP, NP) instead of two, and movement possibilities would become much more restricted.

Under this option, movements within a simple clause would be predicted to be acceptable, as they are in English. Relocating *wh*- to CP Spec crosses only one phase node (TP) before an edge position is achieved:

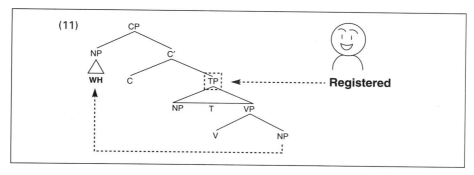

However, any movement out of embedded clauses—even stepwise movement of the kind that English permits!—would be ruled out. Such movement will always cross both a TP and a CP node, with at most one of them registered at an edge:

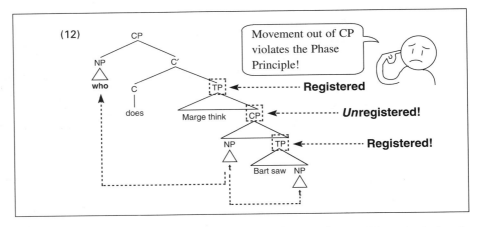

Thus, a language with CP, TP, *and* NP as phase nodes would contrast sharply with English. Like English, it would allow movement in simple clauses or within the matrix clause of an embedded structure. But it would allow no movement out of embedded clauses, ruling out cases of stepwise movement that are perfectly acceptable in English.

 **EXERCISE**   Show with diagrams that a language with CP, TP, and NP as its phase nodes will also block movement from *wh*-islands, complex NPs, and sentential subjects.

Notice now that this constellation of predictions matches the German facts. German allows movement in simple clauses and in the matrix clause of an embedded structure (1a–d). But it forbids movement out of embedded clauses (2a,b).

Language Learning as "Parameter Setting"

The picture arising from this discussion is an attractive one. We can view the human language faculty as endowing learners with a fixed set of principles, each containing parameters subject to a small degree of variation. The learner's task thus reduces to setting or "fixing" the values of those parameters on the basis of the data he or she is exposed to.

In the case of movement principles, all children would come equipped with a Phase Principle "hardwired" in. But their own particular language environment would give them different clues for the correct phase node settings of their language. A child learning English would receive evidence that TP and some NPs are phase nodes. A child learning Italian would receive evidence for CP and NP. And a child learning German would receive evidence showing that TP, CP, and NP are the correct phase node choices. Once these values are determined, nothing else need be said. Possible and impossible movements will simply follow from the Phase Principle applying in the context of those phase node choices. Variation in languages will thus follow from parametric differences of these kinds.

In recent years, this principles-and-parameters approach to linguistic variation has been widely pursued. Linguists are actively searching for fixed, invariant principles determined by Universal Grammar that at the same time leave room for minor variation in their application. Through this model, it is hoped that we may one day be able to answer the question of how a biologically given human language faculty that is presumably common across the species and constrains language acquisition sharply in the way that it must, nonetheless allows for the apparently rich variation in grammatical systems that it does.

There is also a methodological lesson here that is worth carrying away. When we come up against languages that diverge from what we find in English, it is very often far from obvious that the differences are what they seem. Variation can be of a highly restricted kind and can follow from other differences by a rather complex chain of connections—like the effects of phase node choice. Therefore we don't, and shouldn't, discard hard-won principles like our Phase Principle in the face of variation. Rather, we try to generalize the principles in appropriate ways. In modern linguistics, this strategy has been successful to a remarkable degree.

EXERCISES

1. Give justifiable pre- and postmovement structures for each of the following examples. If the example is ambiguous, having more than one plausible tree, then note this and choose one pre- and postmovement structure pair:

    (1) Which brother of a friend of Bart recognized that visitor from Springfield?

    (2) Lisa asked which picture of Maggie in Milhouse's sister's brother's room fell on the floor.

    (3) How proud of Bart does Marge think Homer believes Mr. Burns is?

    (4) Homer put in the basement all of the old trash from the garage sale.

    (5) Homer's claim that the universe was square during that early period made us nervous.

    (6) Marge said Smithers asked when the audit occurred.

    (7) Marge said Smithers panicked when the audit occurred.

    (8) Homer, Marge doesn't think that Burns will ever promote to a supervisor position.

    (9) Lisa thinks that Bart may become a criminal in the future, and Principal Skinner thinks that he may too.

    (10) Under which piece of furniture does Marge think Maggie put her sticky candy?

    (11) Did Bart ask whether Homer knew who might come to his graduation?

    (12) Unfortunately, Homer worded carelessly a very important letter about his job.

    (13) At that time, Marge didn't know whether Homer would lose weight or change to a different job.

    (14) Who knows what who said to who?

    (15) How and why we should draw phrase markers in a particular way is not always obvious.

2. Consider the questions in (1) and (2) and the ambiguous example in (3):

   (1)   Who can Smithers persuade to visit Mr. Burns?

   (2)   Where will Marge expect Homer to put the ladder?

   (3)   Lisa wondered when Bart said she saw Nelson.

   A.   Give the premovement structure for (1).

   B.   Give the postmovement structure for (2).

   C.   Give both pre- and postmovement structures for the ambiguous (3).

3. Consider the following constituent question of English:

   (1)   How will Homer word the letter?

   Now do the following:

   A.   Give a sentence that would be a plausible answer to the question in (1).

   B.   Draw a phrase marker for the underlying form of (1). That is, draw a tree diagram that shows where the *wh*-phrase in (1) is located *before it moves*. (Assume that *how* is an AdvP.)

   C.   Draw a phrase marker for the surface form of (1). That is, draw a tree diagram that shows where the *wh*-phrase in (1) is located *after it has moved*. (Don't forget the movement of *will*!)

4. Next, consider the following constituent question of English:

   (1)   How long will Homer claim that the party lasted yesterday?

   Now do the following:

   A.   Give a sentence that would be a plausible answer to the question in (1), and that follows its form.

   B.   Draw a phrase marker for the underlying form of (1). That is, draw a tree diagram that shows where the *wh*-phrase in (1) is located *before it moves*.

   C.   Draw a phrase marker for the surface form of (1). That is, draw a tree diagram that shows where the *wh*-phrase in (1) is located *after it has moved*. (Use a triangle for the upper part of the structure.)

5. Give postmovement structures for the sentences in (1) and (2), and indicate the path that the *wh*-word or *wh*-phrase follows. Be sure to include all relevant parts of structure (tenses, traces, *PRO*s, etc.).

   (1)   Homer wondered what Bart claimed Lisa said Maggie ate.

   (2)   Marge asked where Homer thought Lisa said she saw Bart.
         (on the reading in which *where* questions the place of seeing)

6. Indicate the phase nodes that are relevant in the movements shown in (1)–(3). You will probably want to draw trees for these cases.

    (1)   Who does Homer think Bart believes that Lisa likes t ?

                                                     ("1-step" derivation)

    (2)   Who did Mr. Burns claim Homer forced t to visit Moe?

                                  ("1-step" derivation)

    (3)   Which person does it appear that Homer wants to talk to t?

                          A   B   ("2-step" derivation)

7. English contains adverbial clauses like *before Bart chased Lisa, while Maggie slept, because Homer likes beer*, and *in case Marge bakes cookies*. What is their internal structure? Two hypotheses are shown here. The first, Tree (1), analyzes adverbial clauses as PPs with P taking a TP complement. The second, Tree (2), analyzes them as PPs with P taking a full CP (containing an inaudible C *THAT*).

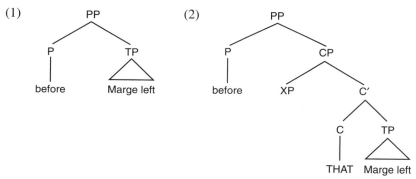

Using the Phase Principle, construct an argument for Tree (1) based on the facts in (3)–(7). Use the four-part form for arguments, making all steps in your argument explicit.

    (3)   a.   Bart ate the cookies [before Marge served the milk].

          b.   *What did Bart eat the cookies [before Marge served t]?

    (4)   a.   Lisa left the library [after she met Milhouse].

          b.   *Who did Lisa leave the library [after she met t]?

    (5)   a.   Bart crept out [while Homer slept in the chair].

          b.   *What did Bart creep out [while Homer slept in t]?

(6) a.   Moe respects Homer [because / although he likes anchovies].

    b.   *What does Moe respect Homer [because / although he likes t]?

(7) a.   Marge carries acorns [in case / unless she sees squirrels].

    b.   *What does Marge carry acorns [in case / unless she sees t]?

8. The question in (1) is ambiguous. It can be understood as inquiring about the time of Bart's claiming or about the time of Milhouse's visiting Springfield.

(1)   When did Bart claim that Milhouse visited Springfield?

By contrast, the question in (2) is unambiguous. It can only be understood as inquiring about the time of Bart's asking.

(2)   When did Bart ask whether Milhouse visited Springfield?

Explain why (1) is ambiguous. Give phrase markers corresponding to its two different readings. Then explain why (2) is unambiguous. Give a phrase marker corresponding to its one available reading, and explain why the reading where it asks about the time of Milhouse's visiting Springfield is not available.

References

Allen, Cynthia. 1980. *Topics in diachronic syntax.* New York: Garland.

Asimov, Isaac. 1965. *A short history of chemistry.* New York: Anchor Books.

Bresnan, Joan. 1982. *The mental representation of grammatical relations.* Cambridge, MA: MIT Press.

Chomsky, Noam. 1957. *Syntactic structures.* The Hague: Mouton.

Chomsky, Noam. 1970. Remarks on nominalization. In *Readings in English transformational grammar*, ed. by Roderick A. Jacobs and Peter S. Rosenbaum, 184–221. Waltham, MA: Ginn.

Chomsky, Noam. 1972. *Language and mind.* New York: Harcourt, Brace, Jovanovich.

Chomsky, Noam. 1975. *The logical structure of linguistic theory.* Chicago: University of Chicago Press.

Chomsky, Noam. 1977. *Language and responsibility.* New York: Pantheon Books.

Chomsky, Noam. 1986. *Knowledge of language.* New York: Praeger.

Chomsky, Noam. 1988. *Language and problems of knowledge.* Cambridge, MA: MIT Press.

Chomsky, Noam. 2000a. Language as a natural object. In Chomsky 2000b, 106–133.

Chomsky, Noam. 2000b. *New horizons in the study of language and mind.* Cambridge: Cambridge University Press.

Chomsky, Noam. 2003. Rationality/Science. In *Chomsky on democracy and education*, 87–97. London: RoutledgeFalmer. Originally appeared in *Z papers special issue*. Available at http://www.chomsky.info/articles/1995----02.htm.

Derry, Gregory. 2002. *What science is and how it works.* Princeton, NJ: Princeton University Press.

Descartes, René. 1972. Discourse on the method of rightly conducting the reason. In *The philosophical works of Descartes, vol. 1*, ed. by Elizabeth S. Haldane and G. R. T. Ross, 79–130. Cambridge: Cambridge University Press.

Freud, Sigmund. 1995. *The Freud reader*, ed. by Peter Gay. New York: W. W. Norton.

Goldstein, Martin, and Inge Goldstein. 1984. *The experience of science.* New York: Plenum Press.

Haegeman, Liliane. 1994. *Introduction to Government and Binding Theory.* 2nd ed. Cambridge, MA: Blackwell.

Humboldt, Wilhelm von. 1999. *On language: On the diversity of human language construction and its influence on the mental development of the human species,* ed. by Michael Losonsky, trans. by Peter Heath. Cambridge: Cambridge University Press.

Jackendoff, Ray. 1977. $\overline{X}$ *syntax: A study of phrase structure.* Cambridge, MA: MIT Press.

Keil, Frank. 1986. The acquisition of natural kind and artifact terms. In *Language learning and concept acquisition: Foundational issues,* ed. by William Demopoulos and Ausonio Marras, 133–153. Norwood, NJ: Ablex.

Kuhn, Thomas. 1962. *The structure of scientific revolutions.* Chicago: University of Chicago Press.

Platts, Marc. 1979. *Ways of meaning.* London: Routledge & Kegan Paul.

Popper, Karl. 1959. *The logic of scientific discovery.* London: Routledge.

Radford, A. 1988. *Transformational grammar.* Cambridge: Cambridge University Press.

Stone, I. F. 1980. *The trial of Socrates.* New York: Anchor Books.

Thrax, Dionysius. 1987. The technē grammatikē of Dionysius Thrax (trans. Alan Kemp). In *The history of linguistics in the classical period,* ed. by Daniel J. Taylor, 169–189. Amsterdam: John Benjamins.

Index